CHRISTIAN MISSION AND INTERRELIGIOUS DIALOGUE

Edited By

Paul Mojzes and Leonard Swidler

Religions in Dialogue
Volume 4

The Edwin Mellen Press
Lewiston/Queenston/Lampeter

Library of Congress Cataloging-in-Publication Data

This volume has been registered with The Library of Congress.

This is volume 4 in the continuing series
Religions in Dialogue
Volume 4 ISBN 0-88946-520-7
RD Series ISBN 0-88946-379-4

A CIP catalog record for this book
is available from the British Library.

For information contact

The Edwin Mellen Press
Box 450
Lewiston, New York
USA 14092

The Edwin Mellen Press
Box 67
Queenston, Ontario
CANADA L0S 1L0

The Edwin Mellen Press, Ltd.
Lampeter, Dyfed, Wales
UNITED KINGDOM SA48 7DY

Printed in the United States of America

For Nancy Krody

who over the years has been essential to the dialogue

that takes place in the pages of the

Journal of Ecumenical Studies

CONTENTS

FOREWORD

THE PROBLEM: MISSION AND/OR DIALOGUE?

Paul Mojzes

A qualitative change took place in the relationship between churches and religions, mostly during this century. While exceptions may be found in previous centuries, as evidenced by book titles such as <u>Twenty Centuries of Ecumenism</u> or studies of some instances of irenic Jewish-Christian or Christian-Muslim relations, most readers will be aware that some genuinely new attitudes and approaches manifested themselves in our own age.

Previously the prevalent Christian concept of mission was that it was Jesus Christ's own command to go out and preach the Gospel to the world. This was interpreted to mean that the sacred task of Christians is spread the good news to non-Christians and turn them into followers of Christ. The consequence of this understanding was that a tiny Jewish sect became the world's largest and most universal religion. Huge masses of people were converted to Christianity, sometimes by witness and occasionally by coercion (note, for instance, Charlemagne's repeated baptism of the Saxons).

As Christianity divided into rival churches, often it was believed that the church's mission consists also of the evangelizing or re-evangelizing of those who had drifted away. Satisfaction was felt when individuals or entire groups were brought into the "right" fold. It was believed that the appropriate targets of mission were the Jews, the "Mohammedans"(as Christians labeled them incorrectly), the "heathens" of various sorts (a corporate name for all the others), as well as the heretics and schismatics.

There was joy during the Protestant and Catholic reformations when segments of population were wrested away from each other. There was a sense of accomplishment of one's mission when Jews were converted to any branch of Christianity, or when lapsed or active members of any church were converted to one's own faith. In the heyday of the missionary enterprise in the nineteenth century when Christian missionaries reached nearly all lands there was high hope, even among the liberals, that the world will be saved in the next generation. On the mission field intense rivalry for converts developed between Lutherans, Presbyterians, Methodists, Catholics, Congregationalists, Baptists, Seventh-Day Adventists, Pentecostalists, Jehovah's Witnesses, and so forth. There was even rivalry of sorts between various Catholic orders and between missionaries of different nationalities belonging to the same church. The targeted population was not infrequently puzzled by these rivalries, and not being keen on the details of Christian doctrine or polity often called the missionaries not by their denominational affiliation but by their nationalities (German, British, American, Italian, etc.). The results were often scandalous as the denominational missionary competitiveness reaped the contempt and ultimate rejection of some of the pecuniary manipulation of what was being "offered" by others as people followed the highest bidder. The case is perhaps slightly over- stated here and certainly these were not universal experiences. There were also salutary examples of cooperation. Essentially, however, the picture drawn here is true enough. Were this not a true picture, the modern ecumenical movement among Protestants may have had a different inception. The fact is that one of the most significant impulses for the eventual creation of the World Council of Churches was the 1910 International Missionary Conference in Edinburgh where missionaries of various Protestant denominations faced up to the scandal of rivalry and pledged a change in approach which affected not all denominations, but certainly those that we now call "main line" in the U.S.A.

This is not the place to trace the history of ecumenism of the twentieth century nor how that intra-Christian ecumenism affected and gave spur to the "wider" ecumenism. One thing is certain. By the last decade of the twentieth century it is evident at nearly every occasion where people of different churches and religions meet that the former zeal for conversion and the attendant lack of respect for the authentic religious experience of others is gone. The notion of dialogue, ecumenical and interreligious (the former more than the latter) has domesticated itself in our consciousness and in our practice.

Volumes have been written since then on the purpose, scope, and method of dialogue, as practice and theory intermingled. Astonishingly great leaps were made in dialogue. If the nineteenth century was the Century of Mission, then the twentieth century is certainly the Century of Dialogue. Likewise, volumes have been written on mission, its changing nature, scope, and method and here also much creativity, dedication, and success is in evidence. However, a certain ambiguity and even tension arose as to the relationship of Christian mission and interreligious dialogue. Was interreligious dialogue to replace mission? Was it either mission or dialogue? Or could they go together? Some even wondered whether interreligious dialogue may not be a more sophisticated approach to mission. Or could the content of the good news be disseminated by dialogue? For many there was a clear switch from mission to interreligious dialogue. For instance, religious orders or agencies that once saw their purpose in the conversion of Jews to Christianity became among the proponents of Jewish-Christian dialogue strongly emphatic that its ultimate purpose is not the of making Jews into Christians. The same has often become true of attitudes toward other religions.

During the last decade this problem, which has been in the making for many years, reached a confrontational stage. Within many churches as well as across denominational lines two positions seem to have solidified. One promotes the missionary activity of the Christian church, giving priority to the task of evangelizing all those not yet reached by the Gospel. Some spell it out as the unabashed call for the conversion of non-Christians to Christ and Christianity. On the opposite end of the spectrum are protagonists of a view that advocates interreligious dialogue as the proper way of relating to others, urging that conversion be renounced as an explicit goal of the Christian mission and declaring that dialogue is the mission of Christians today.

As noted, up to the end of the nineteenth century most Christian missioners went to 'save' the non-Christians or "the heathens" or "pagans"; some harbored hopes that by the twentieth century the world would have accepted Jesus Christ as their savior. However, practically from the outset it became evident that souls cannot be saved without attention given to the body and mind, and thus the missionary enterprise both at home and abroad soon included schools, hospitals, orphanages, old people's homes, and many other forms of charity--in fact, this had been characteristic of Catholic "foreign missions" since the sixteenth century. Increased attention was paid to development. Thus agriculture, crafts, health, education, social services were included in the notion of mission. Mission meant not only sending clergy to lead people in the salvific experience of the true God but also sending educational, medical, agricultural, and technical experts.

Many Christian missioners took a serious interest in the native religions and became increasingly appreciative of the authenticity and sincerity of the search for God or for salvation and liberation among those whom they had come to convert. Serious tensions occurred as it became evident that missionary outreach was often accompanied by colonization and exploitation of the various population by Westerners variously linked to the missions, if in no other manner than by a shared religious affiliation. Further, it became apparent that somehow the mission-sending people saw themselves as the subjects of mission and the people to whom the missionaries went as the objects of mission. This too created resentment as well as a realization that the message of Christ is needed just as much in the mission-sending countries as in those to whom the message was originally targeted. Many are now praying for a reverse mission whereby Christians from Africa and Asia, and perhaps Buddhists, Hindus, and Confucians, would come to the former mission-sending countries to save, to inspire, to heal, and to teach--in other words, to light a fire among jaded "believers."

When in the twentieth century the ecumenical movement produced dialogue first among various Christian missionaries and churches and then increasingly across religious divides, the movement for interreligious dialogue emerged. A new appreciation developed for the values found in other religious approaches as well as an awareness of the failures and hurts produced by the Christian missionary endeavors. Interreligious dialogue produced in a relatively quick time some very satisfactory results and gained an enthusiastic following even among many missionary personnel and leaders. Many predicted an end to the proselytizing and the beginning of the cherishing and valuing of truth, goodness, justice, and peace wherever it was found. Conversion was de-emphasized to a mere by-product, which might be avoided whenever possible.

The conflict has now reached critical proportions in some churches where a battle is waged for what seems to be the very soul of the Christian

Church. Different churches wrestle with the issue in different ways. In some churches where the mission board or agency has emphasized dialogue with people of other faiths rather than conversion, some disaffected church members and leaders created rival mission agencies for the purpose of sending out missionaries who would more aggressively pursue the evangelization of non-Christians. This provokes impulses to oust such proponents of the traditional missionary enterprise, while they in turn charge that the church loses its identity when it stops its assertive spreading of the Gospel. They point to the numerical and institutional growth of those churches that continue their missionary activity at home and abroad unabatedly. In other churches where the sending of missionaries espousing only a certain theological mold, members of more a dialogical orientation are creating their own missionary agencies with a different thrust. In both instances the confrontation is so sharp that it threatens schism. Still other churches battle it out without the threat of overt breakup; nevertheless the differences of opinion are palpable. Nearly all major denominations face this crisis regarding mission over against interreligious dialogue.

While this is not an altogether new concern expressed in writing, no collection of such explorations has been published as yet. We felt the need for adding more light rather than heat to this perplexing and difficult problem. The idea for this volume came when the editors read an address of Jozef Cardinal Tomko, "Missionary Challenges to the Theology of Salvation," that was delivered as the opening address at a missionary congress in Rome in November, 1988. We wrote to him asking for permission to use the article as a springboard for a broader discussion and invited a number of scholars, ecumenical leaders, and missioners to respond to the article and the issues which Cardinal Tomko raised so pointedly. He not only graciously consented but offered to read the responses and write a concluding essay reacting to some of the issues raised by the respondents.

In our selection of respondents we did not try to be comprehensive, but did attempt to provide the balance of a variety of respondents representing different denominations, nationalities, church positions, and viewpoints. Actually when the essays reached us we saw that none of the respondents lined themselves up on an extreme end of the either/or spectrum alluded to above, because Cardinal Tomko's nuanced address elicited nuanced and thoughtful responses. For most respondents it is rather a matter of both/and, but with leanings in either direction, since no one tried an impossibly perfectly centrist position.

Most Christians agree that the Church has a task to communicate the source, the inspiration, the life upon which it lives--God's revelation in Jesus the Christ. The Church cannot change into a society for interreligious dialogue or into a general soteriological enterprise. The Church must proclaim its specific kerygma, but as distinct from earlier ages it can do so dialogically. If the Church holds no distinct, worthwhile message and cause, it need not bother enter into dialogue, because it will have nothing to give in the give-and-take of dialogue. The great Czech Marxist philosopher, Milan Machovec, once wrote that he does not want to dialogue with a Christian who does not want to convert him, namely, with one who holds that the Christian truths have only subjective and thus limited validity, a mere personal preference. Machovec wanted to dialogue with a Christian who is persuaded that the Christian truth has a general validity. He was saying that he would rather meet in dialogue a Christian who was hot than one who is lukewarm. Sharing this valid truth or experience need not be done triumphalistically, intolerantly, and exclusivistically. One may embrace the reality of pluralism with a genuine warmth and enthusiasm and yet not become lukewarm in regard to what one stands for.

Interreligious encounters, study, and living has lifted dialogue as the superior manner to relate to each other. A sort of Copernican turn took place in the traditional understanding of how to deal with the truth claims of other religions. When other religions are taken seriously, appreciatively, and are allowed to impress upon us the significance of their experiences, aims, and truth claims, such new insights affect nearly all our previous perceptions not only of the other religions but also of our own. A shift takes place from, "I used to view and accept unhesitatingly and uncritically that we are completely correct in all things," and "I could not even think of viewing appreciatively and with understanding another religion," to a far more unitive view of all religious experiences and expressions. Naturally this new unitive approach threatens to break the former unitive perception of truth apart.

In this struggle to interpret and reinterpret the fundamental truth claim and message of the Christian religion great cleavages in understanding occur as to how to communicate our mission to those who do not already share it. So with the changed times and procedure it is being questioned as to whether at the end of the twentieth century it is still proper and important to speak of the "mission" of the Church. To this question even the most enthusiastic practitioners of dialogue can answer emphatically, "yes!" though the interpretation and packaging of the mission is likely to diverge from the previous.

Jozef Cardinal Tomko and the fifteen respondents in this volume have gone a long way in reflecting on these fundamental issues, shedding useful insights on the relationship of Christian mission and interreligious dialogue. It is our hope that these insights will contribute to the larger sphere of the mind, heart and life of the Church as it relates to other religions--where the tension between mission and dialogue is being played out--with the hope that they will help make that tension creative rather than disruptive.

INITIATING ESSAY

MISSIONARY CHALLENGES TO THE THEOLOGY OF SALVATION

Cardinal Jozef Tomko

1. INTRODUCTION: IMPORTANCE OF THE THEME

Salvation, redemption, liberation . . . various terms, perhaps with a different coloring, but a single reality that constitutes a central problem for humanity in search of the meaning of its own existence. A problem often submerged by the course of life, but one which emerges with pressing urgency at crucial moments.

So it is a complex reality that immediately presents two fundamental aspects: one negative, which answers the question: salvation or liberation from whom or from what? The other aspect concerns the positive con tents: salvation or liberation for what or in view of what?

Salvation is a vital question for humanity and can bring doubt if not crisis to the woman or man who aspires to clarity, to certainty, indeed to security both on the level of physical existence, and on the spiritual and religious levels.

Salvation involves the fundamental vision of humanity: who are humans? do they need salvation? and which salvation?

And the answers vary: There are those who speak of a purely human salvation: humanity finds self-sufficiency and self-redemption in itself; the aspiration to salvation, so deeply rooted in the human heart, can have a satisfactory psychological and sociological explanation; and there are no lack of ideologies or systems that promise this secularized salvation.

Other replies are religious in nature: In one form or another salvation is considered a central theme in all the great religions of the world. Then for the Christian it is one of the fundamental pillars of faith in God "who wishes to save every human being," "qui vult omnes homines salvos facere" (1 Tim 2:3) and in Jesus Christ, who "who because of us humans and for our salvation descended from heaven," "propter nos homines et propter nostram salutem descendit de coelis" (Creed).

To bring and mediate salvation is also the mission of the Church and so her reason for existence.

So we are at the heart of Christian missiology and of the very missionary activity of the Church. Today more than ever it is necessary to make a thorough study of the problems of salvation, to present the reply the Christian faith gives to the problem of salvation, to clarify the Christian specific remedy in relation to the context of today's world, of the great religions and cultures and also of the world of secularity.

The Congregation for the Evangelization of Peoples and the Pontifical Urban University wanted this Congress on the theme of salvation, because today there are precise reasons for urgency:

a) The first reason is the need for clarity in the missionary motivation of the Church and of the missionaries themselves, who dedicate their life and at least some years of their existence to evangelization. In the past missionaries felt the pressing need to bring salvation to non-Christians with an almost dramatic anxiety. If their reading of the sacred texts was perhaps too fundamentalist, it is still vitally important to establish what is still valid in this motive.

b) Then, salvation is a complex reality. Perhaps also for this reason in the last two decades it has become an ambiguous concept that needs to be explained in the light of the faith.

c) The Second Vatican Council assumed a positive, respectful attitude towards the great non-Christian religions and so encouraged the new reflection on the theology of religions and on the salvation of non-Christians. In view of the dialogue with these religions, Christians must have a clear awareness of their own identity and of the role of the Christian faith in the divine plan of salvation. There are many new ideas in this field, but they need a close examination and a serious critical maturation.

In opening this Congress, I do not intend to rob experts and scholars of theological and humanistic subjects involved in the problems of salvation of their job. Instead I want to present some questions and some challenges that missionary life itself poses to them, in expectation of a reply. They come from direct experience, gathered in various mission lands, behind which are ideas that circulate in the various books and articles on the subject. These experiences above all invite theologians to have the greatest precision in formulating their own theses; a precision that is measured in the light of faith, but also in the light of the practical disruptive consequences that these theses produce in the field of the missions.

2. SALVATION AND NON-CHRISTIAN RELIGIONS

The first concrete experience comes from the Far East, where the great majority profess one of the ancient classical religions, rich in culture and wisdom.

In a meeting of pastoral operators one orator speaks of the respect the Second Vatican Council invites us to have for these religions; he presents them as a great human effort in the search for the Absolute. Then, following the activity of <u>God</u> in history, who spoke through the prophets and, recently, "in these days" "has spoken to us by a Son" (Heb 1:1f.). The Christian cannot lack in respect and gratitude to the Father who was willing to send his own Son so that he might reveal the true face of God to humanity: Jesus Christ as the Incarnate Word is the best Revealer of God and so also the "way" (Jn 14:6), as he himself indicated.

However there is an objection from one group of missionaries that this presentation is not acceptable, because it degrades non-Christian religions to an effort from below and exalts Christianity as the religion coming from above, whereas in truth all religions are equally inspired by God and constitute ways of salvation. This group of missionaries has in fact withdrawn from direct pastoral activities and has devoted itself to socio-economic collaboration with the non-Christian majority, in the spirit of a "dialogue of life." In that region there are many possibilities of evangelization through direct announcing and catechesis; the native clergy is insufficient, but because of these missionaries' conviction of the role of Christian and non-Christian religions in salvation the surge of evangelization has diminished.

This practical attitude is, however, based on ideas. And the ideas revolve around some central points such as:

a. God's plan of salvation

b. Jesus Christ's role in this plan

c. the mission of the Church in relation to salvation

d. the role of non-Christian religions.

Today everyone admits the universal saving will of God, who "wishes to save every human being" (1 Tim 2: 4) even though many stop at this point in the reading of the Pauline text and neglect or consider as less important what follows: "and to come to the knowledge of the truth" (1 Tim 2:4). However it may be, many questions remain open as to how God realized and realizes this universal plan in history: with what means, through which people and instruments.

And here attention immediately moves to the other three points of interest: Jesus Christ, the Church, non-Christian religions. St. Peter, in front of the Sanhedrin, asserts that there is salvation only in the name of Jesus Christ, "and in no one else" (Acts 4:12). This affirmation gives theologians the difficult task of explaining whether and how people were saved before Christ and how, even after Christ, those who do not know or do not accept Jesus Christ are saved. The question of the necessity of the Church for salvation comes as a consequence and in connection with the person and the work of Christ. And so the focal center of the problem is reduced to two poles: Christ and non-Christian religions.

Paul Knitter had the merit of reducing all theological reflection on religions to four schemes or patterns of the Christ--non-Christian religions relationship.[1]

a) The first period that dominated nearly all the history of Christianity was that of hostility towards "pagan" religions: Christ "against" religions.

This hostile attitude was influenced by a rigid interpretation of Origen's and Cyprian's affirmation: "Extra Ecclesiam nulla salus," which limited divine grace to the Church. The geographical discoveries of other continents led other theologians, like Bellarmine and Suarez, to correct this narrow perspective--which Knitter calls "exclusive"--to a rather "inclusive" one: from no salvation "outside the Church," they went to no salvation "without the Church." This perspective remained until our own century in the form of various theories concerning invisible or potential membership in the Church.

---

[1] Paul Knitter, *No Other Name? A Critical Survey of Christian Attitudes Toward the World Religions* (Maryknoll, NY: Orbis Books, 1985; Idem, "La teologia cattolica delle religioni a un crocevia, *Concilium*, Italian ed., 22, 1 (1986), pp.133-143. Cf. also John Hick-Paul Knitter, *The Myth of Christian Uniqueness, Toward a Pluralistic Theology of Religions* (Maryknoll, NY: Orbis Books, 1987).

It has been noted that this schematization is not sufficiently objective[2] It is true that the Fathers of the Church assumed a hostile attitude toward cults, rites and myths considered as idolatry and aberrations; yet it remains to be seen whether they were so in reality! However in the Church there is also positive appreciation of the valid aspects of religions: St. Justin also speaks of the "lógos spermatikós" or "seeds of the Word"; St. Clement of the "illumination of the Logos"; St. Irenaeus of the "divine teaching"; Pope Gregory the Great gives wonderful missionary directives for the evangelization of England; Raymond of Peñafort and Raymond Lulle support dialogue with Islam; St. Thomas Aquinas speaks of "natural religion" which is a "praeparatio evangelica." Then there is the attitude of love and respect towards everything that is not an error in many missionaries, like St. Francis of Assisi, in Ricci and De Nobili, in the famous 1659 Instruction of the Congregation for the Propagation of the Faith. And what can be said of the theologians of at least four centuries who maintained that God's grace operated also outside the visible confines of the Church, but was always mediated by Christ and by the Church, until the thesis that excluded non-members of the Church from salvation was officially condemned in the Holy Office's letter to the Archbishop of Boston, in the case of Fr. Feeney, dated 8 August 1949.[3]

b) The Second Vatican Council (1962-65) and its Declaration "Nostra aetate" opens a decidedly new perspective which Knitter characterizes with the dual concept: Christ within religions.

The positive statements on the possibility of salvation also for non-Christians were "made clear"--according to Knitter[4]--by Karl Rahner.[5] He

---

[2] Cf. D. Colombo, "Missionari senza Cristo?" *Mondo e Missione*, 10 (1988), p. 317.

[3] Cf. Denzinger-Schönmetzer, eds., 33, 3866-3873.

[4] Cf. Knitter, *art. cit.*, p. 135.

maintained that other religions are and can be ways of salvation positively included in God's plan of salvation; it is always the grace of Christ that operates in the non-Christian, offered through the respective non-Christian religion. The person thus touched by Christ is unconsciously directed to Christ and to his Church, he is an "anonymous Christian," who must however be transformed into an explicit, fully ecclesial Christian. Rahner's theory, however, developed above all by Robert. Schlette and by Anita Röper[6] and accepted by Edward Schillebeeckx, does not satisfy Knitter, because it would end up "only in a partial and provisional approval of them."[7]

C) In the last decade, a certain number of theologians have been searching for a new perspective described as "Christ above religions." Not satisfied with Rahner's theory, they maintain that other religions have an independent validity: even if Christ is not, in their opinion, the exclusive cause of saving grace, yet He remains above all religions and all peoples. To preserve the fact of faith in the uniqueness, finality and so on of the normativity of Christ, they give various explanations. Christ is the only "critical catalyst" also for other religions, in the face of our modern world:[8] Hans Küng. Claude Geffré uses the universality of the right that Christ has over all peoples, in that he is the Word of God made flesh, whereas this would not be due to Christianity as a historical religion.[9]

---

[5] Karl Rahner, "Das Christentum und die nicht christlichen Religionen," *Schriften zur Theologie*, vol. 5 (Einsiedeln: Benzinger, 1962).

[6] H. Robert Schlette, *Le religioni come tema della teologia* (Brescia, 1968; German ed. Freiburg: Herder, 1964); Anita Röper, *Die anonymen Christen* (Mainz, 1963).

[7] Knitter, art.cit., p. 136.

[8] Hans Küng, *Christianesimo e religioni universali*, Milan 1986; idem, "Per una teologia ecumenica delle religioni," *Concilium*, 22, 1 (1986), pp. 156–165.

[9] Claude Geffre, "La Mission de l'Eglise à l'âge de l'oecumenisme interreligieux," *Spiritus*, 1987, p. 6.

d) To put Christ above religions does not seem very ethical if an honest dialogue is to be held. This, at least, is what the theologians think who propose a model that sees Christ together with other religions and with other religious figures. According to them, after the abandonment of "ecclesiocentrism," it is necessary to eliminate "Christocentrism" as well and put God at the heart of religion, in a theocentric vision.

Knitter himself upholds the theory of "unitive pluralism" or of "the coincidence of opposites," according to which "each religion (or religious figure) is unique and decisive for its followers; but it is also of universal importance." It is neither exclusive--"against" nor inclusive--"within" or "above"--but is "essentially related to other religions," so, "perhaps...other revealers and saviors are as important as Jesus of Nazareth."[10]

Raimundo Pannikar reaches the same conclusion from the distinction between the Christ-Logos and the historical Jesus. There is more in the Christ-Logos than there is in the historical Jesus, so that the Logos can appear in different, but real ways in other religions and historical figures, outside of Jesus of Nazareth.[11]

The faithfulness of this theology to Christ is assured because it still maintains that God really spoke through Jesus, but it is fully open to God's possible message in other religions.

e) Finally, Knitter crosses also this Rubicon in order to "liberate" the theology of religions. Using the methodological criteria of the theology of liberation (option for the poor, orthopraxis), he resolves to "go beyond theocentrism, towards soteriocentrism," so that "the primary concern of a theology of religions should not be "rightful belief" in the uniqueness of

---

[10] Knitter, *art. cit.*, 139.

[11] Raimundo Panikkar, *The Unknown Christ of Hinduism* (Maryknoll, NY: Orbis Books, 1981).

Christ, but "rightful practice" with other religions, of the "promotion of the Kingdom and of its soteria"; in other words: "This means that the basis and principal interest of every theological evaluation of other religions is not their relationship with the Church (ecclesiocentrism) or with Christ (Christocentrism), or even with God (theocentrism), but rather the degree in which they are able to promote <u>salvation</u>: the <u>well-being of humanity</u>."[12]

This well-being in which the Kingdom, the Reign of God, consists is the Reign of justice and of love to be reached in collaboration or dialogue with all. Exalting interreligious dialogue, Knitter reduces faith in Christ to the level of an ambiguous earthly "well-being." Here at last is a reassuring conclusion for missionaries who are perhaps perturbed: "The missionary goal is reached if the announcing of the Gospel to all peoples makes the Christian a better Christian and the Buddhist a better Buddhist," since "the primary mission of the Church is not salvation business" (to make people Christian so that they can be saved), but the task of serving and promoting the kingdom of justice and of love."[13]

I do not know how far the missionaries I mentioned at the beginning acted on the basis of the opinions explained here. What is certain is that they concentrated on social action, trying to achieve this in dialogue with non-Christians and abandoning the direct announcing of Jesus Christ more and more.

This reduction of evangelization occurred also in other countries and in other continents. It is justified in various ways, but it always starts from at least two presuppositions: first, every religion is a way of salvation; second, it is necessary to seek dialogue with other religions, which must be re-evaluated.

---

[12] Knitter, *art. cit.*, 141–142.

[13] Knitter, *No Other Name?*, 222.

It also presents a common tendency to eclipse or reduce the role of Christ, of the Church and of announcing and to concentrate all the activity and finality of evangelization on the building up of the Reign of God, sometimes undefined and at other times identified with social well-being, justice, peace and love.

3.1 THE "MISSIO DEI"

The most explicit theological motivation of this tendency is found in the most radical derivations of the theory of the "missio Dei."[14] The real protagonist of the mission is God. God's sovereignty or absolute lordship must in the end overcome the "Christomonism" in which the Christian missiology, both Protestant and Catholic, was enclosed (A. van Ruler; M. K. Miskotte). The "extra" promised by Jesus is realized in the building up of the Reign of God. "The real end of the missio Dei is the Kingdom of God, not the ecclesia viatorum," Anderson decrees.[15] God saves as God wants and when God wants; God's action is not bound to the Church. Mission today is the action which tries to discover God's action in the world: to discover God in the world and serve God and not "to bring Christ" to the world. So also the Church, like Christ, must practice kenosis, self-emptying, in this service.

Even more radically opposed to the Church's role in mission is the tendency of "out-churchism." The Reformed Dutch theologian and missionary J. C. Hoekendijk[16] asserts that mission is realized with the proclamation of the "shalom" in hope; so the "missio" is "pro-mission" in the

---

[14] Cf. H. H. Rosin, *Mission Dei* (Leiden, 1972).

[15] Mentioned in J. Lopez–Gay, *Missiologia contemporanea*, in: AA.VV., *Missiologia oggi* (Rome: Urbaniana University Press, 1985), p. 98.

[16] J. C. Hoekendijk, *The Church Inside Out*, (1964); *Die Zukunft der Kirche und die Kirche der Zukunft* (1965).

service of the world, building up peace--"shalom," that leads to intercommunion and participation. With this service to the world people are coagulated and so the Church happens as an event and not as a structure.

Also the Catholic L. Rütti[17] rejects the theology of the Decree on missions of the Second Vatican Council as being too ecclesiocentric and not very realistic when it refers to the trinitarian missions and the mandate of the Lord. For Rütti, mission is the responsibility of Christians before a world in the hope of transforming it, in order to create a new world.

"The commitment of Christians (N.B. not of the Church!), bestowed with a new promise for the world, is not to maintain or spread a church, but it consists in efficacious responsibility for the present hope in the new world."[18]

3.2 THE CENTRALITY OF GOD'S REIGN

The centrality of the Reign of God appears more and more frequently in these theories. And the Reign of God, in the full ambiguity of interpretation, is also the cornerstone of the more recent reflections of some Asian theologians, who were influenced by their experiences of direct contact with the great ancient religions and cultures. Indeed, one of them sees "a Copernican revolution of the theology of evangelization" in the fact that "the centre of the approach moves from the Church to the Kingdom."[19] First he analyses and then relativizes the role of the Church for salvation. He reports the opinion of some who "called the Church an extraordinary

---

[17] L. Rütti, *Zur Theologie der Mission: Kritische Analysen und neue Orientienung* (1972).

[18] Rütti, *op. cit.*, p. 345; cf. J. Lopez-Gay, *op. cit.*, p. 105.

[19] M. Amaladoss, S.J., "Faith Meets Faith," *Vidyajyoti* (1985), pp. 109-117; "Dialogue and Mission: Conflict or Convergence?" *Vidyajyoti* (1986), p. 63.

way in opposition to the other ordinary ways" of salvation represented by religions.[20]

After Vatican II, the relationship between the Church and religions could not be presented in terms of the presence-absence of salvation, nor of light-darkness, and not even with the divine-human or supernatural-natural dichotomy; today the binomial explicit-implicit, or full-partial, is more common. Since "the Church, as she is, is a historically and culturally limited realization of the Good News."[21] he abandons ecclesiocentrism. "The Church does not offer an easier or a fuller salvation . . . because of God's universal saving will and the socio-historical nature of the human person, God's saving encounter with man occurs also through other religions and their symbolic structures: writings, codes of conduct and rituals. . . . The Church is called not only to witness, to proclaim, but also to collaborate in humility and respect for the divine mystery that operates in the world."[22] "Being a member of the Church is not an easier or surer way of salvation."[23] Our theologian recognizes the saving role of Jesus Christ and refuses to set Christocentrism against theocentrism. But here too, with Pannikar, he distinguishes between the cosmic Christ and the historical Christ. The saving mediation of non-Christian religions is linked to the cosmic Christ, whereas the Church's role is linked to the historical Christ and to his paschal mystery. Now we must not take advantage of the "communicatio idiomatum," attributing certain qualifications such as "final, last, unique, universal" to the historical Christ, because they belong not to Jesus, but to the Word. But in the end, how is the divine universal plan of salvation accomplished?

---

[20] M. Amaladoss, "Dialogue and Mission," p. 65.

[21] *Ibid.*, 72.

[22] *Ibid.*, 78.

[23] *Ibid.*, 82.

24

Through evangelization that knows three patterns: the first ecclesiocentric, the second centered on the world and the third on the Reign of God. The author aims at an evangelization in the global sense in which "the new focal point"[24] is the Reign of God, i.e., the building up of a new humanity that will unite all people in a community of love, justice and peace. This is the mission in which the Church must collaborate--with dialogue, with inculturation and with liberation: strangely, but significantly, proclamation, i.e., the announcing, is omitted. The explanation is found, perhaps, in our theologian's extremely radical doubt: "In this context of religious pluralism does it still make sense to proclaim Christ as the only Name in which all people find salvation and call them to be disciples through baptism and to enter the Church?."[25]

Starting from the experience Jesus had of the Father, also another Indian theologian concludes that "the Church's mission is not so much to bring salvation as to bring the manifestation, not to obtain the conversion to the Church as the necessary means of salvation, but to help in the realization of the broader Kingdom of God as it develops in history. This includes the effort to help followers of other religions to follow those religions in a better manner."[26]

These theories are now widespread and beginning to bear fruit in the practical field. One pastoral magazine presented the following program of a missionary insti- tute: "We go out on the missions not so much to plant

---

[24] Amaladoss, "Evangelization in Asia: A New Focus?" *Vidayajyoti*, 51, 2 (1987), pp. 7-28.

[25] Amaladoss, *"Faith meets Faith,"* p. 110.

[26] J. Kavunkal, "The 'Abba Experience'of Jesus: The Model and Motive for Mission Today," *FABC Papers*, 43 (1986), p. 14; idem, *To Gather Them Into One* (Nettetal: Steyler Verlag, 1985).

the Church or to bring the faith, but rather to discover a faith and a goodness that already exist there."[27]

Some missionaries who work among the Indios in Latin America pose the same problem for themselves from a different angle. They were faced with the difficulty of changing the customs with which the Indios live happily and with an easy conscience; so why should they disturb their good faith with the severe demands of the Christian morality which is too hard for them and leads them to continuous spiritual distress? On the other hand following their conscience, the Indios are saved just the same. Some of these missionaries then asked themselves whether it was not perhaps better to try to raise the level of social life and concern themselves more with the physical health of the Indios than with their salvation.

So the need for a clear answer to the problem is felt in many continents. It is even vaster with regard to the relationship between salvation and human promotion in any form (economic, social, political, development, liberation, justice and peace).

3.3 SALVATION AND HUMAN PROMOTION

Several recent theological opinions on non-Christian religions have weakened one of the motives that urged missionaries to sacrifice themselves for the salvation of non-Christians, announcing Jesus Christ and the Christian faith to them. These theories exalt the role of other religions and common commitment for the renewal of the world and for human promotion; some reduce evangelization to this purpose, others include this renewal in the very concept of salvation, yet others give human promotion priority ("first make men, then Christians," or "first feed the hungry, then speak of God"). In this

---

[27] Cf. the article "Maryknoll's Changing Concepts of Mission," *Tripod* (Spring 1988), p. 65.

field all continents feel the need for clarity: mission continents in order to give a correct orientation to missionary activity, other regions in order to direct their animation and cooperation properly.

The radical position that reduces the Church's mission to human promotion is expressed by G. Davies in one concise sentence: "The purpose of mission is not to make Christians, but to help peoples to become men."[28] Also for some liberation theologians mission is a historical practice in the revolutionary process; without this participation mission becomes omission, whereas "participation in the process of man's liberation is already, in a certain sense, the work of salvation."[29] Without adopting Karl Barth's diametrically opposed Puritan opinion, which maintains that the purpose of mission is exclusively eschatological salvation, it is necessary to confirm and deepen the balanced position reached by the Church in the last two decades, but only imperfectly passed into missionary practice and into certain theological theories.

4. CHALLENGES AND QUESTIONS TO THEOLOGIANS

After this vast but incomplete presentation of various opinions about salvation, it is necessary to explain at least some anxieties, challenges and questions the missionary world addresses to experts.

a) The first series of challenges and questions the missionary pastoral addresses to experts and theologians concerns the contents of salvation, i.e.: Which salvation are we dealing with? Salvation/liberation from what--or for what?

---

[28] G. Davies, *Dialogue with the World* (1968), ch. 4; mentioned in J. Lopez-Gay, *op. cit.*, p. 114.

[29] Gustavo Gutierriez, *Teologia della liberazione*, Brescia 1972, 79; cf. also pp. 94; 202; 272.

1. Is it an <u>essentially religious</u> salvation? And if this is so, does it concern only the next world, in the <u>exclusively eschatological</u> sense, as Karl Barth wished, assigning to the mission the task of bringing this salvation and of being a "crisis" of all human, cultural and religious values?

2. According to divine revelation, can it be said that the salvation to which evangelization tends is of an economic, political, social or cultural nature? Or is it limited to service to the "world," for the "well being" of the world?

What are <u>the bonds between the "human" dimension</u> (liberation, progress, development, justice and peace) and the <u>"divine"</u> or <u>"spiritual"</u> <u>dimension of salvation</u>: liberation from sin and from evil (which are its fruit and consequence), the rebirth of God's children to the new life and final participation in the happiness and glory of God in life everlasting?

3. In evaluating the elements of salvation of non-Christian religions, should one not take account of the difference--sustained for example by Hans Urs von Balthasar[30]--between the religions of revelation that profess a personal God (Judaism, Christianity, Islam) and those that believe in an impersonal divinity and thus see the contents of salvation differently?

b) Putting oneself on the level of the Christian faith, another series of fundamental questions concerns <u>the divine plan of salvation</u> in its three pillars: <u>God, Christ, Church</u>.

1. <u>"God desires to save all human beings"</u> (1 Tim 2: 4)--this is clear and is generally accepted in all theologies. It becomes more problematical if what is also revealed and follows immediately in the Pauline text is likewise respected: ". . . and to come to the knowledge of the truth" (1 Tim 2:4). What does this addition mean? Is the solemn <u>mandate</u> to preach the

---

[30] Hans Urs von Balthasar, *Das Christentum und die Weltreligionen* (1979); Italian trans.: *Il Cristianesimo e le religioni universali* (Piemme: Casale Monferrato, 1987), p. 6.

Gospel to all peoples and to baptize those who believe not perhaps the interpretation that Jesus himself gives to God's saving will? How can one explain the solemn and decisive tone of this command (cf. Mt 28: 19f.; Mk 16: 15f.)?

Obviously, what divine revelation understands as "salvation" desired by God for all must be established.

2. Jesus Christ is humanity's only Savior and the only Mediator between God and humans, according to revelation: "And there is salvation in no one else, for there is no other name under heaven given among men by which we must be saved" (Peter's testimony before the Sanhedrin: Acts 4:12). "For there is one God, and there is one mediator between God and humans, the man Christ Jesus, who gave himself as a ransom for all" (1 Tim 2: 5f.); "No one comes to the Father, but by me" (Jn 14, 6). With his death and resurrection Jesus became for all humans "the source of eternal salvation" (Heb 5:9) and "Leader and Savior" (Acts 5:31).

Can the only definitive role Jesus Christ has in the work of salvation perhaps be disputed ("No other name?") without neglecting the facts of the Christian faith? Or is it sufficient to consider them as later Christologies of the New Testament and as emphatic statements on a level with those of the enamored husband who thinks his own wife is the most beautiful and most lovable woman in the world (Knitter)?

3. Does the fact that Jesus Christ is the Son of God made man, the incarnate Word, have some impact on the quality of his message and of the Christian faith? Can the "revelation" brought by him be put on the same level as the "revelations" or "divine inspirations" contained in other religions?"

4. Can he be put "next to" or "together with" other founders? Is he not a savior also for them?

5. Does God save those who do not believe in Christ, without Christ? Does Christ's grace constitute salvation? How does Christ reach those who do not believe in him?

6. What should one think of the difference between the cosmic Christ and the historical Christ?

7. The necessity of receiving baptism and of being part of the Church is also contained in the divine plan of salvation: "He who believes and is baptized will be saved" (Mk 16:16); in fact one cannot enter the Reign of God unless "one is born of water and the Spirit" (Jn 3: 5); through baptism one enters the Church, which is by the will of Christ "the universal sacrament of salvation" (LG 48) and it is only through it "that the fullness of the means of salvation can be obtained" (UR 3).

8. So is it necessary to believe with the Second Vatican Council and in the Council itself when "basing itself upon sacred Scripture and Tradition, it teaches that the Church, now sojourning on earth as an exile, is necessary for salvation" (LG 14)? We are well aware that the obligation to follow the Church belongs only to those who know this necessity (LG 14) and that "those also can attain to everlasting salvation who through no fault of their own do not know the Gospel of Christ or his Church, yet sincerely seek God and, moved by grace, strive by their deeds to do His will as it is known to them through the dictates of conscience" (LG 16).

9. So in what sense is the Church the "universal sacrament of salvation"? Since non-Christians who lead a good life are excluded from formal and explicit membership of the Church, can it still be said that it is necessary for salvation and, in the affirmative case, in what sense?

10. Is complete aversion to the so-called "ecclesio-centrism" theologically justified? Must the mission forego planting the Church as one

of her goals? (Cf. Eph 3:17; 2, 19; AG 6, 9; Evangelii nuntiandi EN 62, etc.)?

11. Have other religions a "sacramental" function for salvation in the same way as the Church which is "the universal sacrament of salvation," or are they only "occasions" of salvation?[31]

c) The specific Christian purpose of the mission also needs to be clarified. The questions have already been partially asked in the first series of questions concerning the contents of salvation. But some theories expounded need a thorough critical examination, above all as far as the Reign of God and dialogue in relation to the mission is concerned.

1. Can it be said that the Reign of God is the center of Jesus Christ's mission (and of that of the Church), separating it from or setting it against the great mandate that obliges us to "teach" and "make disciples of all nations, baptizing them," "teaching them to observe all that (he has) commanded you" (Mt 28, 20); to "preach the Gospel" (Mk 16:15), to preach "repentance and forgiveness of sins" (Lk 24:47); and announce and "testify that he is the one ordained by God to be judge of the living and the dead" (Acts 10:42)? What meaning does the "Reign" have on the lips of Jesus Christ?

2. Following the text and context of the Gospel, does the Reign of God precisely mean earthly social well-being? Are "the values of the Reign" reduced to justice, fraternity and peace?

3. Is "the Reign of God" not at the same time "the Reign of Christ"?

---

[31] Cf. S. Maggiolini, "Le catholicisme et les religions non chrétiennes," *Nouvelle Revue Théologique*, 109 (1987), pp. 509-520.

4. Has "the Reign of God" no relationship to the Church?[32]

5. If "the proclamation of the Reign of God is evangelization,"[33] according to Evangelii nuntiandi (8-10), is it not also true that evangelization is a complex and rich reality? and that among other things it includes the "plantatio ecclesiae" (AG 6; CIC c. 786; EN 59, 62)? And yet is it not equally true that "evangelization will also always contain--as the foundation, center and at the same time summit of its dynamism--a clear proclamation that, in Jesus Christ, the Son of God made human, who died and rose from the dead, salvation is offered to all humans, . . . and not an immanent salvation, . . . but a transcendent salvation" (EN 27)?

6. Does the fact that God operates with grace also on non-Christians release the Church from the obligation of announcing the Gospel?

7. Does dialogue replace the announcement-proclamation? Does the announcement eliminate dialogue? Or do both belong to the "complex and rich reality" of evangelization?

CONCLUSION

The challenges and questions presented do not exhaust the expectations, nor the tasks that lie before this Congress, but they do show how important its theme can be at the present moment.

Because today, even more so than in 1974-75, the years of the Synod of Bishops and of Paul VI's Apostolic Exhortation Evangelii nuntiandi, which was the fruit of it, the words of this document are extremely true:

---

[32] The "Conference of Catholic Bishops of India," C.B.C.I., recently expressed "concern about some theological tendencies in vogue among religious. There is a tendency to preach the Kingdom while dissimulating the Church, to preach the values of the Gospel, overlooking the person of Jesus in his capacity as Christ. The Christology of St. Paul and of St. John seems to be ignored."

[33] M. Amaladoss, "Risposta alle obiezioni," quoting EN 8, Vidyajyoti, 10 (1985), p. 478.

The presentation of the Gospel message is not an optional contribution for the Church. It is the duty incumbent on her by the command of the Lord Jesus, so that people can believe and be saved. This message is indeed necessary. It is unique. It cannot be replaced. It does not permit either indifference, syncretism or accommodation. It is a question of people's salvation. It is the beauty of the Revelation that it represents. It brings with it a wisdom that is not of this world. It is able to stir up by itself faith--faith that rests on the power of God (cf. 1 Cor 2:5). It is truth. It merits having the apostle conse-crate to it all his time and all his energies, and to sacrifice for it, if necessary, his own life (EN 5).

At this point I would add: it is also fitting that this Congress should dedicate a deep reflection to it.

ROMAN CATHOLIC RESPONSES

THE HOLY SPIRIT AS POSSIBILITY
OF UNIVERSAL DIALOGUE AND MISSION

Maria Clara Lucchetti Bingemer

The question of universal salvation and the huge interpretations it brings to the missionary task of the Church is certainly a very central one. It seems difficult to reconcile God's universal desire of salvation with the commitment to announce the Gospel of Jesus Christ and to promote belonging to a particular Church. Christology and ecclesiology will not help us very much at this point. Perhaps it would be useful, however, to take pneumatology as our point of departure because of the guarantee and the evidence that we have of God's universal desire of salvation is the Spirit of God who is poured out over the whole creation as Spirit of Life.

The history of the Holy Spirit as active among God's people, as we find it in the Hebrew Bible and New Testament and in the narratives of the early Church, displays certain characteristics which enabled the people to discern its presence and recognize that presence as divine.

The first of these characteristics is the "production" of life. When the Spirit is active the mist and disorder of chaos become an organized and harmonious cosmos (Gen 1: 1 ff.); the wilderness is transformed into a garden (Is 35: 1-6); and dry bones are changed--before the astonished eyes of the prophet, himself possessed by the same Spirit--into a strong and mighty army (Ezek 37).

By contrast, when the Lord God takes away the Spirit, the creatures die and return to the dust from which they came (Ps 104: 29-30). The Spirit's absence, or any attempt to restrict, stifle or grieve the Spirit, results in a diminution of life and an increase in the predatory, destructive power of death.

The Spirit, who was outpoured over the whole creation, and not only over the Church and determined religious spaces and confessions, is the Person and the Divine Force who, after the death and resurrection of Jesus, brings salvation while--because--it brings life. The Spirit is also the One who since the origin of Creation, gives life and breath to everyone and everything that lives. Thus the production of life is the sign of the presence of the Spirit. Likewise where life grows and increases, we must search and find the Spirit of God. Because of this, the Spirit is the only possibility of a mission which is really universal, as well as of a dialogue among different religions--starting from this common point: life. And life, before, and because it is a theological question, is an anthropological one.

1. THE PNEUMATOLOGICAL SUBVERSION OF ANTHROPOLOGY

The presence of the Spirit of God within human beings provokes important consequences: it alters and affects their deepest and most essential constitutive anthropological categories, by radically subverting the foundations of their being.[1]

---

[1] By *altered* we mean a deep transformation caused by the presence and manifestation of the other (*alter*). Alterity is today one of the most important and central categories in anthropology, both at the philosophical level and at the theological. On this theme of alterity see, among others, E. Levinas, *Totalité et infini* (La Haye, Martinus Nijhoff, 1971); E. Dussel, *Metodo para una filosofia de la liberación* (Salamanca: Sigueme, 1974). The question of alterity, however, has also been elaborated in the discourse about God, both within and outside Christianity. See, on this point, U. Vazquez Moro, *El discurso sobre Dios en la obra de Emmanuel Levinas* (Madrid: Univ. Comillas, 1982); L. Bodd, *A Trindade, a sociedade e a libertação* (Petrópolis: Vozes, 1986); X. Pikaza, *Dios como Espiritu y persona* (Madrid: Secretariado Trinitario, 1989).

The first characteristics of this pneumatization is that the Holy Spirit provokes in human persons an exodus, a going out of themselves and moving towards the other or others.[2] The first movement caused by the Spirit which announces its presence in humankind is, therefore, a movement of drawing out of the person his/her immediate interests and attachments so that s/he becomes open and serviceable to all, capable of facing the most adverse situations, dangers and tribulations, rejection, suffering and death.[3]

This is true not only in those people who are conscious of the presence of this Spirit in the Christian way of being and believing, but in every man and woman who lives in this earth. Taking this anthropological fact from the Christian faith point of view, we can affirm that on that we can see the trinitarian movement of God, the exodus of the Spirit who is constantly being sent out by the Father and by the Son, the "other" Paraclete, who was present at the beginning of the whole creation (Gen 1: 1) and now fills the earth with its divine presence and can be recognized by the fruits of life it produces in the middle of that same Creation.

That presence of the Spirit in creation, in humankind and within each human being makes of those human beings pilgrims, who find themselves not in their own selves, but rather in the other, or in the others. That is to say, people in constant "mission" towards the others, perhaps not to announce the Gospel or to share religious beliefs, but to announce and make happen

---

[2] By "exodus" from one's self I mean the experi-ence of going out of one's self as it takes place in all human beings reached and influenced by the Spirit of God and guided by towards love and service of the other. Love and service cannot be offered or practiced without a profound act of self-denial, or rejection of all which in the self is rooted in sin, selfishness and self-sufficiency. It has always, therefore, that painful dimension of the exodus, of a departure, of leaving behind what is known to venture into unknown land, into the mystery of the other. All mission must go through this exodus; this is the condition for the possibility of undertaking mission. But also it is true among non-Christians, who feel compelled to go out of themselves to love and serve others.

[3] Cf. biblical texts such as 1 Cor 9: 22; 2 Cor 1: 44 ff.; 4: 7-15; 5: 1 ff.; 8: 2; Phil 4: 14; Gal 2: 19 ff.; 6: 17; 1 Cor 2: 1-5.

the most fundamental belief, common to all human beings: the faith in life as something beautiful and worth doing, the greatest of all gifts, the most precious good.

That is why the Spirit draws the human beings out of themselves, of their categories, their deepest prejudices, their most entrenched habits, comfort, securities, in order to live with and for others, and to make them aware of their potential for living. And this consequently, provokes in them, no matter which religion they belong to, a need to work for more life, which is equal to saying, for salvation for others, for everyone.

2. THE SPIRIT ALTERS HUMAN SPACE

This process is the beginning of the subversion of the anthropological categories that belong to all human beings. It will alter their deepest and most constitutive egos to the extent that they will now understand themselves in the life of the other, from the other's point of view, both the Other who restructures the being through its re-creator breath, and the others who hope for their participation in the praxis of the construction of life. That is to say, the Spirit at work in the whole of creation and within all the creatures draws them out of themselves and alters their inner and outer space.

Anthropologically, that means living in the space of the other and letting the other live in their own space. Several important consequences at all levels, for mission and interfaith dialogue follow from this. The permanent change of this space means, on the one hand, having to move always towards the unknown and to be open to the invasion of the unknown. The other remains a mystery which will never be fully revealed. To be willing to live in the other's space means to accept being eventually rejected, choked, saddened, offended and even destroyed. It means also having to live in anonymity or obscurity. It means accepting the characteristics, culture and the categories of others in order that Life may happen within the frame and categories of the other, and not as an imposition of foreign categories which will hinder the communication started by the Spirit in order to produce Life in a different way that we are used to.[4]

The consequence of this world presence of the Spirit on the other hand are positively felt also in the creation of an alternative space for human beings. The Spirit who alters the anthropological categories in order to produce life at all levels, subverting the same notions of mission, religion and salvation, is the same Spirit who draws human beings out of their selves in order to place them in another space. Space is one of the fundamental ways of human self-understanding. The loss of site, of place, of land, of space--in other words, atopia--is always felt as a source of anguish and despair, disgrace and malediction, menace to life, death.

So, by altering and subverting the human space in the process of producing life, the Spirit prevents the human beings from constantly understanding themselves in the light of their own selves and from their own geographic situation, and from defending, tooth and nail, a space of their own. The Spirit allows, even when there is not an explicit consciousness of it, the space to be a common space, the space of everyone, where sharing and flavoring the fruits of creation is a normal practice and where anthropology is subverted and reconstructed, inside and outside, by a new concept of life wider than the limits imposed by determined religious creeds and a narrow idea of mission. Where there is life, where human life and creation can grow and develop themselves, there is the presence of the Spirit

---

[4] I think here about the fact that America as a whole is getting prepared for the Assembly of the Episcopacy, at Santo Domingo, in 1992, on the theme of Evangelization and Cultures. Christian people in America are now called to take very seriously this question of inculturation, of the incarnation of the Gospel in different cultures; in our continent, specially, this question constitutes a great challenge to evangelization. See, on this question, *REB* 49, n. 196, Dec. 1989; see also AA.VV. *Cultura y evangelización en America Latina* (Santiago de Chile: Paulinas-Ilades, 1988).

of God. And those situations which produce life that way, altering the space of human beings should be stimulated, even if not explicitly in the name of some determined religion--for to stimulate life is to stimulate the life of God to fulfill the whole earth and the whole created space.

3. TRANS-FORMATION AND CON-FORMATION BY THE SPIRIT

Besides altering the anthropological space, the Spirit alters the human form as well. The New Testament is full of passages where the change of form undertaken by the Spirit in the human beings appears under different names: seal (Eph 1: 13; 4: 30), image (2 Cor 3: 18), dressing (Col 3:, 10; Eph 4: 24). It is, in fact, a true transformation, a metamorphosis of the human beings which takes place with the presence of the Spirit. And that process of transformation gradually alters vitally and essentially the form of human beings by giving them a new configuration, in fact, Christ's configuration.

Therefore, the transformation accomplished by the Spirit in human form is, in fact, a conformation--conformation to Jesus Christ, the Son of God, the most beautiful of the children of Man, the one who came in order that everyone have life, and abundance of life. So, when the Spirit conforms human beings to Jesus Christ, the Son of Man, the Son of God, that makes them more fertile and generators of life for everyone and everything who surround them by the simple practice of charity and love of one another, by coming out of their selfishness and showing before the face of the world the form of that historical person who was love in himself, who passed through life only doing good (Acts 10: 38).

Thus the presence of the Spirit--even when men and women are not conscious of it--is a presence of love, for only love produces life. If God is love, God can be the supreme object, not of necessity, nor of rationality, but only of love. The whole course of the life of God in the middle of creation and in the heart of humankind can only be motivated and permeated by the flame of love. The whole history of intolerance and religious persecutions, trying to imprison the Spirit of God into determined patterns, was not able to suppress the Great Love, nor stifle the divine "Pathos,",which from all eternity has broken across the unbridgeable gap and opened up a way, kindling in its turn in the hearts of men and women an irresistible insatiable love, which was at the origin of all things and is the destination of every human life.[5]

4. SALVATION: A GIFT OF THE SPIRIT FOR ALL CREATURES

In this way the Spirit, who is the source and driving force of love, and is itself divine love, is poured out on history and humankind, and finds favorable and fertile soil for its divine creative imagination, which calls forth and kindles the flame of love and life in its fullness against all that threatens to quench it, and keeps it burning without its being consumed. It renews and brings the whole of reality, which has been injured by the sin of discrimination and evil in all their forms, back to the Great Love whence they came and by which they were brought into being.

Life is the other name of salvation. As all admit today the universal saving will of God, it is necessary to recognize that God accomplished and accomplishes every day this universal will by sending constantly the Spirit, producer and doner of Life, who does not end nor is limited within a determined religion or church, but is given as a graceful gift to every creature.[6]

---

[5] Cf. my article "The Holy Spirit creator of a community of life" in: *Women in a Changing World* (World Council of Churches), 28 (December 1989), pp. 3-5.

[6] In Latin America and other parts of the Third World, where life is under menace every day, the presence of the Spirit of God as doner of life is felt when the poor and the oppressed organize themselves in order to build new situations of life from within the situations of death which oppress them.

That is the deepest sense of the "missio Dei": to seek God's action everywhere in the world by the fruits of true life this action produces, and then proclaim that <u>there</u> is the presence of the Living God, even if it cannot identify itself with a specific creed of religion.

That does not mean that it is no longer necessary to evangelize explicitly, to announce the Good News of Jesus Christ, or to build the Church. But if we really believe in the Spirit of God as a source of "subversion"--and a subversion which brings salvation--of anthropology, we must admit that where that anthropology is altered in order to be more lively and a producer of life, there salvation is happening, the Spirit of God is in action. The mission should be, thus, primarily to make that explicit and announce this with the force of a <u>kerygma</u>.

This is the real Good News: God is "in mission" everywhere. And to collaborating in making this mission of life grow in every place or situation it exists is the commitment of all men and women, and also of the Church, which will then be called to a humble and kenotic recognizing of itself only as a community within the human society which is conscious of the wonderful things and the universal work of salvation the Spirit of God is realizing everywhere. That will not diminish the mission of evangelization given to the Church, but, on the contrary, can help it accomplish it with new force and truth. "The Church is called not only to witness, to proclaim, but also to collaborate in humility and respect for the divine mystery that operates in the world."[7]

---

[7] M. Amaladoss, "Dialogue and Mission: Conflict or Convergence?" *Vidyajyoti* (1986), p. 78 (cited by Cardinal Tomko).

NO, YES, AND NO

Denise Lardner Carmody

Cardinal Tomko's paper, "Missionary Challenges to the Theology of Salvation," provoked three basic responses in me, two negative and one positive. Let me present them in dialectical order: one negative, one positive, and another negative.

1. SEXIST LANGUAGE

Throughout this paper, the language is sexist: written with male pronouns, to the linguistic conclusion that the humanity being discussed has men as its prime instances and women as secondary. I don't know whether this paper was delivered in English, or subsequently translated into English. Perhaps the sexist language should be attributed to the translator, but in the version I received, the flaw is egregious, and my suspicion that Roman authorities would be puzzled by this charge makes me think it important to state very baldly that such insensitivity is a major reason that a growing number of women, and men, find the pronouncements of Roman Catholic authorities unpersuasive, if not incredible.

This is a paper about the theology of salvation, as missionary circumstances spotlight such theology. It is a paper wrestling with the question of what salvation, liberation, redemption, and the like mean--how we ought to understand such terms, in view of both traditional Christian faith and current circumstances in missionary situations. Yet this paper begins, in its first full sentence, with language that either positions "salvation" as patriarchal, and so deliberately rebuffs feminist sensibilities, or is ignorant of the whole manner of patriarchy, and so is even more problematic: "Various terms [salvation, redemption, liberation] perhaps with a different coloring, but a single reality that constitutes a central problem for man in search of the meaning of his own existence." Does the Cardinal mean that salvation concerns only men? Surely not, though by his language one cannot be metaphysically certain. Does the Cardinal not care about the sensibilities of those, women and men both, who think that language reveals the user's assumptions and shapes the hearer's sense of reality, so that language depicting the world as though men stood for all human beings does a double disservice? Who knows? Has the Cardinal even made himself aware of women's concerns, or of the significant impact that feminist thought now has on all the humanistic disciplines? Again, who knows? It is hard to believe, though, that in a Roman Curia considerably troubled by what it considers "radical feminism," and considerably concerned to tell women what the genuine feminine virtues are, no glimmer of the question of linguistic usage has appeared on the horizon.

From the outset, then, I read the Cardinal's paper with a jaundiced eye. Here was a voice most likely little concerned with the sensitivities of the people inhabiting the situations it was discoursing about. Here was a voice most likely speaking from the pulpit on high, little inclined to come to grips with actual human experience, little troubled by the need to translate theology into experiential terms. 50% of the people implied as the referent of missionary outreach are women. Their needs and hopes may be the same as those of men regarding the essence of salvation that one can abstract, if one's theological tendency is essentialist and abstractive, but their concrete, daily needs--the ones that a truly incarnational theology would long to meet--are not the same as men's. Men are not burdened with children, treated as sex objects, subjected to clitoridectomy, kept in thrall to fathers, husbands, eldest sons, raped, and spurned as unclean the way that women are. Men are not barred from the priesthood and other tokens of Catholic Christian institutional authority the way that women are. To ignore these differences, and despise women's linguistic and conceptual sensitivities, is to show oneself unequipped for the task at hand. If one wants to discourse about salvific missions to today's human beings, one had better develop some interest in where those human beings are, how they actually live, what their real needs (in possible contrast to the needs that lecturers find convenient) actually are.

2. CHRISTOLOGICAL ORTHODOXY

The whipping boy in the Cardinal's speech is Paul Knitter and others who have proposed a radical rethinking of the missionary venture, such that neither the Church, nor Christ, nor even the Western God would be the primary focus or touchstone of the enterprise but the worldly needs of human beings would hold primacy of place. I doubt that Paul Knitter is happy with the interpretation of his thought offered in this paper, and I am sure that his position holds more nuance than what the Cardinal, because of either spatial limits or misunderstanding, suggests.

But I agree with some version of the worry that the Cardinal puts forward. I agree that a missionary venture willing to put the significance of Christ on the back burner and not convinced that the story of Christ is the axial good news, the narrative best able to communicate the force of divine love that is the gist of salvation, is dubiously Christian. If orthodoxy is the desire to sing in chorus with the great Christian thinkers who have preceded us, to worship and opine as the doctors of the Church, the great saints (men and women, East and West, ancient and recent) honored for their large hearts and keen minds, have done, then I want my missionary theology to be orthodox. Moreover, I want my Christology, which at some point is bound to be the crux of a missionary theology that is Christian, to be orthodox--one that presents Jesus as not simply the most admirable of human liberators but also as truly divine. The language of Chalcedon may be troublesome nowadays, but I find the intent plain: full humanity, and full divinity. Both terms are fully mysterious, wrapped in the counsels and infinite being of God. But, in my opinion, if one does not tie salvation to the unique event and person of Jesus Christ, one is not speaking with the grand Christian tradition.

Now, there are many ways to try to make this tie. One can use a variety of languages. Many of the liberation theologians who have come under a cloud in Rome seem to me to be working valiantly to make a valid, effective translation of orthodox intentions. One can focus on what Jesus implies, and pioneered, for political, economic, sexual, social, cultural, and other human relations needing salvation. The missionary venture that an orthodox Christology implies need not be from the top down, or dogmatic in the pejorative sense of more interested in consecrated formulas than in experiential realities. But, in my view, it does have to be a venture in cross-cultural translation of a passionate commitment to Christ as the personal place where the glory of God shone round about (I write in the Christmas season) in a way that, for the followers of Christ, it has shone nowhere else. This man has words of eternal life that Christians do not find in Buddhism, Islam, or secular humanism. Christians may find other words of eternal life in those or other places. They may revere the Buddha or Muhammad or even Karl Marx as fountains of wisdom and power. But, if they know what they are doing and saying, they are Christians because Jesus is their master, their beloved, the place where the world holds together for them and God has shown divinity to be incomparably parental.

One doesn't forget this kind of conviction when one enters upon the construction of a missionary theology. It is not something one can bracket because one is dealing with people who hold other primary allegiances. Naturally, one should not be obnoxious, or superior, or chauvinistic about it. Naturally, it does not imply any historical or cultural superiority of the Christian Church. The theological claims it makes for the Christian Church should be modest, because that is how the bride of Christ should comport herself. But I believe that it has to develop some cognate to Rahner's theory of Anonymous Christianity, some way in which the human maturity and integrity that all people are moved by their best cultural and personal impulses to seek comes to fruition and stands most fully revealed in Jesus Christ. Again, I repeat that his need not put Buddhist, Muslim, Marxist, or other views of salvation in the wastebasket. It need not mean overlooking other people's non-Christian allegiances, which frequently have excellent credentials and sometimes are colored by Christians' historical failures. But it does mean taking seriously, as a datum of faith to which one has to be faithful, the Christian sense of the divinity of Christ, which entails his being the uniquely adequate revelation of God and center of God's salvific activity.

However, theologians need the freedom to ponder how Christ can be the center of an economy of salvation that embraces people who don't consider themselves dependent on Christ, and some of such pondering rightly can focus on the liberations that the love Christ incarnated imports in the social order. Relations between the sexes, between the classes, between the races, and between human beings and the other creatures with whom they share the ecosphere all can be much better than most people have experienced them to be--if God truly is who and what Jesus presented God to be. Jesus's own criterion--the fruits a messenger or message produces--

suggests that bringing about perceptible changes in human relations is a fine standard for missionaries to try to meet. Such changes have to be social, economic, educational, and medical, as well as matters of prayer and fasting. They have to recall the interpretation Jesus gave to the Isaiah passage (61:1-2) in the synagogue at Nazareth, at the beginning of his ministry: "Today this scripture has been fulfilled in your hearing" (Luke 4:21). By the logic of the Incarnation itself, the grace of God has to seize eyes, ears, mouths, stomachs, brains, hands. The anointing that conveys salvation is credible in the measure that it brings people fully alive, in the measure that it makes them credits to their Creator and Redeemer. We know that our Redeemer lives when our bodies and souls alike feel blessed. We take the salvation of Christ to heart when it keeps alive our hopes for a communion of saints, a seeing of God face to face, a wiping away of every tear from our eyes. Without this language of incarnational salvation, Christianity might be merely another gnosticism. The implication for missionary theology and practice is plain: the words have to lead to transforming deeds. The message is cultural and political.

However, to found the cultural and political imperatives of Christian missiology in any but the unique power revealed in Christ would be to short-change those to whom one is preaching and ministering. The Gospel is not wise by human standards, powerful the way the powerful of the world tend to be. Ours is a Gospel whose wisdom is the crucified Christ, on his way to the resurrection for which faith can bring all people to hope. So, inasmuch as reflections and challenges such as Cardinal Tomko's remind us that the great thing Christian missionary efforts have to offer is the unsurpassable demonstration of divine love that Christ himself makes present, they do us a great favor. The riches of Christ are so great that we should never feel the need to dilute the Gospel. The riches of Christ are so humanistic, so radically enfleshed, that we ought to be able to do into any situation, any non-Christian culture, with the modesty that comes from a profound confidence. How we proceed in dialogue with representatives of a given non-Christian culture, what programs we decide will best incarnate the gospel--these are matters of prudence, best worked out by those who know local conditions well. But what the substance of the salvation we are offering ought to be is completely unambiguous: the fulfillment of human potential made known and available by Jesus the Christ.

3. STYLE

My third reaction to Cardinal Tomko's paper concerns the style, the tone, in which it is cast, and this reaction is negative. Perhaps the best way for me to conclude my response would be to ruminate about this issue gently, in a spirit more sad at opportunities missed or deficiencies revealed than antagonistic or condemnatory. In dealing with Paul Knitter and others laboring to rethink Christian missiology, the Cardinal does not create the impression that he views them as members of the family, brothers and sisters with whom he shares much more than what divides him from them. He does not offer much evidence that he appreciates the profound sympathy for God's presence in non-Christian religions and cultures that has led theologians such as Knitter to back away from traditional Christian claims. If we use the dictum that the style is the message, the message is that a pre-Vatican II sense of the relations between a Cardinal and a theologian, or an ordinary church member, prevails, such that the bond among all Christians, the democracy created by baptism and morality, means less than the different stations the Cardinal and the ordinary Christian possess in the

Church. This is sad, because it places such a burden on the one assuming a higher station, a magisterial role. He has to have the lion's share of the wisdom, and common sense tells us that frequently he cannot, because he has not lived in the situation being discussed, or he has not had the experience that is crucial. Were he to present himself as duty-bound to speak for Christian tradition, or to mediate the papal view that is only available to those called to care for the entire Church, who could object? The democracy created by baptism and human mortality does not obviate the possibility of different roles in the Church. It does not destroy the possibility of obedience and fidelity to customary authority. But it does humanize all of this. It does move it from the institutional model, which is impersonal, and bring it to something more Christian, the family of God.

Christians will only create the good conversation they need to fulfill all their commissions from God, missionary and other, when their first instinct is familial rather than institutional. They won't have the full contribution of all the members the Body requires if it is to flourish unless all members can feel they are receiving a prejudgment of good will. These are simply the laws by which human communities operate, as the Holy Spirit makes them plain. Where there is charity and love, God abides. Where there is charity and love, there is a presumption of good will, good work, intellectual offering that seek to forward the mission of Christ, the mission of the Church, the good of all the human beings God has created and holds close as the apple of the divine eye. I miss the tone of such love in the Cardinal's paper; I don't find my faith nourished by his presentation. I would not feel invited to put forward my views, to reveal my own theological hypothesis, to make known anything that I was not willing to guard and fence about.

This is a lamentable feeling to have, and certainly Cardinal Tomko should not be held fully responsible for it. It stems from the whole freeze that has come over curial authority and theology since the death of Pope John XXIII. We have become a Catholic Church more inclined to criticize, discipline, reprove than to support, nourish, encourage. We have become more an institution driven by fear than a family confident of its Father's love, its Mother's understanding. And so, all of our missions are much less effective than they ought to be. All of the joy and peace that ought to be the great signs to the world of God's presence and power has atrophied. Certainly, the Spirit is not defeated by our human failures, but the Spirit must be weeping over our faithlessness, as Jesus wept over Jerusalem. A Pharisaism afflicts us. We don't seem to know or exploit the freedom for which, Paul said, Christ has set us free.

Freedom is the other side of the love that is the crux of salvation, redemption, liberation. Freedom is the outbreak of the Spirit of Christ is our minds and hearts, our bodies and assemblies. Without a robust freedom that makes us trust one another, support one another, correct one another with a pointedness that is kid, we cannot be the great sign lifted up for the nations. We cannot serve the Christ who is our pearl of great price. I hope that more discussion of missionary challenges to the theology of salvation will move us toward conversion.

THE REIGN OF GOD AND A TRINITARIAN ECCLESIOLOGY
AN ANALYSIS OF SOTERIOCENTRISM

Gavin D'Costa[1]

INTRODUCTION

Jozef Cardinal Tomko's address poses some pertinent questions to a swelling current of opinion in the theology of religions. The scope of his questions are wide ranging. I will restrict myself to a single task, that of analyzing the shift that Cardinal Tomko charts, fol-lowing Paul Knitter's schematization, of the moves from <u>ecclesiocentricism</u> to <u>Christocentricism</u> to <u>theocentricism</u> to the current emphasis on <u>soteriocentricism</u> with its conco-mitant implications for mission. As Knitter is an articulate exponent of this new approach, I will focus my analysis on his work, although many of my observations are applicable to others who share his presuppositions. I will argue that a coherent Christian soteriocentricism, with its important emphasis on liberating action, requires for its intelligibility and critical usefulness an underlying theocentricism, Christocentricism and equally so, ecclesiocen-tricism. Otherwise, such an unfounded soteriocentricism is in constant danger of masking vacuous or alien ideologies, that are then elevated to criteria for truth and subject Christian revelation to their control. If it is

[1] I am grateful to Dr. G. P. Loughlin for his helpful criticisms of a first draft of this essay.

argued that these criteria are not alien to Christianity then we are inevitably driven back to Christ, God and the Church for their grounding. If they are alien then they may rightly be questioned as to their usefulness and intelligibility for use within a Christian theology of religions.

In short, I believe a Trinitarian ecclesiology offers the best and most intelligible justification for a soteriocentric approach.[2] Such an approach facilitates the acknowledgement of the Holy Spirit within the world religions--in a manner that cannot be specified a priori--and an attentiveness to the critique of Christian practice and theology by the Holy Spirit acting within the world religions. This latter point is sadly neglected in Cardinal Tomko's paper. A Trinitarian ecclesiology also facilitates a justification for mission.

THE SOTERIOCENTRIC REVOLUTION

I shall use Knitter's texts cited by Cardinal Tomko.[3] First we need to understand the history by which Knitter's soteriocentricism arose. In replacing "old" approaches Knitter tries to steer clear of affirming the Church, Christ or God as a <u>normative criterion</u> for truth, as such an approach "seems to contradict our present experience" (A:143). This experience involves four affirmations: "1) the relativity of all revelations and religious truth claims, 2) the truth and goodness of other religions, 3) the encounter with other believers who also state that their experience of revelation is a message for all times and all peoples, 4) the demands of dialogue

---

[2] This is the thrust of *Lumen Gentium*. Thus Grilmeier notes: "the ecclesiology of Vatican II is pneumatological, just as it is christocentric and ultimately theocentric." Ed. H. Vorgrimler, *Commentary on the Documents of Vatican II* (London: Burns & Oates, 1967), p. 142.

[3] Paul Knitter, *No Other Name?* (London: SCM, 1985), = A; "Catholic Theology of Religions at the Crossroads," Hans Küng, Jürgen Moltmann, eds., *Christianity Among the World Religions, Concilium,* 1983, 1986, pp. 99-107 = B; "Towards a Liberation Theology of Religions," in John Hick & Paul Knitter, eds., *The Myth of Christian Uniqueness* (London: SCM, 1987), pp. 178-200 = C.

that require that no one enter the conversation with a prepackaged final word." (A: 143, my numbering added).[4] I do not think that any of these four affirmations, the first and fourth being highly questionable, require the abandonment of the normativity of Christian revelation.

By normativity, I mean the claim that through the revelation of God in Christ, Christians are confronted with the self-disclosure of God in the particularities of history. Regarding Knitter's first point, there is no way in which God's self-disclosure can be relativized, i.e., to say that this disclosure is only true for Christians. If Jesus Christ is really God's irreversible eschatologicial self-disclosure, as is confessed by most Christians, then this revelation is true, whether it is accepted or not, for all men and women. (The mode of articulating this revelation is of course subject to the relativity and particularities of history). Such a claim need not conflict with assertions 2), that truth and goodness is found in other religions; and 3), that other religions make similar universal claims.

Regarding 2), Vatican II affirmed the normativity of Christ, while positively endorsing truth and goodness in other religions (See Nostra aetate.) It is arguable that, unless one has some sense (not exhaustively, but normatively) of what truth and goodness are, it will be impossible to joyfully acknowledge their existence anywhere--within or outside Christianity. If Christians are confronted by the normative shape of grace in history through the contours of Christ, the doctrine of the Holy Spirit equally facilitates the recognition that this grace is not limited to Christianity. But the discernment of this explicit extra-ecclesial grace requires a christocentric criteria, which thereby implicitly relates it to the Church, the body of Christ. So when

---

[4] These are not his only reasons. I have dealt more fully with the issues in *Theology and Religious Pluralism* (Oxford/New York: Basil Blackwell, 1986, ch. 2; and *John Hick's Theology of Religions. A Critical Evaluation*, London/New York: University Press of America, 1987, esp. ch. 5.

Knitter quotes Maurier approvingly, that if we view other religions "from within" a Christian perspective, the result is that "fundamentally the other religion is . . . disqualified" (A:142), I find the latter comment problematic. It is imperative that other religions must define themselves in dialogue, in the same way that Christians would wish to define themselves to their dialogue partner. It would seem that from Knitter's use of the quote, other religions are "disqualified" by virtue of the fact that they are viewed, in the final analysis, from a viewpoint they may not share. However, if such a procedure is rendered illegitimate, then logically we must allow that Hitler's claim to be guided by God can only be judged according to Hitler's own criteria, and thereby taken as true!

All religions construe the world from within their own normative paradigm. There is no neutral free zone. Such is the internal logic of religious worldviews, profoundly demonstrated in William Christian's study.[5] The real issue for Christians is the complex hermeneutical task demanded by Christian faithfulness, of understanding the other, so as to learn, share, be criticized, and when necessary pose questions to the other. Furthermore, it is required that the Christian approach should provide theological reasons for why it is not a hermetically sealed paradigm (which would be idolatrous), and why it should therefore be open to the world while also being a source of judgement upon the world and itself.

Assertion 3), that all religions make universal claims, amounts to a descriptive statement that poses the question of how such claims (e.g., Buddhist) are to be understood within another religion (e.g., Christian), rather than abandoning such claims for the sake of a spurious unity or harmony. Such claims are internally required and sanctioned within the

---

[5] William Christian, *Doctrines of Religious Communities* (New Haven/London: Yale University Press, 1987).

religions--although in differing ways. While partly endorsing Knitter's suggested move away from an exclusively "either-or" truth claim model, to an emphasis upon a "both-and" understanding, he is surely in danger of minimizing the possibility of genuine conflicting ontological assertions regarding both theory and practice. William Christian's earlier work rightly indicates many instances of genuine conflicting claims.[6] Again, Nazism viewed as a religion in relation to the Barmen Declaration, highlights this genuine problem. Although Knitter admits the ontological import of New Testament Christology (A: 184), he falsely softens the tensions when he says "that every discovery, every insight, must be corrected or balanced by its opposite." (A: 221) This is true to an extent, but being corrected or balanced, or indeed totally challenged to conversion, by other religious insights, is surely different from asserting that all "differences are, fundamentally, not contradictions but 'dialogical tensions and creative polarities'." (A: 220)

The final assertion 4), espouses <u>imperialist</u> "demands of dialogue" that "no one enter the conversation with a prepackaged final word." (A: 143) On what legitimate grounds can Knitter stipulate such a criteria for Buddhists, Muslims and others? Certainly for Christians, normativity in the way I have specified, requires that dialogue on the Christian side can only be undertaken in fidelity to God's self-disclosure. In this respect, dialogue is indivisible from mission, when mission is understood as different modalities of witness (i.e., through deeds, thoughts and words). This self-disclosure is not a "prepackaged final word" in as much as it is, by its own logic, constantly open to development and enrichment. The notion of the "development of dogma" within the Roman Catholic Church preserves both the normativity of revelation and its continual openness to development and

---

[6] William Christian, *Oppositions of Religious Doctrines* (London: Macmillan, 1972).

enrichment--and as a source for self-criticism of the community who live by it.[7]

Having indicated some problems with Knitter's reasons for soteriocentricism, we are now in a position to ask what this soteriocentricism amounts to. In his initial reflections Knitter sought a criterion by which "human liberation" could be discerned by "general guidelines or criteria" (A: 231) that did not draw on the normative claims of any religious tradition-- thereby implicitly importing a new normativity in his attempt to bypass normative Christianity. His new normativity draws heavily on Jung! (A: 231, 269). It states that personally a religious belief must move and satisfy the human heart. Intellectually, it must satisfy and broaden the mind, and practically it must "promote the psychological health of individuals." (A: 231). Only in a footnote (on p. 240) does Knitter allude to the complex epistemological and ontological problems raised by the nebulous notion of "psychological health," entailing such fundamental questions as "what is the fulfillment and goal of human nature," a question which inevitably draws us back to Christology, God, the Spirit and the Church. One can also imagine a variety of contradictory, rather than complimentary, set of truth claims fulfilling Knitter's vague Jungian criteria. Clearly a Marxist, a Theravadin Buddhist, a Nazi, and Christian could all plausibly argue that their beliefs satisfy these requirements!

In his later writings he drops all reference to Jung and concentrates (as he had already begun to) on liberation theology in order to justify his emphasis on "human wholeness." I mention his earlier excursion in order to indicate the way in which soteriocentricism cannot ultimately escape the question of normativity and the frameworks of meaning which inform the

---

[7] See Karl Rahner, "The Development of Dogma," *Theological Investigations*, vol. 1, (London: Darton, Longman & Todd, 1961), pp. 39-77; and Edward Schillebeeckx, *Revelation and Theology*, vol. 1, (London: Sheed & Ward, 1967), pp. 13-15, 66 ff.

question of normativity and the frameworks of meaning which inform the notion of "soteria." Knitter equates "kingdom-centeredness" with soterio-centricism and suggests: "For Christians, that which constitutes the basis and the goal for interreligious dialogue, that which makes mutual understanding and cooperation between the religions possible . . . that which unites the religions in common discourse and praxis, is not how they are related to the church . . . or how they are related to Christ . . . nor even how they respond to and conceive of God, but rather, to what extent they are promoting soteria (in Christian images, the basileia)--to what extent they are engaged in promoting human welfare and bringing about liberation with and for the poor and non-persons." (C: 187; B: 105). Such an approach is apparently more satisfactory as it "does not impose its own views of God or the Ultimate on other traditions" (C: 187), even if it does impose its soteriocentricism upon them!

There are a number of problems with Knitter's suggestions, most of which arise from his undialectical promotion of liberating practice without attention to the theological justification for doing so, or the theological implications embedded in any understanding of "liberation."[8] Firstly, because he is striving for a common meeting place where differences of doctrine are bypassed, he fails to account for the way in which the paradigmatic and normative sources of a tradition shape their understanding of what the human condition is and what it ought to be. Hence, promoting human welfare is an unhelpful common denominator as it specifies nothing in particular until each tradition addresses itself to what is meant by "human" and the "welfare" of human beings.

---

[8] Stanley Hauerawas makes the important point that "liberation" itself is too limited an image to express the fullness of "Christian salvation," as well as criticizing its "fatal abstraction" (p. 71) in the work of Gutierrez. Both comments are applicable to Knitter; see "Some Theological Reflections on Gutierrez's Use of 'Liberation' as a Theological Concept," *Modern Theology*, 3, 1 (1986), pp. 67-76.

To take one example: if Christianity is to address this agenda (promoting human welfare), it does so by reference to its shaping normative paradigms. There are no a priori reasons why the poor and nonperson should be preferential, or that poverty needs to be eradicated. Such views rely on frameworks of meaning and paradigmatic viewpoints. The "Reign of God," although it is not a full blue-print for the exact shape of a future society, certainly entails a form of life requiring self-giving love in conformity to the patterns of "service" and "love" instantiated in Christ. It is only in relation to the teachings and practice of Christ that the contours of the Reign of God become clearer. Through his praxis, in the power of the Spirit, we glimpse what it is to "preach good news to the poor . . . to proclaim release to the captives . . . to set at liberty those who are oppressed, to proclaim the acceptable year of the Lord." (Lk. 4:18ff.). The fact that Jesus' life and teachings embody the Reign of God, although only proleptically, makes Luke add to his account of Jesus' reading of the Isaiah passage cited above: Jesus sat down and said "Today this scripture has been fulfilled in your hearing" (v. 21). But, and this is all important, Christianity still looks to the future for the consummation of the Reign of God and in this respect is committed to a shared praxis heralding in the Reign of God. While it cannot claim a monopoly on the Reign of God, which is within the prerogative of God, it can certainly state and enact normative patterns by which the Reign of God can be dimly recognized. And it can only do this, not by virtue of the superiority of Christians, but by the attentiveness to God's self-disclosure in the Son, through the Spirit. In fact, this requirement of discernment demands first and foremost a self-criticism in as much as Christians constantly fall short of their calling. In this sense, soteriocentrism has radical ecclesiological implications.

With Knitter, I want to stress the importance of common action, but I also want to indicate the implicit normative criteriological issues for

Christianity in this approach. Liberating practice cannot be divorced from its revelatory grounding within Christianity. Hans Küng responds to Knitter's soteriocentricism in a similar vein, pointing out that "Practice should not be made the norm of theory undialectically and social questions be expounded as the basis and centre of the theology of religions." (B: 123) It is for these reasons that it is difficult to make sense of Knitter's claim that "the absolute, that which all else must serve and clarify, is not the Church or Christ or even God--but rather the kingdom and its justice." (C: 190) I have tried to show that the "kingdom and its justice" is a vacuous phrase if it is not given some normative content, be it Christian, Jungian, or Buddhist. How, for a Christian, can one serve this absolute, or even speak of the "kingdom" and its "justice", without reference to God's Reign/Kingdom (theocentricism) instantiated in Christ's life (Christocentricism), through the power of the Spirit which is active through creation (pneumatocentricism)? And how, for a Christian, can he or she speak of the Reign of God and its justice without experiencing, however imperfectly, the meaning of these words in worship, prayer and action (ecclesiocentricism)?

In Knitter's wedge between theory and practice, he misses a real opportunity not only to properly justify his soteriocentric approach, but also to make it a radical theological question for Christians. For, in proportion to the promotion of the "Reign" by people from other religions (in ways that cannot be specified a priori), the Christian is radically questioned both in his or her own restricted understanding of what is the Reign of God; and also called to recognize the ways in which God may be working through other religions. Also, if we take seriously the possibility of the Spirit's activity within the other religions, as I think we must, then Christians need to be attentive to being judged by the Spirit in a way which can facilitate a deeper and more authentic faithfulness to the Gospel. This latter feature of mission and dialogue is neglected by Cardinal Tomko.

I have given such detailed attention to Knitter's turn toward soterio-centricism in order to suggest that, without a Trinitarian ecclesiology, it falls into theological incoherence. Striving to promote the Reign of God cannot be reduced to a form of liberal humanism concerned only with the material and social welfare of the human person. However, it must of course involve this in as much as the material conditions and structures within which we live can structurally preserve injustice, suffering, and violations of the dignity of the person--all of which are an affront to the Gospel. Salvation is ultimately eschatologically consummated, while also being a reality in the present order. In promoting the Reign of God, the Christian through dialogue will be called to a radical self-questioning in his or her meeting of the Holy Spirit in the non-Christian's life. The Christian may also be called to challenge and question the ways in which another religion may actually stifle the Spirit and detract from the dignity of the person and subvert the Reign of God (although the latter requires an honest, informed and living knowledge of the religion in question). Therefore, striving to promote the Reign of God cannot involve the redundancy of mission for in so much as Christians are called to serve the Reign of God, they are called to witness and proclaim through their words, thought and actions, the rule of God the Father, instantiated in history through his Son, in the power of the Spirit. This Trinitarian mystery is both the basis of the Church and its inspiration for its self-questioning, its reason for mission and its reason for a humble, respectful and critical attentiveness to the world religions.

CHRISTIAN UNIQUENESS AND INTERRELIGIOUS DIALOGUE

Claude Geffré

Religious pluralism has become the inescapable destiny of our faith and our theology. Contrary to the naïve optimism of the nineteenth and the beginning of the twentieth century--the great missionary epoch--Christianity has not conquered the entire planet, and the significant religions of the world give every indication of increased vitality. This is true of Islam, which continues to grow in Africa and Asia. It is also true of the so-called "pagan" religions of the East, which not only maintain their hold in Asia but also exercise a new attraction for the West.

Since Vatican II, Catholic theology has sought to go beyond an absolutist conception of Christianity that correlates with a narrow, church-centered understanding ("Outside the church no salvation") to adopt an attitude of respect and esteem toward the other religious traditions. Without going so far as to consider the non-Christian traditions as "ways of salvation," the Catholic teaching office has recognized them as bearers of "salvific values." The word "dialogue" has become a key word, one must even say a slogan, for an entire Catholic literature, particularly in writings on missions.

There is no doubt, even at the highest levels, that the unavoidable consequences of a true dialogue have not immediately been taken into account. In this regard the famous Assisi Conference of October 27, 1986, which sought only to be an "object lesson" in regard to the teaching of

Vatican II, proved to be a revelation. The fact is that the extreme reaction of those who, following the lead of Archbishop Lefebvre, have chosen to become schismatic rather than subscribe to the Church's teaching about the multiplicity of the religious world has made clear that it is not so easy to engage in a new dialogue with other religions without compromising the uniqueness of Christianity in its claim to be the one true religion. In the following brief reflections I should like to draw on my experience of encounter with non-Christians to call to mind the necessary requirements for an authentic interreligious dialogue. One must, at one and the same time, repudiate the illusions attending dialogue and underscore the inadequacy of solutions that do not safeguard the uniqueness of Christianity, thereby risking a compromise of the Church's abiding mission. This will serve as a response to the serious questions posed by Cardinal Tomko in his opening remarks before the Roman Congress on "The Church's Mission."

1. THE CONDITIONS OF ALL TRUE DIALOGUE

There is such an excessive use of the word "dialogue" in ordinary Christian speech that one ends up forgetting the elemental demand of this fundamental human attitude. I limit myself here to three essential presuppositions that concern all dialogue, including that between non-Christians and Christians. First, the otherness of the speaker must be respected in his or her own identity. With this necessarily goes an interest in the convictions of the other, the more so as they are culturally and religiously foreign to me. I have to try to leave my spontaneous prejudices behind and guard myself especially against assuming as already known whatever strikes me as being similar to elements of my own universe of thought.

Second, I must define myself in terms of my own religious and cultural identity. If, under the pretext of complete openness and universality of outlook, I stand precisely nowhere, there will be no dialogue. In the current context of incertitude and relativism, one risks ending up with a set of agreements deceptive in their appearance. It is pure demagogy to pretend that one is a "citizen of the world" without roots in any one place. It is from the depths of one's particularity that one has a chance to manifest the universal opening out of all that is authentically human. Thus, in an issue of interreligious dialogue, one's fidelity to oneself--put otherwise, one's own faith commitment--is the condition of true encounter. It is essential to forgo even the illusion of being able to bracket one's faith or simply suspend it temporarily to respond to the other party.

Third, a true dialogue assumes a certain equality between the partners. It is here, unquestionably, that the major difficulty lies in dialogue between Christians and members of other religions. There is the factual, fundamental tension between the very demands of dialogue and the inmost conviction of Christian participants that they already possess the truth, referring everything to the only true and absolute religion. It is worthwhile to state clearly the terms of this dilemma. Where does it leave my Christian faith if I consider Christianity as one religion among others, if the Christian revelation is not a definitive and absolute manifestation of God, if Christ is only one mediator among others and not the coming of God as a human being? At the same time, how is one still to speak of dialogue on a plane of equality if from the start I am convinced that I already possess the truth, if I claim for my religion that it not only is the only religion but the absolute religion?

2. THE IMPASSES OF INTERRELIGIOUS DIALOGUE

Despite all the protestations of openness and understanding, experience has often convinced me that our non-Christian dialogue partners are not fooled by our latent superiority feelings. In Jewish-Christian dialogue, for example, even if Christian theology has proceeded toward a decisive new look at things and accepts the fact that the "Church-Israel" duality constitutes an irreducible duality, we continue to affirm that only Christianity fulfills the promises to Israel. Moreover, we have very badly understood the fundamental asymmetry of the two religions issuing from Abraham: Christianity cannot conceive of itself apart from Judaism, whereas Judaism is clearly conceivable apart from Christianity. Likewise, I have often heard my Muslim friends tell me that dialogue with us was flawed from the start. For, while it is true that Islam does not recognize the divine sonship of Jesus, he is nonetheless a figure entirely basic to the Muslim faith: he is the "Seal of Holiness," and his message is the very Word of God. By contrast, most Christians hesitate to recognize the authenticity of the prophecy of Muhammad as one sent by God. Further, in the dialogue with the representatives of the major Eastern religions, Christians have trouble conceiving of how they can be radically challenged and enriched--even in the matter of faith in a personal God--when they try to understand better the Heaven of Confucius, the Brahman of those committed to Vedanta, and the Nirvana of the Buddhists.

It is not the goal of the present essay to write this page of the history of theology, but it is well known that for a decade now theologians have been spawning attempts to go beyond an absolutist conception of Christianity and recognize in the other religions legitimate ways of salvation. No longer able to identify Christian unity with the unity of <u>exclusion</u>, we prefer to speak of a unity of <u>inclusion</u>. Going back to the Church Fathers' theology of <u>semina Verbi</u>, we will gladly say that the great religious traditions of humanity are carriers of a certain number of "seeds of the Word" and that they are as such--according to the pedagogy of the divine plan--"preparations for the Gospel." These can assist the various adherents to other religions in recognizing the fullness of the truth to be found in Christianity.

Following many theologians, I perceive ever better how much this inclusivist position makes authentic dialogue difficult because it does not take seriously the differences of other religious traditions. It continues to imply a form of secret imperialism as if all that is true, beautiful, or holy in other religions is implicitly Christian. I therefore attempt to reconcile Christocentrism with a more radical theocentrism in virtue of which the great religions of the world are seen as different responses to the unique divine Reality.

All theology must begin by reflecting on religious pluralism as a historical fact permitted by God, an occurrence whose significance escapes us. Whatever the case, it is not to be attributed only to the limitation of the human spirit or deviations in religious consciousness. It may also be the expression of the spiritual "riches" given by God to the nations (see Ad gentes, 11). Without yielding to relativism, that is, without putting in question the uniqueness of the mediatorial position of Christ as the cause of grace, I am prepared to recognize the other religious as "independent ways of salvation" (Hans Küng). I understand the permanent vocation of the Church as being to disclose and advance the "Reign" of God, which had its inception in the first instant of creation and continues in the religious history of humanity well beyond the visible frontiers of the People of God.

At his conference, Cardinal Tomko asked whether there is not currently among Christian theologians an overextended use of the word "Reign" to the detriment of the Church of Christ, and whether the values of the "Reign" are not often reduced to justice, brother/ sisterhood, and peace. The abiding mission of the Church as clear witness to Jesus Christ would then be at risk of being compromised. It is clear that the Church must not renounce its primary mission, which is the proclamation of the Gospel and the call to conversion, but I would quickly add that the conversion of people's hearts is not without an impact on the transformation of social relations. Following Christ, we cannot, in Christian life, disjoin the mystical pole from the political. In the missionary activities of the Church, we must go beyond the opposition between "evangelism" and "social action." All Christians are called to evangelize by their words and actions. With or without special ministries, all the baptized are responsible for evangelization, without which their actions will be reduced to purely temporal tasks. They have the duty not only to render witness to Jesus Christ throughout their lives but also to incarnate the Gospel in the structures of society and the new areas of modern society.

All human-service tasks for development, for peace, for sister/brotherhood, and justice are therefore an integral part of mission as the incarnation of the Gospel in history. Whether it be by the Church's official rhetoric or the witness of Christian communities, the Church cannot fall in with society's status quo over which flies the banner of violence and profit. In all circumstances and all places, the Church must testify that the proclamation of the "Reign" of God coincides with the refusal of all absolutization of human power, whether it be a matter of political power, money, a privileged race, or a particular people or social class. This new consciousness of the complexity and diversity of the tasks at the center of the unique mission of the Church is clearly expressed in the balanced formula contained in the final report of the Extraordinary Synod of Rome in 1985: "The saving mission of the Church with respect to the world must be understood as integral. For, while spiritual, the Church's mission implies the promotion of the human in the temporal domain as well... It is necessary, therefore, to set aside and to go beyond false and useless polarities, such as that between spiritual mission and service for the world."

3. CHRISTIAN UNIQUENESS

The already courageous stance of God-centeredness appears too timid to certain theologians, especially those rooted in the religious traditions of the East. According to them, this notion still retains an unacceptable asymmetry at the heart of interreligious dialogue. The requirements of a true dialogue thus invite us to bring about a truly Copernican revolution in our vision of other religions. Beyond exclusivism and inclusivism, it becomes a question of opting for a pluralistic theology of religions. Clearly, what is being said is that we must renounce the traditional Ptolemaic vision according to which all religious traditions revolve around Christ and Christianity as their center and adopt a vision in which all religions, including Christianity, revolve around a solar center that is the mystery of God as ultimate Reality. In concrete terms, this takes us beyond the theocentric model that continues to maintain the normativity of the Christ-event in interreligious dialogue.

I am sensitive to the seductiveness of such a position, inasmuch as it favors the practice of dialogue on a level of equality. At the same time, I have not succeeded in seeing how we do not already compromise the very identity of Christianity, which has throughout the centuries claimed the uniqueness of the mediation of Christ, inseparably human and divine, as the definitive and normative revelation of the face of God.

It is true that there is no authentic dialogue if each participant is not willing at the start to renounce claims to a monopoly on the truth. But, as we have seen above, the first requirement of interreligious dialogue, like all dialogue, is for each partner to be faithful to its innermost selfhood. The question then deserves to be raised: why is it that only a radical theocentrism would respond to the requirements of authentic dialogue? It seems to me that a deepening of Christology would open up more fruitful ways that respect at the same time the requirements of a true pluralism and those of Christian identity. Without ending in a ruinous dissociation between the eternal Word and the incarnate Word, in other words, between the "cosmic" Christ and the "historic" Christ, it allows--in conformity with the vision of the Church Fathers--a consideration of the economy of the incarnate Word as something more vast, namely, the economy of the eternal Word, which coincides with the religions of all humanity. I will not go so far as to say, with Raimundo Panikkar, that the historical Jesus does not exhaust the Christ-Logos--as Cardinal Tomko has remarked, this dissociation risks compromising the realism of the unity of the incarnate Word--but it seems to me legitimate and traditional to admit that the humanity of Jesus of Nazareth does not exhaust the mystery of Christ in his eternal preexistence, at once as divine and human.

In any case, in the encounter with the representatives of the non-Christian religions, our principal concern must always be to show clearly that one does not confuse the universality of the right of Christ as Word made flesh with the universality of Christianity as a historical religion. We must guard against making Christianity an absolute religion that includes all that is good in the other religions. Neither historical Christianity nor the Church that people see is absolute. The only absolute is the "Reign," of which Jesus Christ is at the same time both the messenger and the future. It would be traitorous to the Christian faith inherited from the apostles to make of Christ one mediator among others of the Absolute.

Finally, to live the faith in the age of interreligious dialogue teaches us to think of the absolute to which we lay claim as a relational absolute and not as an absolute of exclusion or inclusion. We can, without compromising the absolute engagement inherent in all true religious faith, consider Christianity as a relative reality, but not in the sense in which relative is opposed to absolute; rather, in a relational sense that resembles the possible locus of a mutual agreement among religions. The truth that Christianity witnesses to is neither exclusive nor inclusive of all other truth: it is relative to that which is true in the other religions. Accepting the designation of the uniqueness of Christianity as a relative uniqueness, not as a uniqueness of excellence and integration, does not compromise its singularity among the religions of the world. Faith demands an absolute engagement of all believers, but there is a limiting principle that is immanent in faith itself and that must lead us to a "cordial recognition of otherness" (St. Breton) in our dialogue with the faithful of other religious traditions. I do not see how this acceptance of the relativism of Christianity as a historical religion--that is to say, our effort to purify our vision of Christianity of its connotations of excellence and integration--could lead us to sacrifice the Christian difference. On the contrary, our reading of the inescapable aspirations of human conscience calls on us to affirm with conviction the uniqueness of Christianity in the symphony of the religions of the world. In accord with its own genius, Christianity must be said to be incomparable with any other religion. It defines itself essentially in reference to the Gospel, that is to say, the good news of a liberation, not from sin only but from all religious codes, whether prescriptive or ritual, that would lay claim to being acceptable to God.

In insisting on this uniqueness of the Christian religion, I obviously affirm the uniqueness of the mediation of Christ. I likewise maintain the necessity of the Church as "sacrament of salvation" for all the nations. At the same time, there is a large theological consensus in favor of acknowledging that the Church as historical reality does not have a monopoly on the signs of the "Reign" and the means of salvation. Especially since the Second Vatican Council, we are often reminded that the means necessary for salvation are promised to people beyond the visible borders of the Church, that it is, moreover, possible to forfeit salvation within the Church. "Even if a person is incorporated into the Church, that person is not saved who fails to persevere in love, remaining in the midst of the Church, 'as of its body' but not 'as of its heart'" (Lumen gentium, no. 14). At issue is a traditional teaching Cardinal Tomko never dreams of raising. Many of the questions formulated at the end of his conference, however, betray the fear that the current insistence of many theologians on the demand for interreligious dialogue diminishes the urgency of the explicit mission of the Church. It is, however, commonly admitted, arising even in the document of the former Secretariat for Non-Christians, that dialogue is not only a preamble to but also an authentic form of mission. An obvious condition of this is that dialogue never be separated from or opposed to the other essential form of mission, which is proclamation. We read, for example, in the document Dialogue and Mission, published in 1984 on the twentieth anniversary of the Secretariat: "In the Church's consciousness mission appears as something unitary but with complex and interconnected elements: presence, witness, involvement in the service of people, liturgical life, dialogue, preaching, and catechesis" (DM, no. 13).

Mission as explicit witness given to Jesus Christ, therefore, loses nothing of its urgency if it is not concentrated on the conversion of the non-Christian at all cost. Often we find ourselves in situations of fact where explicit witness to the Gospel is not possible. At that point, mission as incarnation of the Gospel in time preserves its meaning. In fact, silent witness--through adoration, association with the lowliest, the practice of the beatitudes, and recognition of the seeds of truth and goodness that can exist within the members of other religions--continues to exercise the Church's proper mission as sacrament of the "Reign."

4. CRITERIA FOR AN INTERRELIGIOUS ECUMENISM

Absurd as it would be, under the pretext of openness, to decree that all religions are equally valid, so would it be contrary to the rules of dialogue to presume to establish a hierarchical principle of religions that begins with Christianity identified as the absolute religion. The question remains, nonetheless, how to seek a plane of understanding built on common bases and criteria that permit the speakers to make progress in their very divergences.

The chief key of Christian ecumenism, knowing <u>how to seek unity in diversity</u>, is a fruitful principle that can be extended to what some do not hesitate to call a "global ecumenism." I certainly mean to guard myself against mixing confessional ecumenism and interreligious ecumenism. The situations are at most analogous. In the former, each church can question the pretensions of the other churches to being absolute, but all are agreed on the absoluteness of Christ. In the case of interreligious ecumenism, other religions call into question not only the pretensions to absoluteness of Christianity but also the very absoluteness of Christ. This is why dialogue between Christianity and other religious systems on the doctrinal level is so difficult.

While practicing total respect for differences, we cannot give up on the search for certain ecumenical criteria of convergence. Experience teaches that there is no general rule. We have to proceed case by case in exploring this or that religion. Thus, we must begin by focusing on the dialogue of the three monotheist religions, then move on to the much more extensive dialogue among the principal religions of the world, which the Assisi Conference symbolized superbly. Even if Christian monotheism, as trinitarian monotheism, is radically different from the other two monotheist religions, Christians share with Jews and Muslims a common heritage in matters of belief in "one God, living and subsisting, compassionate and all powerful, creator of heaven and earth, who has spoken to the human race." But, if we take the pains to recall that in the past the monotheist religions have been more intolerant among themselves and with regard to the other two than with the great "pagan" religions, we cannot pretend that belief in a personal God is a criterion that automatically favors interreligious dialogue.

We go deeper, no doubt, by invoking the anthropology of homo religiosus (Mircéa Eliade) to which all authentic religions testify. Each religion aspires to be an inquiry into ultimate Reality, whether this Reality be recognized as a personal God or not. In every religion we can distinguish a fundamental faith (see Tillich's ultimate concern) and then a collection of beliefs that bear on particular truths and on the rules of life. The ultimate Reality can be the personal God of the biblical tradition, the transcendent Absolute of Hinduism, a hidden force in things (Brahman) that coincides with the hidden force in me (Atman), or even Nothingness as in Buddhism. It is in their fundamental faith that the different religions resemble each other, and it is in their beliefs that they are distinguished from each other, even confront each other because of fundamental disagreements.

Finally, if it is true that each religion has its own criteria of truth (divine revelation, sacred texts, myths, etc.), which are not necessarily accepted by other religious traditions, it must be possible to come up with a basic ecumenical criterion of the ethical order that coincides with what is genuinely human, of a kind acknowledged by universal human consciousness.

Whatever the plurality of ethical systems, the global human community shares a certain number of "convictions in depth" that are made the object of juridical codification, such as the "Human Rights." At the end of the twentieth century, more than forty years after the Universal Declaration of Human Rights of 1948 (United Nations), it does not seem excessive to affirm that all religions, which under one aspect or another are inhuman, are under sentence of either self-transformation or death. And, we spell out a minimum of negative criteria for determining whether a religion, by its rites, its institutions, its dogmas, and its ethics, violates the dignity of human persons and contradicts the quite legitimate aspirations of human conscience.

4. BEYOND DIALOGUE

There are several forms of dialogue. There is, first of all, the silent dialogue of prayer where each religious tradition makes an appeal to its own resources deriving from its spiritual experience. In this matter, the Assisi Conference was the first expression of what could be a global ecumenism of the world's religions. Prayer is a universal language, more universal even than belief in a personal God. Next, there is dialogue concerning the contribution of each religion to constructing a better world and building world peace. This sort of dialogue is effective in many areas of the world and is the objective of the World Conference on Religion and Peace. The third is ecumenical in the proper sense; even if it is the most difficult form of dialogue, it is necessary to reach out toward it. In it, each religion presents to the others its particular beliefs and deepest spiritual experiences. Only such a dialogue can help us overcome the centuries of ignorance and prejudice regarding other religions. At the same time, this dialogue invites us to discern better the originality of the message we confess and believe in, and it stimulates us to a renewed search for the God beyond God--that is to say, of the inadequate representations within which we enclose God.

Thus, dialogue as examination of truth leads us to a reciprocal conversion. In the experience of dialogue, I can discover that I do not prove, either intellectually or existentially, the truth that I claim for myself. Conversely, my partner in dialogue can come to another insight into the religious truth to which she or he witnesses. There is no authentic dialogue without personal communion or without a common celebration of a truth that transcends them. This is why a dialogue between members of different religions generally leads beyond dialogue, to a mutual transformation of the religions that meet. The American theologian John B. Cobb, Jr., has demonstrated this in an exemplary way with regard to the dialogue between Christian and Buddhist: "A Christianity which has been transformed by the incorporation of the Buddhist insight into the nature of reality will be a very different Christianity from any we now know. A Buddhism that has incorporated Jesus Christ will be a very different Buddhism from any we now know."[1]

The dialogue among the three monotheistic religions is already well under way, and we cannot know in advance the fruitfulness of such exchanges for the new understanding each religion has of its own tradition. Must we go so far as to speak of a mysterious complementarity of the three Abrahamic traditions in expectation of the "Reign" of God? We know in any case that the historical encounter between Israel and the Church is as decisive a theme for Christian theology as for Jewish. On the other hand, we have not finished verifying how much the critical challenge of the intransigent monotheism of Islam invites us to a better understanding of the

---

[1] *Beyond Dialogue: Toward a Mutual Transformation of Christianity and Buddhism* (Philadelphia: Fortress Press, 1982), p. 52.

fundamental dogmas of the Incarnation and of the Trinity. However, inversely, I have often ascertained among Muslim friends how much our Christian understanding of the Bible as the word of God may directly challenge a certain qur'anic fundamentalism.

In our relations with the major religions of the East, we must be ready for a longer journey, serving our apprenticeship, even a departure from our own context, before announcing prematurely any convergence. In comparison with religions that are religions of the One, and of nondistinction between ultimate Reality and the reality of the self and the world, it is incontestable that the biblical revelation testifies to some things radically new, as to decisive characteristics of the divine image, to the relation of God and humanity, and to the privileged relation between God and history. At the same time, we must not forget that at the center of the monotheist religions, especially of the Christian tradition, there has always been a strain at once mystical and theological that seeks to go beyond what is overly anthropomorphic in the dialogic relation of a created "I" and a divine "Thou." Prayer, in its freest and most spontaneous expression, testifies to a unity in origin more radical than the external relations between the creator God and the created self. Meister Eckart is the boldest and at the same time the profoundest witness to this ultimate quest into the human interior. In his words, "If I were not, God would no longer be." His words have to do with the spiritual person's becoming free of all the things that comprise God for us, as is suggested by the title of his famous sermon, "Why must we rid ourselves even of God?"

This emancipation even from God of which the Rhenish Master speaks puts us on the road to a theme that presses to its logical extreme that of utter gratuity. It is the theme of <u>death</u> as the expression of the excess of love. At issue is a theme altogether essential to Christianity as a religion of the paschal mystery. In fact, though, and this will be the provisional conclusion to this brief reflection on interreligious dialogue, Christian uniqueness has universal import. The religious person does not encounter in silent meditation the final Reality of the universe without passing through death. Speaking of the paschal dimension of prayer as the expression of the most radical gratuity of love refers us back, it seems to me, to a fundamental anthropological datum underlying all spiritual experience, whatever be the infinite diversity of its modalities in the world's different religions. Prayer attests that people do not define themselves solely by their need and their fulfillment of that need. They also define themselves by longing and the transcendence of longing--the quest, in other words, of the Ultimate.[2]

Translated from the French by
Jack Nelson, Temple University

---

[2] On this particularly complex subject of the encounter between religions, let me list a number of my previous works that can shed light on my current thinking:

"Le coran, une parole de dieu différente? *Lumière et Vie*, vol. 32, no. 163 (July-August, 1983), pp. 21-32.

"La théologie des religions non chrétiennes vingt ans après Vatican II," *Islamo-Christiana*, vol. 11 (1985), pp. 115-133.

"La mission de l'Eglise à l'âge de l'oecuménisme interreligieux," *Spiritus* (February, 1987), pp. 3-10.

"Mission et inculturation," *Spiritus* (December, 1987), pp. 406-427.

"Pluralisme religieux et absolu de l'Evangil," *Jésus*, no. 59 (December, 1988), pp. 19-22.

MISSIONARY ACTIVITY REVISED AND REAFFIRMED

Paul F. Knitter

The theological community owes Cardinal Jozef Tomko a great debt of gratitude. In the questions he has raised, and in the manner in which he has raised them, he offers both a challenge and an example to all those committed to the task of aiding the Christian communities to live the Gospel in a manner that will both speak to "the signs of the times" and be faithful to the original message. While Cardinal Tomko did not impose his authority on the theological discussion about the Church's missionary activity and other religions, he did speak with clarity and with impassioned concern about issues that must be addressed by theologians. He has not just called for theological conversation but has given that conversation both import and direction. I am happy and honored to respond to his call and to converse with him.

I understand Cardinal Tomko's central questions and concerns to be the following: new theological models for understanding other religions and the Church's mission have led to: a) a lessening of missionary motivation and commitment to the cause of Jesus Christ, and b) a reduction (I counted the world "reduce" or "reduction" six times in the Cardinal's address) of missionary activity to either the promotion of human well-being or to dialogue with other religions. These dangers result especially from the theological models which call themselves "soteriocentric" and "pluralistic"--that is, which a) propose soteria or the Basileia tou Theou as the primary purpose of the

Church's mission and the basis for dialogue and which b) see Jesus Christ as "together with," rather than "within or above" the other religions and thus do not insist on the finality or exclusive normativity of Christian revelation over all other religions.

In what follows I hope to respond to Cardinal Tomko by showing that these pluralistic and salvation-centered models, if properly understood (and that means, if explained more clearly than their proponents have done), lead not only to a revision but to a reaffirmation of missionary activity. I hope to make clear my own conviction that the Cardinal's concerns to maintain commitment to Christ and to announce the Gospel and plant the Church are not only respected but affirmed and strengthened by the new pluralist views of Christ and other religions. In other words, if there had indeed been a movement in Christian theology of religions from ecclesiocentrism to Christocentrism to theocentrism, and now to soteriocentrism, this growth has not been an Ablehnung (denial) of what went before, but rather an Aufhebung (a sublation). The meaning of the Church is not lost in Christocentrism, but clarified and reaffirmed. In the theocentric model, the role of Christ is not watered down or minimized but understood differently and reappropriated. In the soteriocentric approach, God is not reduced to humanity but affirmed as the very condition for the possibility of saving humanity.

I will try to make this clear by showing first how the motivation for and then the purpose of missionary activity is reaffirmed in a pluralist-soteriocentric theology of religions and mission. In doing this, I hope to clarify what may be certain misunderstandings of this theology on the part of the Cardinal and others.

I. MOTIVATION FOR MISSION

In this first section, I will be responding to Cardinal Tomko's christo-logical concerns that the new recognition of the validity and saving power of other religions and religious figures has jeopardized or diluted the validity and saving power of Jesus Christ. We can approach this issue in two ways: theological-Christological and personal-existential.

1. **Theological-christological:** Contrary to wide-spread misunderstand-ings, while the new pluralist views of other religions do not insist that Jesus the Christ is absolute and final, most of them do continue to hold that he is <u>universal</u> and <u>decisive</u>. Or, in the terms of a recent study, though Christians may be hesitant to say that Jesus is <u>unsurpassable</u>, they can and must continue to affirm him as <u>indispensable</u>.[1] In other words, the pluralist-soteriocentric model is in no way saying that Jesus is savior "just for me" or "just for Christians or Westerners." Nor is it suggesting that Buddha is just as good as, or the same as, Jesus. Such relativistic pap is the death-knell of both personal religious commitment and interreligious dialogue and is recognized as such by most theologians. In this new model, therefore, both the <u>uniqueness</u> and the <u>universality</u> of Jesus and his Gospel are maintained. There is no other like him. His message is meant for all time and can make a difference, a vital difference, for all peoples.

Edward Schillebeeckx elaborates such a position in a recent essay in which he seeks to confront more honestly the reality of religious pluralism; in doing so, he seems to move beyond his previous understanding of the uniqueness of Jesus. On the one hand, he staunchly affirms that universality is essential to the Christian witness of Jesus; if this is lost, so is the Gospel and Christian identity. Yet Schillebeeckx also insists that universality does

---

[1] Richard Viladesau, *Answering for Faith: Christ and the Human Search for Salvation* (New York: Paulist Press, 1987), pp. 242-45.

not mean absoluteness or superiority over all other expressions of truth. In other words, the Christian conviction that Jesus offers "the definitive and decisive revelation of God" does not necessarily mean that "that revelation then is normative for other religions." So he bemoans the historical and present-day fact that "a proper claim to universality was twisted imperialistically into an ecclesiastical claim of absoluteness." Signaling his own pluralist turn, he then rejoices that "At the moment, Christianity is not dropping its claim to universality, but is letting go both its exclusivist and inclusivist claim to universality." According to Schillebeeckx, therefore, missionaries can maintain the universality and uniqueness of Jesus, without, however, insisting that Jesus is the norm that must exclude or include (i.e., fulfill or subordinate) all other religious truths.[2]

The missionary will therefore proclaim the universality of Jesus without proclaiming his superiority. With such a Christology, one is still utterly committed to announcing this universality to the ends of the earth. But at the same time, one is open to the possibility/probability that as one explores the ends of the earth, one may well find other universal messages--other revelations or religious figures who also have a unique and universal message that might lead Christians to a fuller grasp of God's inexhaustible truth. A pluralist missioner, therefore, can affirm what might be called a "complementary uniqueness" for Jesus. Jesus' uniqueness, universal and indispensable as it is, can be complemented, enhanced, yes "fulfilled" in other unique revealers. Such missionaries are confirmed both in their full commitment to the particularity of Jesus and at the same time to the universal God who is ever greater than Jesus. And, as we shall see in a

---

[2] "The Religious and the Human Ecumene," in *The Future of Liberation Theology: Essays in Honor of Gustavo Gutiérrez*, Marc H. Ellis and Otto Maduro, eds. (Maryknoll, NY: Orbis Books, 1989), pp. 179-180, 182.

moment, this makes missionary activity a matter of both proclaiming and listening.

2. **Personal-existential:** The implications of such a pluralist Christology for a personal missionary spirituality are important for correcting what have been certain excesses in a pluralist theology of religions. Because Jesus remains unique, universal, decisive, and indispensable, missionaries remains "absolutely" and "fully" committed to him in their spiritual lives. For such missionaries, there is indeed "no other name" like that of Jesus, even though there may be other names that claim their attention and admiration and response. If I may resort to the analogy of marriage: while the commitment one had to one's spouse does not prevent one from appreciating and enjoying the company and friendship of other persons, the marriage commitment remains unique, special, focal, and in a certain sense, exclusive (especially in the sexual expression of the relationship).[3] A   s Harvey Cox has pointed out in his recent book <u>Many Mansions,</u> not all of the new pluralist approaches to other religions have properly maintained the unique role that Jesus plays in Christian commitment <u>and</u> witness. Cox, in other words, would endorse many of Cardinal Tomko's concerns. As Cox peruses the pluralist literature, he finds that the pluralists, in so stressing the universal, have too often lost touch with the particular. He calls it a "soft-pedaling [of] the figure of Jesus himself," which has led to "the loss of the personal voice" in Christianity's encounter with other believers. Christian pluralists are no longer speaking sufficiently from their own commitments

---

[3] See Paul Knitter, *No Other Name?* (Maryknoll, NY: Orbis Books, 1987), p. 185. In this regard, Schillebeeckx in the essay quoted above has, I fear, misunderstood the way I used the analogy of marriage to understand the meaning of the New Testament affirmations of Jesus as "one and only." I did not mean to suggest that just as my spouse is the one and only "for me," Jesus is God's truth only "for me." Rather, I was trying to point to the possibility or necessity that one can have a unique and special relationship and commitment to one person without removing the possibility of learning from the beauty, truth, and goodness of others.

and passions; and that means that they are soft-pedaling an essential aspect of dialogue--the need to <u>denounce</u> as well as announce, to disagree and oppose as well as to embrace and share. Hence, Cox urges his fellow pluralists not to forget that after Jesus announced that there are "many mansions" in his Father's kingdom, he immediately added that he was "the Way" to those mansions. (John 14: 2, 6) All authentic Christian dialogue must maintain this paradoxical balance between the universality of "many mansions" and the particularity of Jesus as the Way, Truth, and Life, for" without the radical particularity of the original revelation, we would have no faith to share."[4]

Christians who endorse a pluralist-soteriocentric view of other religions can, and should, maintain this balance and preserve the "radical particularity" of Jesus Christ, in both their own spirituality and in their witness to others. This will require of them, I suspect, an even deeper and more demanding faith than in the past. The "paradoxical balance" between universality and particularity calls for an <u>absolute</u> commitment to truth which one realizes, at the same time, is always <u>partial</u> and relative. To balance <u>particularity</u> and <u>universality</u> therefore means that Christians must also balance <u>absoluteness</u> and <u>relativity</u>: on the basis of their experience of the truth and power of the particular Jesus, missioners are totally committed to this Gospel, ready to go forth and sacrifice all for it; at the same time, because this Gospel has made known to them the universality of God's love and presence, they will realize that what they are totally committed to is only a part of this divine fullness. Faith, therefore, remains a matter of <u>absolute commitment</u> but it is no longer a matter of <u>absolute security</u>; a

---

[4] Harvey Cox, *Many Mansions: A Christian's Encounter with Other Faiths* (Boston: Beacon Press, 1988), chapter 1.

missionary can confidently say "Scio in cui credidi" (I know in whom I am trusting), but s/he cannot say just where that trust will lead. (2 Tim 1:12)

So faith is the paradoxical living out of absolute commitment to relative truth. Or, in terms of dialogue and mission, it is, as John Macquarrie has put it, a matter of full commitment to Jesus Christ and at the same time a genuine openness to others.[5] Just what this means, or just how this is done--that is, how to combine absolute commitment with the realization that one's "truth" or one's "savior" is relative and not final or absolute--this is one of the greatest challenges facing the Church in a pluralistic age. As Langdon Gilkey has said, it is a challenge that will first have to be lived out in praxis before we can properly reflect on and understand it in theology.[6]

II. PURPOSE OF MISSIONARY ACTIVITY

1. In trying to clarify how a pluralist-soteriocentric theology/missiology reaffirms the purpose of missionary activity, I shall try to respond to Cardinal Tomko's concerns that these new perspectives reduce mission to either "an ambiguous earthly 'well-being'" or to a conversational exchange with other believers. Such a reduction, I want to strongly maintain, is not at all a necessary result, or even a likely danger, of what I take to be an essential ingredient in post-Vatican II Roman Catholic ecclesiology--namely, the new understanding of the relationship between Church and God's Reign.

Most ecclesiologists today maintain that there is a difference, though an essential bond, between the Church and the Reign of God, that the Church is not to be identified with the Reign of God, that the Reign is

---

[5] John Macquarrie, *Principles of Christian Theology* (London: SCM Press, 1966), pp. 155-58.

[6] Langdon Gilkey, "Plurality and Its Theological Implications," in *The Myth of Christian Uniqueness*, pp. 37-50.

larger and, yes, "more important" than the Church. The Church, therefore, lives out its true nature when it is Reign-centered, not self-centered. To question this difference-yet-relatedness between Reign and Church is not only to place oneself outside of Roman Catholic and Protestant thinking, it is also, willy-nilly, to open the door to the idolatry of identifying the Church with the Reign of God.

But let me address the Cardinal's concerns more directly: to say that the Reign of God is "more important" than the Church, or that the primary purpose of missionary work is the Reign of God not the Church, or that "the center of the approach [of the theology of evangelization] moves from the Church to the Reign"[7] does not mean that the Church is unimportant, or that "primary" means "only," or that if the Church is no longer in the center it is outside the circle.

Michael Amaladoss clarifies what his "Copernican revolution" in mission theology entails: "It [the Church] is called to a twofold service; one is to witness to the Kingdom and to promote its realisation in the world; another is to proclaim Jesus and to build up a community of disciples. The second is a means of serving the first."[8] So in order to promote the Reign of God, missionaries must be about many things, such as planting the ecclesia, establishing the community, proclaiming the Word, dialoguing with other faith communities. All of these tasks, it must be said, are essential to the purpose of mission. But in insisting that they are essential, we recognize that they are subordinate to the primary, focal goal of working for the Reign of God. They are essential means to the primary end. Thus the distinction and the subordination between Reign of God and Church does not make for a separation; on the contrary, the relationship between the two is one of

---

[7] Michael Amaladoss, as quoted by Tomko (Original: p. 547)

[8] "Faith Meets Faith," *Vidyajyoti*, March, 1985, p. 112.

dipolar unity: each calls to the other. The Church needs the Reign of God for its identity, and the Reign needs the Church for its realization. (Of course, it needs other things besides the Church as well.)

And though the Reign of God, as preached by Jesus the Nazarean, represents a reality that will always be beyond our comprehension, we can be sure of one of its essential characteristics. On the basis of his extensive study of the New Testament witness and of recent New Testament exegesis, Edward Schillebeeckx concludes that when we say that the purpose of Jesus' preaching was the Reign of God, we mean that Jesus' primary concern was "the well-being of humankind."[9] Gloria Dei vivens homo--the glory of God is the well-being of God's creatures (Iraeneus). Thus, in Jon Sobrino's more biblical terms, the Reign of God means life--God's intent that there be life, that all peoples (and we can add, all creatures) may have life and have it more abundantly.[10] So although the Reign of God cannot be "reduced" to earthy well-being, it must include, or strive for, such well-being. Otherwise it is not the Reign preached by Jesus.

If the well-being of humanity is to be promoted, if there is to be ever more abundant life, clearly this world must be changed, for as is painfully evident, so many of the practices and structures of nations and of the international community are death-dealing, rather than life-giving, for millions of people. The well-being of humanity and of the earth demands "social transformation," "development," "political liberation," yes, in some instances, "revolution." But again, as Cardinal Tomko reminds us, this is not enough. What is also needed is internal, spiritual transformation. While it is not sufficient to change individual human hearts in order that the Reign of well-

---

[9] Edward Schillebeeckx, *Christ* (New York: Seabury Press, 1980), Part 4.

[10] Jon Sobrino, *The True Church and the Poor* (Maryknoll, NY: Orbis Books, 1984), idem, *Spirituality of Liberation: Toward a Political Holiness* (Maryknoll, NY: Orbis Books, 1987).

being be realized, still, unless hearts <u>are</u> changed and unless people recognize and experience a power of transformation which is as much beyond them as within them and without which they cannot create new structures of justice and love--unless such internal conversion takes place, we build the Reign of God on foundations of sand.

The Reign of God therefore might be defined as the utopian vision of a society of love, justice, equality, based on an inner transformation of humans. It is a society in which people will <u>act</u> and <u>live together</u> differently because they will <u>be</u> and <u>feel</u> themselves differently. Such a Reign is both socio-political and spiritual. Its realization demands both "development" and "evangelization." Again, we are speaking about a dipolar unity between these different dimensions.

2. If the Reign of God is the focus of missionary activity, what does this mean for our understanding of other religions? What is the relation between the Reign of God and the religions of the world? For both <u>theological</u> and <u>phenomenological</u> reasons, we can say that other religious traditions of the world can and should be considered possible "agents" of what Christians call the Reign of God.

Theologically, when post-Vatican II Catholic theology announces that the religions are <u>viae salutis</u> (ways of salvation), this means that they are <u>viae regni</u> (ways of the Reign). Anyone who accepts Karl Rahner's persuasive argument that God's salvific will and saving grace operate, not despite, but because of the religions, not outside but within their beliefs and practices, will recognize--perhaps more clearly today than Rahner did in the 1960s--that grace is a force that transforms not only the heart but society. Grace is present in its full potency only when it is creating a new world of love and justice out of the present world of injustice and oppression. Therefore, wherever there is grace, there is the borning of the Reign of

God. If Christians are to look upon other religions as vehicles of grace, they must also consider them as co-workers for the Reign. This, of course, is not to deny the all too evident and ugly reality that the religions of the world often have been and still are obstacles to the well-being of humanity; they have served as opium for the oppressed or as ideological tools for the oppressors. But this is as true of Christianity as of other faiths. To recognize the reality of sin is not to cancel the possibility of grace. As Augustine argued against the Donatists, grace can also flow through sinful conduits. The Reign of God can be built with imperfect instruments. Like the Christian Church, the religions of the world can be simul justus et peccator, both sinful and justified, both impediment to and instrument of the Reign of God.

Phenomenologically, I think a case can be made that the basic vision and teachings and utopian dreams of the religions of the world have an immense potential for helping to "build a new humanity" and for inspiring and directing persons in the daunting task of working for peace, justice, and ecological sustainability.[11] As Cardinal Tomko has correctly observed: "In one form or another, salvation is considered a central theme in all the great religions of the world." Today we see that there are movements within all the major religions of the world to express this central theme in terms of earthly well-being; growing numbers of believers throughout the world are responding to the "common human experience" and "common threats" of our times: the reality of oppression and suffering and the need for liberation. The confrontation with so much suffering and injustice that had given rise to the theology of liberation within Christianity is having similar effects in other traditions. Ordinary believers and religious leaders are reexamining

---

[11] See *Education for Peace: Testimonies from World Religions* (Maryknoll, NY: Orbis Books, 1987); Denise Lardner and John Tully Carmody, *Peace and Justice in the Scriptures of the World Religions* (New York: Paulist Press, 1988).

their traditions and sacred scriptures and are performing what Christian theologians call a "hermeneutics of suspicion," by which they lay bare the ideological and oppressive abuse of their religion, and then a "hermeneutics of retrieval" by which they seek to rediscover and reactivate the liberative content of their scriptures and central beliefs. Such this-worldly, liberative revision is taking place especially within Hinduism, Buddhism, and Islam.[12]

Christian missionaries and liberation theologians are recognizing, ever more clearly, the importance of this "liberative potential" in other faiths and are realizing that other believers can offer new ways of understanding and effecting what Christians call the Reign of God. Asian theologians are reminding their Latin American colleagues that if there is going to be a world-wide liberation and renewal of humanity, it will have to be the work of many different religions; it will have to be the fruit of a world-wide dialogue and cooperative effort among all the religions. Building the Reign of God is too big a job for any one religion. Such is the growing awareness and challenge emanating from spokespersons for the Asian Churches such as Aloysius Pieris, Michael Amaladoss, Samuel Ryan, Stanley Samartha, Felix Wilfred, Ruben Habito, Tissa Balasuriya, and the recently assassinated Michael Rodribo.

This refocused view of other religions as instruments of the Reign of God means therefore that though missionary work can never be "reduced" to interreligious dialogue, it must include such dialogue as part of its essential task. More explicitly, though there is a clear difference between evangelization/witnessing and dialogue, there is no contradiction between them; indeed, they need each other. In a pluralistic-soteriocentric understanding of Church and other religions, missionaries experience the

---

[12] See *Religions for Human Dignity and World Peace* (Proceedings of the Fourth World Conference on Religion and Peace--WCRP), John B. Taylor and Günther Gebhardt, eds. (Geneva: WCRP, 1986) and other publications of the WCRP.

Divine Word in Jesus to be a focal part of a larger, liberating conversation of God with humanity; they recognize, therefore, that they cannot really speak the Word of God in Jesus unless they do so in conversation with the Word of God in other mediations. Especially according to Roman Catholic tradition, the Word of God in Jesus is in basic (that doesn't mean total) continuity with the Word of God throughout creation. Only if this continuity is recognized and sought after can this Word be truly heard. Thus, both to understand the Divine Word in Jesus and to make it understood to others, missioners must listen to and understand this Word in the words of others.

Recognizing that dialogue is an essential part of evangelization, the Thirteenth General Chapter of the Society of the Divine Word prophetically announced that "dialogue is at the core of the missionary activity of our Society."[13] Only if dialogue and evangelization are joined together in a holy--though sometimes tense--marriage can either bear fruit. Alone they languish.

3. But a final concern of Cardinal Tomko must be raised: with the Reign of God as the primary purpose of missionary activity, how do we handle the question of conversions? Does building the Reign of God include working for converts? In the Cardinals words: "Must mission forego planting the Church as one of its goals?" Or even more trenchantly: "Can it still be said that it [the Church] is necessary for salvation?"

From the perspective of a pluralist-soteriocentric theology, missioners can clearly affirm that yes, conversions are important--conversions not just to the Reign of God but to the Christian community! Because they are convinced, as disciples of Jesus Christ, that the Reign of God or the well-being of humanity requires that the vision and the empowerment of Jesus

---

[13] *Following the Word* #1, August 1988 (Rome: Generalate of the Society of the Divine Word), p. 17.

and his Spirit become part of the human project, missioners will preach the Gospel. And that means they will seek to establish communities of Gospel-followers and preachers. In this sense, then, one can say that the "Church is necessary for salvation": the Christian community must make its necessary, its universally meaningful, contribution to the task of building God's Reign. Where this contribution is lacking, the formation of the Reign of God will be, in Christian convictions, incomplete, and so the missioner will be eager to increase the numbers of those how are committed to making the Christian vision of the Reign of God known to their neighbors, both across the street or across the seas. Conversions to the Christian community are not just welcomed, they are sought after.

But in stating this, and in trying to realize it in their ministries, soteriocentric missionaries will also "keep their priorities straight." Such conversions are not an end in themselves, but, rather, a means to the primary end of serving the Reign of God. There are other means for attaining this primary end. If through their preaching and example, the values of the Gospel are understood and assimilated into a different culture or a different religion, then the missioner is achieving the purpose of being sent--even if this does not result in conversions to the Christian community.

This means that it is necessary to clarify and expand the traditional notion of conversion. The assimilation of Jesus' message by another religious community may result in conversions that are real but that do not make for new members of the Church. We are talking here about a genuine, but an "inner," conversion by which the Hindu, for instance, is really different, changed, transformed through her encounter with the Gospel and the Christian community; and yet she remains a Hindu--perhaps a different kind of Hindu, but still a Hindu. Such conversions are real. And they satisfy the purpose of missionary outreach. Examples of what we are talking about abound. Gandhi is perhaps the most notable instance of someone whose Hindu religious identity was deeply changed but at the same time confirmed by his encounter with the Gospel. A more recent example of such a "convert" might be the Zen Buddhist scholar Masao Abe, who has admitted how much his understanding of Buddhism has been affected by his encounter with Christians, especially in the area of the meaning of history and social ethics.[14]

But if conversion is still a valid and necessary goal of missionary activity, it becomes, in the soterio-centric model, a beneficial two-edged sword. The pluralist-soteriocentric missioner will also recognize that the purpose of mission is not only to bring about the conversion of the other but also the conversion of the missionary and of the Church. Missioners go forth to expand the Church not only through the increase of members but also through the increase of new truth, new cultural identity, new challenges within the Church. The Church, in other words, needs missionaries not just to change others but to change itself; without missionary activity the Church would not be able to carry out the vital principle of its well-being: ecclesia semper reformanda (the Church always in need of reform).

So in proclaiming the Good News, missionaries realize that others may have Good News to proclaim to them. And they know this not simply on the basis of some philosophical principle, but because of what they have discovered in Jesus Christ--that this God of Jesus, in God's love and wisdom, is always more than what they already know through Jesus; and because of Jesus they can search for and receive the truth wherever it may present itself. More concretely, because missioners are so committed to the Reign of God revealed in Jesus, they are ready to have their knowledge of the

---

[14] See Masao Abe and Paul Knitter, "Liberation and Spirituality: A Buddhist-Christian Conversation," *Horizons*, 15 (1988), pp. 347-64.

Reign clarified, perhaps corrected, through their encounters with others. The most effective missionaries are those who have been converted by their converts.

CONCLUSION

I sincerely believe that a more open, pluralistic, and "soteriocentric" dialogue with followers of other religions is in no way an impediment to missionary activity; on the contrary, it is a condition for the possibility and for the renewed vitality of our missionary efforts. Unless we Christians reach out to and dialogue with our fellow pilgrims on other paths in a shared effort to promote the well-being of our people and our planet, we will not be truly and adequately faithful to the present-day demands of our missionary vocation.

A LETTER FROM THE MISSION FIELD

(to Leonard Swidler)

Robert McCahill

Dear Leonard,

Greetings to you from Islampur, a section of Netrakona town in north-central Bangladesh. It is raining here as I begin this letter with the illuminating help of a hurricane lamp.

Some weeks ago you sent an invitation my way requesting that I read and comment on Cardinal Tomko's thought-provoking discourse at the International Congress of Missiology, entitled "Missionary Challenges To The Theory Of Salvation." When I received your invitation, a Bangladeshi major seminarian had just begun living with me in Netrakona for a period of exposure to mission among Muslims. It was not possible to find time to comply with your request during the six weeks of Prashanto's stay because we were busy with mission, service, reflection, prayer, and the chores of daily survival, e.g., shopping in the bazaar, drawing water at the well, going to the river to bathe, repairing our bamboo hut. Prashanto returned to the seminary this morning, and I am turning to the Cardinal's discourse.

At the end of his presentation, the Cardinal asks, "Does the fact that God operates with His grace also on non-Christians release the Church from the obligation of announcing the Gospel?" Briefly stated, I believe the obligation remains with as much urgency as it ever had, but that the interpretation we give to "announcing the Gospel" needs to be broadened.

That question is related in my mind to another question raised by missioners in another part of the world, namely: "If God saves non-Christians, if it is not necessary for one's eternal salvation that one enters the Church, then what is the future of mission? What are missioners to do?"

I cannot speak for all mission areas of the world because I have lived in only two of them during these past twenty-five years. However, based on that experience, and especially upon these past fourteen years in mission among Bangladeshi Muslims, I believe there is no diminishment of the need for missioners. But, their task does have a new focus, at least in this area of the world.

Why a new missionary focus? For one reason, because of the history of these people. The people of this Indian subcontinent were colonized by Englishmen during two hundred years, from the mid-18th century to the mid-20th century. The English were Christians. Until now, these terms are nearly synonymous in the Bangladeshi mind: Englishman, white man, colonist, foreigner, Christian. At present, Bangladesh has 110 million people, 85% Muslim, 14% Hindu, 7/10 of 1% Buddhist, and 3/10 of 1% Christian. Most of the adult population perceives, either through stories, dramatic presentations, education or literature, that the white Christian colonists abused their forebears and their homeland. They perceive that colonists subjected their ancestors, ruined the local economy, and treated this beautiful, rich, fertile Bengal area in a purely selfish way. They suspect that white folks are still colonists at heart, that they are abusive (e.g., liquor and sex), and that they despise the poor. They suspect that missioners come here to change the Islamic faith they love and convert them to a religion whose main benefit is material assistance.

How does a missioner announce the Gospel in such circumstances? One way is by simply trying to live according to the Good News he or she believes in. As the letter of assignment I have from my Bishop states it, there are five priorities for me to attend to in Netrakona. I am encouraged to: live among the poor as a brother to them; serve the sick so that they may live; show the respect which our Christian religion has for Islam and Hinduism; explain to those who inquire about the reason for my lifestyle and good works; contact the Christians in the area (a scattered few) and encourage them to lead good lives.

A missioner's task of announcing the Gospel should vary from place to place, i.e., what the missioner does and says. Here, for example, it won't do to proclaim to Muslims "Jesus Christ is God. Repent and believe in Him." Nobody is listening to that. (And if they are, I am told by those who have preached to them, it is in view of their expectation of material benefits. More on that, later.) After all, Muslims already have a clear idea of who Jesus is for them. Jesus is one of the very greatest of their prophets. They are not asking to hear who we Christians think Jesus is. However, they are indeed asking, insistently and intensely: "Who are you? What are you doing here? Why?" I reply: "I am your Christian brother. I am here as a servant of the sick-poor because Jesus came to serve and to heal. The answer to all your ways is simply: Jesus. That is, because Jesus went about healing, so do I. Because Jesus was celibate for the love of God, so am I. Jesus is the reason for the lifestyle you are wondering about, and for the good works you observe. God inspires me to follow Jesus. Jesus is my model."

"How much will you give me if I become a Christian?" is the blatant way Muslims ask me about joining the church. The question has a basis in fact. Some Christian denominations have and do use material benefits to entice Muslims and Hindus into the fold. Also, it sometimes happens that a Christian sect "raids" a village where another Christian denomination is already established in order to change their affliction. For example, the Seventh Day Adventists recently introduced themselves into a village 20 miles away from here where a Baptist community had lived unitedly for several decades. That village is now split. The Christians are inimical to one another. Non-Christians in the area view those Christians' disharmony with mild contempt. It is a source of mirth for them. Countless Muslims of this country could relate stories similar or even more unfortunate than this example.

That example describes a mission effort made by some non-Catholic Christians. What has it got to do with the activity of Catholic missioners? A great deal. In the minds of most Bangladeshi Muslims and Hindus, Christians of all sects and denominations are one. In their minds, Catholics, Baptists, Seventh Day Adventists, and others are one in their purpose. By association Catholics share a reputation. The reputation is that Christians buy followers. In that circumstance, a sensible mission method for a missioner to pursue towards persons who approach and inquire "What will I receive if I become a Christian?" is to treat it as a joke, chuckle with the inquirer, and then explain to him what Catholic Christians believe about other religions. That is, we respect them.

The Church since Vatican Council II projects a new attitude about non-Christians. One of the key statements reflecting that attitude is quoted in the Cardinal's paper: "Those also can attain to everlasting salvation who through no fault of their own do not know the Gospel of Christ or his

Church, yet sincerely seek God and, moved by grace, strive by their deeds to do His will as it is known to them through the dictates of conscience." (LG 16) Who will demonstrate this new Catholic Christian attitude towards Muslims, Hindus and others? In Bangladesh, missioners are the first persons who must exemplify this teaching of the Church towards people of other faiths. Why depend on missioners, and not on the faithful in general, to incarnate the new attitude? Because Muslims regard missioners as the official representatives of the Christian religion. They conclude that as the missioners behave, so their faith teaches. Thus, if missioners are primarily concerned with efforts to convert Muslims, it means that the Christian faith devalues Islam, has little respect for Islam, and is by dialogue merely trying to catch and transform believing Muslims into the foreign religion. But if the alleged new openness of Christians towards Muslims is sincere, then Muslims will be able to judge the truth of that by observing the missioners' lives and dealing with Muslims.

Cardinal Tomko's final question asks: "Does dialogue replace the announcement proclamation? Does the announcement eliminate dialogue? Or do both belong to the complex and rich reality of evangelization?" Both approaches, it seems to me, are authentic forms of evangelization. I believe that if in a certain place at a given time--for example in Netrakona during this year--dialogue is needed, then dialogue constitutes a proclamation. Dialogue in that instance proclaims concretely, by witness and example: I appreciate your faith. I am with you as a fellow-pilgrim on earth. I value your life, your culture, your religion.

However, in another place, the other approach could be more fitting. From what I've heard others say, Korea comes to mind.

The several biblical quotations in the Cardinal's discourse are apt encouragement for mission. Nevertheless, I believe that one text that is deeply relevant for mission today--as it is relevant to the whole of Christian living--has not been mentioned. "God is greater than our hearts" (1 John 3:20).

Missioners and other Christians who strive to pray, reflect, and live as Jesus lived can, in consultation with the local Church, decide on the form of evangelization that is needed in a particular place and time. We believe that God is at work among Christians and among our neighbors of other faiths. The divine plan is being fulfilled. Souls are not pelting into hell like monsoon raindrops because these people do not and probably never will profess the beliefs we hold dear. But God is greater than our hearts. We can rest assured that God's wonderful and surprising will is being accomplished. "Fear not" is another apropos reminder.

Most people, I've found, are pretty good. It has never made sense to me to speak of the condemnation of these good, non-Christian folks, especially those among them who are suffering so much, now. I am reminded of a meeting. Some months ago a letter was sent out to numerous Christians inviting them to a meeting whose theme would be "The Suffering Servant." Those invited were requested to submit the names of other persons sympathetic to the theme so that they also could be invited. One person submitted numerous names, names like Fatima, Ayesha, Hashina, Iasmin, Johura, Khaleda, etc. This missioner reasoned that there are no persons in Bangladesh who are more closely conformed to The Suffering Servant than are Muslim women. The 68,000 villages of this country are teeming with suffering servants. Is our Christian vision broad enough to encompass that fact?

One man's view of the Church's mission, cited in the Cardinal's paper, is that "The purpose of mission is not to make Christians, but to help people to become men." Similar to that is a statement I've heard here in

Bangladesh: "The purpose of mission is to make Muslims better Muslims." I cannot agree with either statement. It would make better sense to me to say that the aim of mission in this country is simply to build trust and friendship between followers of Jesus and followers of Mohammmed. (When I say "simply" I do not mean to imply that it is easy. Building trust in an environment of suspicion is not easy.) In fact, I did not come to Bangladesh to make others better people or better Muslims. The principal reason, rather, was that Christian faith moved me to come, to show love for the poor, to offer service to Muslims and Hindus, to be useful to them in their needs. In short, I was and still am inspired to live as a Christian among the Muslim poor in order to help my neighbor.

A missioner, having inserted him or herself into the environment of another faith, attempts to grow with the followers of that faith in mutual respect and love. The missioner is a sign of the unity of humankind.

Does the fact that Muslims suspect Christian missioners of having the intention of converting them affect the way missioners announce the Gospel? Yes, and rightly so. I believe it may be grace that inspires Muslims to question missioners about their motives for coming to them. I believe, further, that it is Good News when I tell Muslims: "We Christians believe that all people are equal in the eyes of God. We believe that Muslims must be good Muslims, Hindus must be good Hindus, Buddhists must be good Buddhists, and Christians must be good Christians. We believe that all persons can be saved by doing good according to the teachings of their own religions."

However, as important as it is to declare those truths openly, it is even more important for missioners and for all Christians to be and behave as Christians, that is, to live the Good News. Living the Gospel in a Muslim milieu is every bit as difficult as preaching it. Besides, an oral presentation can easily be misconstrued, e.g., "The missioner is just saying those things to attract you. Watch out; he wants to snare you." On the other hand, compassionate behavior, fraternal treatment, and selfless service are surer paths into the Bengali Muslim's heart. Such Christ-like behavior can also be misconstrued, but not as easily as things merely spoken. The impact of disinterested Christian love for the poor is, for Muslims, the most powerful statement of Christian faith imaginable.

In a critical context the Cardinal mentions the "programme of a missionary institute: 'We go to the missions not so much to plant the Church or to bring the faith, but rather to discover a faith and a goodness that already exists there.'" I think this is a good example of the misunderstanding that can easily arise when a missioner tries to say something significant about mission in just a few words. I can well imagine that the missioner-author of the quoted remark was not attempting to outline a program for missionary action, but rather to inspire a broader vision among Christians. The point he makes is important for anyone concerned about the Catholic Church in developed countries. His observation beckons Christians to an awareness of the spiritual riches present among persons of other faiths and places. It is a service to the Church whenever a missioner from the developed world attempts to impress upon his or her fellow Christians the enlightening fact that grace is found among peoples of all faiths, in the technologically backward and problem-beset developing countries as much as in the developed ones. One of the roles of this reverse mission is to expand the hearts and minds of the Christians who send missioners, so that the senders will appreciate truth, goodness, and spiritual beauty that is readily discoverable by their missioners in countries where good communications, sanitary toilets, and a host of other standard conveniences are scarce. Our fellow Christians, our sponsors, deserve to hear that. It can broaden their horizons. It can free their hearts to hear first hand evidence from the mission field that non-Christians are also good folks. You can trust them. You need not approach them defensively. We are all brothers and sisters.

Nowadays it is more urgent than ever to speak up about the goodness missioners find among followers of other faiths. Why? To use a current example, because of the recently departed Ayatollah Khomeini. In the view of some Christians, all Muslims are guilty of fanaticism by association with him. These Christians do not distinguish between the excessive Shiite Muslim leader and the huge majority of the world's eminently tolerant Sunni Muslims. (Why then should we Christians expect Muslims to differentiate between Christians belonging to various sects and denominations?) It is one of the duties of missioners to reach out to members of their own faith community, to help them resist negativism and to think well of other faith communities.

The rain has stopped. Someone just called at the door. I pushed it aside. The neighbor lady--mother of five children, she is the second of two living wives of Abdul Ali--presented me a plate of freshly prepared cakes. Gladly I received the unexpected sign of hospitality. Her husband watched approvingly from their doorway. It was a small thing, but more than enough to make me conscious of God's presence in others. Trust and friendship are growing. The increase of friendship and trust gives evidence that we are all growing in knowledge of the truth. (1 Tim 2:4) The truth of human oneness, long obscured by our pettiness and exclusivity, shines forth through persons of diverse faiths who are reaching out to one another.

> Fraternally,
>
> Bob McCahill 25 Feb., '90

INTERRELIGIOUS DIALOGUE, MISSION, AND THE CASE OF THE JEWS

Michael McGarry

1. INTRODUCTION

His Eminence Cardinal Jozef Tomko has done us all an enormous service by outlining carefully the contours of the contemporary conversation about mission. I believe that he has touched the heart of the discussion where he marks "the need for clarity in the missionary motivation of the Church and of the missionaries themselves." (my emphasis) The confusion which searches for "clarity" flows from the abandonment, I submit, of the traditional doctrine of "extra ecclesiam nulla salus." Cardinal Tomko gravely underestimates the power of Origen's and Cyprian's affirmation to motivate Christians to be missionaries. He claims "extra ecclesiam" was subject to a "rigid" interpretation. On the contrary, the affirmation says what it says. Everyone--not least of all, missionaries--knew what it meant. Only with mental and linguistic gymnastics can one avoid its obvious conclusion--those who are not baptized Roman Catholics will not go to heaven. For example, St. Francis Xavier did not shrink from using its harsh conclusion in preaching to the Chinese. Thousands of this millennium's missionaries courageously ventured to foreign lands precisely to save the pagans from the fate of eternal damnation--not an unworthy goal. If anything, this affirmation constituted the very bedrock of the Church's missionary motivation. And the missionaries carried with them the scriptural quotations which supported the "rigid" interpretation of "extra ecclesiam." As arcane as "extra ecclesiam nulla salus" may sound to contemporary eras, as recently as 1948 its strict reading had to be repudiated by Pius XII in his letter to Cardinal Cushing about Father Feeney.

In the post-Vatican II church, when one admits, and even rejoices in, Christ's bounteous salvation extending far beyond the Church's borders, it is clear that the "edge" for missionary motive has suffered severe dulling. Indeed, that is the very problematic addressed in Cardinal Tomko's talk and in his and others' efforts to shore up the foundation for mission with other theological buttresses. Today virtually no Catholic missionaries believe that upon their presence or absence rests the eternal fate of non-evangelized peoples. So the modern debate is enjoined with a question unthinkable only fifty years ago: "Why are we here?"

Let me mention two other brief points from Cardinal Tomko's address before I outline my primary contention. First, in parts of Cardinal Tomko's address, evangelization seems to be equated with proclamation and/or convert-making. In Evangelii nuntiandi, Pope Paul VI was more nuanced and variegated: evangelization is one part of mission, and proclaiming Christ (for the purpose of conversion) is one element of evangelization. Secondly, obedience to Christ is surely critical in every Christian's life. However, simply repeating the Great Commission (Matthew 28:19-20) without attention to historical-critical issues distorts the Catholic missionary exigence as much as simply repeating those scriptural quotations that indicate one will be eternally lost without explicit faith in Christ. We need to explore more deeply what "Go teach all nations" means, both in

terms of the content of what we teach and the beneficiary, "all nations."[1]
Both these points deserve more attention.

However, my primary concern with Cardinal Tomko's fine address is
more limited and focused. I fear that speaking of the "theological opinions
on non-Christian religions" in general obscures the more particular, indeed
unique, place which Judaism holds for the Church among world religions.
Certainly, Vatican II's decision to include its reflections on religious relations
of the Jews within the Declaration on Non-Christian Religions did not help
in this matter.[2] Understanding the Church's relationship with the Jewish
people simply as a subset of its relationship with other world religions
ignores, and therefore distorts, the covenantal uniqueness of Judaism.
Christians believe both that God has not abrogated the covenant with the
Jewish people and that God continues to hold them dear. These beliefs are
not comparable, or even analogous, to what can be affirmed about other
world religions.

---

[1] See Douglas R. A. Hare and Daniel Harrington, "'Make Disciples of all the
Gentiles' (Mt 28:19)," *Catholic Biblical Quarterly (CBQ)* 37 (1975):359-69, who
conclude "that *matheteusate panta ta ethne* [of Mt 28:19] means 'make disciples of all
the Gentiles' and that *panta ta ethne* does not include the nation of Israel . . . [Their]
position is that for Matthew the *ethne* and Israel are two distinct entities in salvation
history . . . Although the divine plan required that the gospel be preached first to the
Jews (10:5; cf. 15:24, 26), for Matthew the time for the mission to Israel as Israel is
over. See also, John P. Meier, "Nations or Gentiles in Matthew 28:19?" *CBQ* 39
(1977):94-102. Also, see the dialogue among Gerald Sloyan, Lewis John Eron,
Timothy Lincoln and Eugene Fisher in the *Journal of Ecumenical Studies (JES)*:
Gerald Sloyan, "Outreach to Gentiles and Jews: New Testament Reflections," *JES* 22
(Fall 1985): 764-69; Timothy Lincoln, "Outreach to Gentiles and Jews: Further New
Testament Reflections," *JES* 23 (Fall 1986): 667-70; Lewis John Eron, "Outreach to
Gentiles and Jews: A Jewish Reflection--A Response to Timothy Lincoln," *JES* 24
(Summer 1987):440-44; Timothy Lincoln, "Outreach to Jews and Jewish Christianity:
A Response to Lewis John Eron," *JES* 24 (Fall 1987):644-49; Eugene Fisher,
"Outreach to Gentiles: A Response to Timothy Lincoln's Response to Lewis John
Eron," *JES* 25 (Spring 1988):269-72; Timothy Lincoln, "Of Mount Sinai and Mount
Calvary: A Response to Eugene J. Fisher," *JES* 25 (Summer 1988): 445-48.

[2] On the placement of the Church's relation to the Jewish people in the Vatican
II documents, See John M. Oesterreicher, *The New Encounter between Christians and
Jews* (New York: Philosophical Library, 1986), 158ff.

2. CHRISTIAN MISSION AND THE JEWISH PEOPLE

Since the Vatican II, at least in some scholarly circles, many have been exploring the Church's missionary posture vis-à-vis the Jewish people similar to how others (as outlined by Cardinal Tomko) have sought clarity in the missionary motivation in general. Vatican II called Catholics to a new relation with their Jewish brothers and sisters, a neighborly dialogue. In that dialogue, Catholics have grown to appreciate anew their own roots and the rich spiritual development which the Jewish tradition has enjoyed since the Second Temple's destruction.[3] Indeed, the achievements of the modern Jewish-Catholic relationship are mind boggling, especially when viewed from the perspective of two thousand years of polemics, pogroms, and theological disdain.[4] Preliminary to the specific discussion, then, on mission and the Jewish people, let us review a few moments of Catholic missiology vis-à-vis the Jewish people. Then we will review contemporary achievements of Catholic-Jewish dialogue.

a) Missions and the Jewish People.

For the first few hundred years of our Common Era, relations between Christians and Jews ran the gamut from mock debate to attempts at forced conversions to regularly organized drives to separate and ghettoize the Jewish people. Often evangelization among the Jews took the form of baptisms by coercion as, for instance, in the early part of this millennium with the Jews of Spain. In France, rabbis were forced to take part in public

---

[3] See Hayim Goren Perelmuter, *Siblings: Rabbinic Judaism and Early Christianity at Their Beginnings* (New York: Paulist Press, 1989).

[4] See Edward H. Flannery, *The Anguish of the Jews: Twenty Three Centuries of Antisemitism* (New York: Paulist Press, Rev., 1985) and Marc Saperstein, *Moments of Crisis in Jewish-Christian Relations* (Philadelphia: Trinity Press, 1989).

disputations where they were facile in their arguments, but not <u>too</u> clever lest they embarrass or outmaneuver their Christian counterparts. In the early part of our century, in response to the Zionist Theodor Herzl, Pope Pius X stated, "The Jews have not recognized our Lord, therefore we cannot recognize the Jewish people. . . . And so, if you come to Palestine and settle your people there, we shall have churches and priests ready to baptize all of you."[5] Given even these snapshots of how Jews have endured Christian missionary efforts, one can understand why many of them see Christians only as people bent on converting them.

b) Vatican II's Invitation to Dialogue.

Over against this history of missionizing the Jewish people, Catholics have responded to Vatican II's call for dialogue with their Jewish brothers and sisters; they have begun to listen. They have learned not only facts and history, but also the feelings of their Jewish partners. A rabbinic tale is relevant here.

> "Master, you know that I love you."
> "Ah, yes," the master replied. "But first, tell me: What hurts me?"
> "Master, I know what pleases you. And I will do it, and you will know of my love."
> "My child, until you know what hurts me, you do not really love me."

Certainly two hurts Catholics have heard in the dialogue are the ways Christians have tried to convert Jews and how Jews have been traumatized

---

[5] Quoted in Conor Cruise O'Brien, *The Siege: The Saga of Israel and Zionism* (New York: Simon and Schuster, 1986), p. 104. See also Frederick M. Schweitzer, "The Nature of the Christian Mission: A Historical Inquiry," *Face to Face: An Interreligious Bulletin*, 3/4 (Fall/Winter 1977):3-6 and Eugene J. Fisher, "Historical Developments in the Theology of Christian Mission," in: Martin A. Cohen and Helga Croner, eds., *Christians Mission-Jewish Mission* (New York: Paulist Press, 1982), pp. 4-45, and my "Contemporary Roman Catholic Understandings of Mission," in the same volume, pp. 119-46.

by the Shoah. Hearing these two hurts, many Catholics resonate with Gregory Baum's observation:

> After Auschwitz the Christian churches no longer wish to convert the Jews. While they may not be sure of the theological grounds that dispense them from this mission, the churches have become aware that asking the Jews to become Christians is a spiritual way of blotting them out of existence and thus only reinforces the effects of the Holocaust.[6]

Many Christians, though, are beginning to retrieve and construct the "theological grounds that dispense them from this mission" to convert the Jews. They are beginning to see something more substantial and theologically coherent than simply a "gut feeling" to justify not targeting their programs for the conversion to the Jews. Before turning to this emerging missiology vis-à-vis the Jews, a brief review of the fruits of the Jewish - Catholic dialogue is in order.

c) Fruits of Catholic Dialogue with the Jewish People   Some of the foundation for a new theology of mission must include the fruit and discovery of twenty-five years of Jewish-Catholic dialogue; these might be summarized as follows:

1. The Jews remain the beloved of God; indeed, God has never abandoned them (Ps 94:14; Rom 11:1), nor has God reneged on the covenant given to them through Moses. They are "still the heirs of that election to which God is faithful."[7]

---

[6] Gregory Baum, "Rethinking the Church's Mission after Auschwitz," in Eva Fleischner, ed., *Auschwitz: Beginning of a New Ere? Reflections on the Holocaust* (New York: KTAV Publishing House, 1977), p. 113.

[7] Pope John Paul II, Address to Jewish Leaders in Warsaw, June 14, 1987, in *L'Observatore Romano*, August 3, 1987.

2. Catholics appreciate anew Jesus' own Jewishness and the complex process which gave them the Scriptures which include even some anti-Judaic themes.

3. The Jewish tradition has continued to grow in spiritual riches after the time of Jesus.

4. Jews and Catholics' living together in many countries should not be "a mere 'coexistence,' a kind of juxtaposition, interspersed with limited and occasional meetings, but let it be animated by fraternal love."[8]

5. The Jews enjoy a special place in Christian self-understanding, unique among religions of the world.

Thus, in the words of Pope John Paul II:

> The first [dimension of Nostra aetate to be noted] is that the Church of Christ discovers her "bond" with Judaism by "searching into her own mystery".... The Jewish religion is not "extrinsic" to us, but in a certain way is "intrinsic"' to our own religion. With Judaism therefore we have a relationship which we do not have with any other religion. You are our dearly beloved brothers and, in a certain way, it could be said that you are our elder brothers.[9]

3. A RENEWED MISSIOLOGY VIS-À-VIS THE JEWS

Catholics are pulled in different directions. On the one hand, they hear the Church's missionary exigence, and, on the other, they appreciate anew the sad history of Christian efforts to convert the Jews and the trauma of the Shoah. They wonder, "Do we, in one context, value the faithfulness of the Jewish people to their covenant, and, in another, seek to move them away from that covenant? Has our dialogue with the Jewish people

---

[8] Idem, Address to the Synagogue of Rome, April 13, 1986, in Eugene Fisher and Leon Klenicki, eds., *Pope John Paul II on Jews and Judaism 1979-1986* (Washington: United States Catholic Conference, 1987), p. 84.

[9] Ibid., p. 82.

revealed that Jesus saying 'no one comes to the Father but by me' excludes the Jews because they are already with the Father? Since God is already in covenant with the Jews," many conclude, "our mission efforts should be aimed only towards those without any religious affiliation." Christian reluctance to missionize the Jews, therefore, is not simply a matter of timid faith.

Cardinal Tomko has more than adequately represented the Church's general missionary exigence and questions around its modern application. I have attempted to outline some of the fruits of the interreligious dialogue with the Jewish people. I propose the following as a fruitful direction for Catholic theological thinking to proceed in making a positive exception in the Church's conversionist dimension of its mission:

Since the Shoah, Christians ponder ever more deeply the meaning of Jewish survival in the world. In many ways, the Jews survive despite Christians' best (or worst) efforts at eliminating them through ghettoization, conversion, and pogroms.[10] Furthermore, the atheistic Nazi effort to annihilate the Jewish people was unsuccessful--they survived. What does this mean for the Christians? Part of Christian and Jewish faith is that God is revealed through history. Not everything in history reveals God, nor is all history revelatory. But when God speaks, it is in and through history that the Divine Voice is heard. The survival of the Jews to this day--even and especially through the Shoah--must now be interpreted as a positive sign that God continues to love them and call them his/her own. The Christian answer to the "why" of Jewish survival must be that God wants them to survive, not as a pawn in a Christian theological chess game, but as a people called and chosen. Simply put, Christians are coming to believe that God does not want a world without Jews. After Auschwitz, following the

---

[10] See Schweitzer and Flannery cited above.

will of God, we Christians do not want a world without Jews. Indeed, we have already noted that one of the most sacred retrievals of the new Catholic-Jewish relationship is the affirmation that God has not abrogated God's covenant with the Jewish people. This belief bears, I believe, a consequence--indeed, a mandate--that Christians are not to eliminate the Jews from the face of the earth, even by conversionist programs. The Jews are the sign, a sacrament, that our God is faithful to his/her covenant, and we Christians must begin to honor that choice by not seeking to convert them.[11]

Furthermore, in a post-Auschwitz world where the possibility of European Jewish annihilation almost became a reality, would it serve Christian belief in the God of Jesus that there be no Jews, even by all of them becoming Christians?[12] I suggest not--for the following reasons.

Christians hold, with all their heart, that Jesus stands as the forever valid sign and sacrament of God's saving action. That they are called as individuals to respond in community is the particular privilege and vocation of the Church, which itself stands as the sacrament of this belief. But as believers of both Testaments know and proclaim, God calls people not only as individuals, but also as communities. The Holy One's call in and through community is as irrevocable and unavailable-to-renegotiation as God's call to the human heart is. Thus, must we not now affirm that God's-call-in-community requires a sign and sacrament to be real to and for the world?

---

[11] This is surely an echo of Emil Fackenheim's 614th Commandment that the Jews are to survive *as Jews*, in *God's Presence in History: Jewish Affirmation and Philosophical Reflections* (New York: Harper & Row, 1972), p. 11.

[12] Here I admit that I am slipping into what I wished to avoid; namely, making the Jews part of a Christian theological chess game. Perhaps this pitfall is unavoidable. But I think that it can be argued that one ironic byproduct of the Church's not seeking to convert the Jews is that it serves the Church's larger mission. See also Robert E. Willis, "Why Christianity Needs an Enduring Jewish Presence," *JES* 25 (Winter 1988):22-38.

The Jewish people, I submit, stand as the necessary sacrament and sign of this fuller message.[13] God's electing them through Moses does not end, even with the definitive coming of salvation which Christians recognize in the Jew Jesus. If they today seek to convert the Jews, Christians are systematically attempting to eliminate the sacrament and sign that the Holy One calls humans communally as well as individually.

Furthermore, if by a convert-making enterprise Christians ever eliminate the Jews as a recognizable people in the world, as a nation faithful to the call they hear through the Torah, then Christians will obscure their own doctrine of God's faithfulness to election. That is, if the world sees an end to the Jewish people, then the world may rightly conclude that God's election is only for a time until some other groups obliterates it by conversion. What Christians witness to is that, by the gracious love of the Holy One, Jewish election has been opened to the nations (thus, "Go teach all nations"--see footnote 2) through Christ--a branch grafted on, as Paul put it. (Rom 11:17f.)

From a theological perspective such as suggested above, the Church can--must--make the Jews an exception in evangelization not because of any timidity or lack of faith, not because of guilt or interfaith politeness, but precisely because it believes passionately what has been revealed: that salvation is God's work, not human work, that God chooses whom God wills for the Reign of God and that the Holy One has chosen the Jews and has not gone back on that word. To repeat: if the Church ever came to believe that the Holy One has withdrawn his/her choice of the Jews, then the Church might have reason to despair that God's choice of them, in Christ, is an eternal one. The God of Abraham and Sarah, Moses and Miriam, and

---

[13] Here I acknowledge the influence of Martin Buber, *Two Types of Faith* and Franz Rosenzweig, *The Star of Redemption* with Karl Rahner, "Theology of Symbol" and Edward Schillebeeckx *Christ the Sacrament of Encounter with God*.

Jesus is a faithful God. Simply speaking, God chose the Jewish people first, and God has never turned back. Christians do not now missionize them because they profoundly cherish that doctrine.

THE CHRISTIAN CHALLENGE FOR THE THIRD MILLENNIUM

Raimundo Panikkar

I

The rich and balanced Questionnaire of Cardinal Tomko represents a very positive step in the direction of that old adage: <u>ecclesia semper est reformanda</u>.

As I have dealt elsewhere[1] with most of the individual questions raised, I would like to address myself here to a perhaps more fundamental question: a reform in the ways of thinking.

I should not apologize for taking this wide perspective. It is a contemplative insight into the situation of humanity today rather than a sociological analysis of present trends. Nor do I apologize if I take here a metaphysical stance and show an Asian mentality. This is precisely my point: there are other ways of thinking besides the "Christian" one. I feel that this perspective is called for, if we take seriously the issue raised by Cardinal Tomko and are ready to overcome the <u>inertia of the mind</u>.

Authentic contemplation, which implies involvement and non-attachment, theory and praxis, is required to properly approach the present

---

[1] I would like to single out only three publications of mine because they are practically unknown: "Christianity and World Religions" in *Christianity* (Collective work), Patiala, Punjabi University (1960), pp. 78-127; "The Supername: Salvation in Christ. Concreteness and Universality." Lecture held at the Inauguration of *The Ecumenical Institute for Advanced Theological Studies*, Tantur, Jerusalem the 25th of September 1972; *Transforming Christian Mission into Dialogue*, a collection of seven articles published in *Interculture* 97 (Fall October 1987), pp. 14-45.

situation of the world. Not even Christian theology can proceed today with "business as usual."

As I have argued elsewhere, Christian theology today should not try only to elaborate answers. It should also try to listen to the perhaps embarrassing questions that the "two-thirds world" is putting to the Christian tradition.[2]

II

I may try to sum it all up by a <u>Nonary of Sûtras on Christian Language</u>:

1. <u>During two millennia the Christian language has been the biblical language received and interpreted within a predominantly Hellenic matrix</u>.

Christian theology (or theologies) is an astounding monument of human culture. An insignificant seed, which could not be found even in an Empty Tomb, has grown into a mighty tree nourished by a double and vital sap of a <u>fides quarens intellectum,</u> and an <u>intellectus quarens fidem</u>. It has produced a many-faceted and extremely rich theology as <u>logos</u> of God in the double sense of the genitive: our <u>logos</u> of (about) <u>Theos,</u> and our listening to the <u>logos</u> of <u>Theos</u>. It is one of the most extraordinary phyla of human history.

Concerned with its inner growth and self-understanding, and fruit also of historical circumstances, Christian thought has been rather introverted. It has developed its theology within the cultural boundaries of the Western world and its colonies. Hinduism offers another splendid example of a similar introverted growth. But the human world is wider. The Abrahamic

---

[2]Cf. my article "L'interpel. lació de l'Asia al cristianisme," in *Teologia i Vida* (collective work) (Barcelona: Claret, 1984), pp. 81-93.

phylum, together with all its enrichments, is not unique. Nor the Indic one for that matter.

2. The present-day's increasing awareness of cultural and religious pluralism radically challenges the very nature of Christian theology. It challenges:

a) Its Method:

The belief that God has spoken to Christians, and the conviction that God has imparted a secret to them alone, do not exclude the possibility that God may have, disclosed the same or the other aspects of the divine Mystery to other peoples.

Even the most immediate experience of divine revelation does not weaken the dictum that "Whatever is received is received according to the mode of the one receiving," quidquid recipitur ad modum recipientis recipitur.

Unless we make of revelation a crass anthropomorphic caricature we cannot curtail divine initiative. God is free to tell a secret, and even a different secret, when and to whom God pleases.

In short, the method for approaching the divine Mystery in order to understand as much as possible what it means, requires knowledge of the context in which that Mystery discloses itself. Christian theology implies constitutively a "theology" of "religions"--whereby these two words cannot even be presupposed as normative.

b) Its Contents:

God might have spoken a particular language. By language I understand not just grammatical idioms but the whole range of human communicable intelligibility. Now, this language has to be 1) understood, 2) transmitted, and 3) eventually translated. It is a triple mediation which prevents us from absolutizing any human statement.

116

We mentioned "God" and we might as well have said "History" as another example of what Christian theology called preambula fidei.[3] Now, other cultures and religions have other languages, other perceptions of reality. These cultures cannot be called into question without understanding them; and they cannot be understood without somewhat sharing in the presuppositions of such cultures. Further, we cannot legitimately criticize those presuppositions alone from our own assumptions, or from a presuppositionless (nonexisting) viewpoint.[4]

To assume only one valid kosmology is perhaps one of the most deleterious cultural blunders of Modernity--even if we call it the "scientific" world-view.[5]

In sum: Is the Christian "Revelation" tied to a single conception of the universe? Are the others wrong by virtue of a divine imperative? Should we speak of cultural Pelagianism?

3. This is the challenge of the third Christian millennium: Concreteness versus universality.

The very affirmation that Man is a natural animal--and thus that there is a universal common human nature--is already a cultural statement. Man is a cultural animal as well, and cultures have different self-and world-consciousnesses.

---

[3] Cf. my assertion that *Fundamental Theology* should not assume fixed *preambula fidei*, but study the possibility of using any cultural *preambula* as a basis for an incarnated theology, in "Metatheology as Fundamental Theology" *Concilium* VI, 5 (June 1969) reprinted in my book *Myth, Faith, and Hermeneutics* (New York: Paulist Press, 1979), pp. 321-334.

[4] An assumption is something we set at the start of our thinking about something. A presupposition (*prae-sub-position*) is something we uncritically or unreflectively take for granted. It belongs to the *mythos*. Cf. my cited "Metatheology," p. 324.

[5] By *kosmology* I understand not a different view of the world (cosmology) but a different world; not a different discourse about the universe but a different *universe* (also of discourse).

The challenge is this: Is Christianity a concrete religion or does it bud forth into a more universal Christianness?[6]   In the first case it is one religion among many and needs to be evaluated both according to its own intrinsic norms and according to agreed upon common features. In the second case, notwithstanding the fact that Christianity may continue as a concrete religion, it bursts, as it were, and liberates a metaconfessional core not confined to a particular tradition.[7] This Christianness is the name for humanness as Christians would understand it.

In other words, the catholicity of Christianity can be interpreted as a geographical and cultural category or as a quality which like salt enhances the taste of the food, or like light illumines in different colors the body it touches according to the very nature of those bodies.[8]

4. This challenge is a dilemma: either the circumcision of the mind is a requisite for being Christian or such a requirement is abolished.

We can no longer hold that the "soul is naturally Christian, anima naturaliter christiana, and interpret it as anima culturaliter christiana in the sense of one single culture--broadly as this culture may encompass many subcultures. It has to be recognized that there are non-biblical ways of thinking, that the very patterns of intelligibility of the human race are different, sometimes mutually irreducible and often incommensurable.

---

[6] Cf. my notion of Christianness as different from Christendom and Christianity in John Hick and Paul Knitter, eds., *The Myth of Christian Uniqueness* (Maryknoll, NY: Orbis Books, 1987), pp. 104-107.

[7] While Kierkegaard believed that Christendom is distorted Christianity, I am not saying that this latter is the distortion of Christianness. I affirm that the christic seed carried by Christians is growing now outside the boundaries of Christianity like centuries ago it grew outside the walls of Christendom. I speak of the three kairological moments.

[8] Cf. Raimundo Panikkar, "The Crux of Christian Ecumenism": Can Universality and Chosenness be held simultaneously?" in *Journal of Ecumenical Studies*, 26, 1 (Winter 1989), pp. 82-99.

Putting it briefly. The praeparatio technologica or even culturalis cannot be a praeparatio evangelica--whatever this latter may be.

As I have put it elsewhere: Does one need to be spiritually a Semite and intellectually a Greek in order to be Christian?[9]

It goes without saying that I say this in full admiration for Abrahamic spirituality and Hellenic thinking, further recognizing that these two notions are broad enough to cover a great variety of interpretations. But they do not exhaust the humanum, I submit.

The dilemma should be taken in its depth. It is a fact that in order to understand the biblical revelation, as it has been interpreted so far, one needs a forma mentis which is alien to most Asian mentalities. There is nothing wrong with circumcision, either of the body,, or the mind, or both. But we should be aware of the fact that it remains circumcision, and draw the consequences. The problem is, tellingly enough, not to cross the Rubicon, but who crosses it. The challenge is not another conquest, another territory, a new expansion. The problem is Julius Caesar. It is a great thing teste Paul, to be a civis romanus. The problem is that many a culture does not aspire after that citizenship or even grasp what it may mean to the people of those cultures.

5. Either horn of the dilemma is legitimate: No major theologumenon would be lost in either answer.

Circumcision, like baptism or any other initiation, may be a symbol either of particularity or of concreteness. The human existential way for universality is concreteness. The proper love for one's parents, children, spouse, vocation, people and religion entails neither abhorrence for the other nor even the belief that those loved ones are objectively the best. Reality

---

[9]Cf. my article in Hick-Knitter, op. cit.

is a fabric of relationships. Anything real is concrete and it is in its concreteness that it is connected with the whole universe.

Christianity, in our case, could be catholic, not in a geographical or cultural sense, but qualitatively, as St. Augustine suggests when he translates "catholic" not as universal but as <u>secundum totum</u>, i.e., as that religion which to its believers offers them all they need for their fulfillment and salvation. It is existentially complete--perfect, if we remember the etymology.

<u>Non-circumcision</u> could be a symbol either for universality or for generality. The latter is an abstraction. The former is an urge of the human soul. But urge for universality belongs to the order of the <u>mythos</u>, not of the <u>logos</u>. It is unfolded and often unspoken. It cannot be verbalized in concepts. Everybody wants to know, to quote Aristotle, or to be happy, to cite Thomas Aquinas, but the notion and the contents of such knowledge or happiness vary, and therefore also the means to reach them or the places to find them.

Christianness, in our case, could be catholic as universal, or rather as transcendental, i.e., as the concrete (Christian) way of embodying humanness. It would be, not a particular doctrine, but a concrete realization of what is transcendentally linked to the fulfillment of the <u>humanum</u>.

In sum, each religion has a claim to concrete catholicity and to mythical universality. Seen from another angle, each religion is a dimension of the other. We could speak, with all due qualifications, of a certain religious <u>perichoresis</u>. Did not Nicholas of Cusa describe all religions as "a certain expression of the word of God or of eternal reason," <u>quaedam locutiones verbi Dei sive rationis aeternae</u>?

What should we then understand by Christianity? Perhaps the Christian hologram?

6. <u>But the consequences are different: Christianity or Christianness.</u>

The present state of the question allows us to make a Vishnu stride. Cardinal Tomko's Introduction itself is an encouragement to this. Hardly anybody today defends Christian exclusivity and many are worried by the claim of inclusivity. Christianity is becoming more and more open and is being purified of the inertia of the past--in spite of understandable fundamentalist backlashes.

But how far can the openness go? Where do we draw the line of Christian identity?[10]

The approach to the answer may offer us an example of the Semitic and the Indic ways of thinking--provided we remain well aware of the oversimplification. For the former, based on the primacy of the principle of non-contradiction, a Christian is not a non-Christian. The Christian has to be distinct and eventually separated (sanctus). For the latter, based on the primacy of the principle of identity, a Christian is anyone who does not explicitly confess to being a non-Christian; anyone who does not choose excommunication from the Christian.

We have here two different ways of Christian self-understanding. The consequences are obviously different. On the one hand, we have a religion called Christianity, distinguishable from all others. On the other hand, we have a set of experiences (love of God and of neighbor, truthfulness, fidelity, humility, openness to, freedom, . . .) which for Christians have Christian symbols and for other sets of homeomorphic equivalents. Christian-ness is then not a "religion" in the sociological sense of the word, but the Christian way of experiencing the religious dimension of Man.

7. Only a kenotic and dekerygmatized Christ can sustain the second alternative.

---

[10] Cf. my contribution at the Annual Meeting (1976) of the *Pacific Coast Theological Society*: "Christian Identity in Time of Pluralism."

It has been said time and again, mainly from Asian sources, that Christian self-consciousness will never be able to take experience as paramount, to accept that every single being has Christ-nature (equivalent to Buddha-nature), to recognize that God is only a concrete and not universal symbol, to overcome the belief in an exclusively homogeneous evolution of dogma, that it will never apply metanoia to itself, not only as changing the dogma, but as transcending it.

I submit that if Asian Christians ever come to have a non-secondary place in Christian theology these issues may trigger a theological mutation.[11]

The kenosis of Christ would be here understood not only as an act of humility,[12] but in an ontological sense for which Christian metaphysics is little prepared. Emptiness (in Pali, śûnyatâ) is not annihilation. Nothingness is the horizon of Being . . ., the potentia out which the actus emerges.

Similarly, dekerygmatization does not mean that the injunction to chant, witness, proclaim is no longer valid. It means, however, that we do not confuse the vital attitude of sharing joy and life with the intellectual contents with which we also need to express that deeper motion of the Spirit.

In sum, the kenosis of Christ rescues Christian theology from falling into the danger of christomonism. The dekerygmatization of the Christian experience saves it from falling into being just an ideology. The work of the Spirit cannot be subordinated to the Logos.

8. This amounts to passing from a tribal Christology to a polychromic Christophany.

---

[11] Cf. Raimundo Panikkar, "Indian Theology: A Theological Mutation" in Amaladoss, Gispert Sauch, T. K. John, eds., *Theologizing in India* (Bangalore: TPI, 1981), pp. 23-42, and in general the entire volume.

[12] The (King James) Authorized Version goes so far as to translate *exinanivit semetipsum* (Phil. 2:7) as "made himself of no reputation."

Christian scholars do not find it abusive language to speak of Yahweh as a tribal God previous to the purification of its notion effected mainly by the prophets of Israel. One may as well foresee that to the third Christian millennium is reserved the task of overcoming a tribal Christology by a Christophany which allows Christians to see the work of Christ everywhere without assuming that they have a better grasp on or a monopoly of that Mystery which has been revealed to them in a unique way.

In other words, the mystical Christ is not the same as the cosmic Christ. The cosmic Christ is a cosmological hypothesis. The mystical Christ is the Christian belief in the resurrection which allows the Christian to experience a Christophany in any manifestation of Reality, although, as any belief, it has also kosmological assumptions. "The Unknown Christ of Hinduism" is not the Christ known to Christians and unknown to Hindus, but that Mystery unknown to Christians and known to Hindus by many other names, but in which Christians cannot but recognize the presence of Christ.[13] The same light illumines different bodies polychromatically.

This does not imply that everybody is a member of Christianity, but at the same time it does not split human ultimate consciousness into incommunicable compartments. On the doctrinal and even intellectual level, systems may be incompatible, religions may be incommensurable, but not by bread alone, not by logos alone does Man live. There is also the Spirit enlivening Man--and the universe.

I have said that for a Christian mystical theology every being is a Christophany.[14] But this is only a particular language. It is the language in which the epiphany of Reality discloses itself to the Christian. The

---

[13] Cf. the second edition of my *Unknown Christ of Hinduism* (Maryknoll, NY: Orbis Books, 1981), which spells out what was cryptically written in the first.

[14] See already my Preface of 1959 to my work *Mâyâ e Apocalisse* (Rome: Abete, 1966), p. x.

Christophany is apophatic. The epiphanies are epiphenomena, but the phenomena are real.

Another example may clarify this point. There is much talk about inculturation today. I am not here entering into the discussion.[15] I am saying only that one cannot dismiss too quickly the assertion that the dogma of the Incarnation is already a sort of inculturation. In fact it has a coherent and plausible meaning only within a certain cultural framework.

9. The problematic calls for a Second Council of Jerusalem--held at Râjagrha, if need be.

The two options are legitimate, we said. The deepening of the first will purify Christianity. The striving for the second will liberate Christians and establish trans-religious fellowships without necessarily breaking religious affiliations.

The history of humanity is also left to human initiative. In this decisive moment of the world the urgent problems of present-day civilization are also religious issues. Peace, justice, freedom, ecology, hunger, military and technocratic depletion, . . . are all theological problems as well. To be exclusively concerned with intra-ecclesiastical matters is short-sighted and may distract the Church from its mission as traditionally understood since the Greek Fathers. Religions, for all the benefits they have brought, have also been the cause of strife and war.

The great problems of our present time cannot be evaluated, let alone solved, within one single religious or cultural perspective. We need one another. No religion or culture is self-sufficient to alleviate the human predicament.

---

[15] Cf. my paper at the Annual Meeting of the *Indian Theological Association* (1989): "The Perspective of Inculturation in an Indic Christian Theology of Religious Pluralism" to be published shortly.

Private opinions and prophetic attitudes are necessary, but not sufficient. Divine interventions are always human events as well.

All this leads me to call not for an exclusively Christian Council, say, Vatican III. Geneva N, or Chicago I, but a Council, a <u>Concilium</u>, a Calling to <u>Reconciliation,</u> of the human races. Too long have we been fighting under all types of pretenses, often with religious justifications; too long have we built private empires, religious as well as political and economic. War is no longer about a port or a ritual. It is simply a criminal act. Wars begin not only in Man's mind, they mature in the religious heart of humanity. Religious reconciliation is THE mission of the religious bodies on earth.

The Christian symbol is Jerusalem II (after <u>Jerûŝâlayim</u> I, where circumcision was discussed). Circumcision was no longer valid for Christians, but it remained valid for Jews. Baptism may not be the only sign of salvation. Jerusalem is only a symbol. This Council could equally be called at Râjagrha, where the first Buddhist Council took place.[16] I would make space in it for all living beings, for all is alive and every being has a function to perform, a cosmotheanthropic council, as the Gâthàs, Vedas, and Bible, . . . suggest.

The actual gathering is still a utopia, but not the actual calling for it, the preparation of peoples, the awakening to the need. Not United Nations of States, but a <u>Concilium</u> of Peoples, <u>harmonia mundi</u>.

III

"Missionary Challenges to the Theology of Salvation" was the title of the Meeting in which Cardinal Tomko pointedly said that salvation,

---

[16] Many indologists have doubts about the first Buddhist Council (*samgiti*) near Rājagrha around 480 B.C.E. soon after the Buddha's *mahâparanirvâna*. The second council at *Vaisâli* some hundred or hundred and ten years later is historically certain.

liberation and the like refer to "a central problem for man in search of the meaning of his own existence."

For this "search" Man needs what many religions will call inspiration, grace, a divine impulse. But, concomitantly, we need each other. The Christian mission is specific. It is part of the human mission. The Christian will word it in Christian language: to collaborate in the redemption of the world, to co-redeem with Christ, to proclaim the Joy and glad News of Life and New Life. No one would object to this. Provided, of course, that one had paid heed to what the ancient Buddhist masters have said, as Śântideva and later Atîśa remind us, that it is not only foolish but criminal to dare to preach that one knows the Gospel (dharma) by study alone and has not acquired the connaturality with it, the superknowledge (abhijña) of practical holiness. "How can it be not madness, to preach before even learning one's own measure?" wrote At śa. "Hypocrite! Take the plank out of your own eye first," said Jesus. "Only the uttermost sincerity can effect any change," uttered Chuang Tsu.

I have, on purpose, given another framework to the problems. I have not fallen into the technological frame of mind to jump to find solutions. I have meditated on the questions--and reformulated them. The "expectation of a reply" (Tomko) is here converted into the hope of a new awareness.

RELIGIONS, SALVATION, MISSION

Samuel Rayan

1. CRITICAL QUESTIONS

Cardinal Josef Tomko's address to a Rome Congress on the theme of salvation and mission is a critical contribution to the emergent theology of religions. The speaker's purpose is to present some questions and challenges which missionary life poses to scholars "in expectation of a reply." That, however, does not mean that the speaker has no position of his own. His criticism of some new theses on salvation, mission and the role of other religions comes through clear enough. He finds the new ideas ambiguous, disruptive of missions and a reduction of faith in Christ and Christ's role in salvation.

The Cardinal is disturbed over the relativization of the historical Jesus and the Church, over the bypassing of the direct proclamation of the Gospel, over the redefinition of mission in terms of God's Reign, the discovery of God's action and of already existing faith, and the transformation of the world in justice, peace and love in collaboration with all who are committed to "human promotion." He pleads for a confirmation and deepening of "the balanced position reached by the Church in the last two decades": a balance between new ideas concerning mission and old ones aiming exclusively at eschatological salvation. Yet his language is often the language of European missions much older than the last two decades. After more than two decades of "mission in all six continents," Tomko still talks of "mission continents" (objects of missionary activity, announcing catechesis) as against "other regions" (agents of animation and cooperation). He recalls with nostalgia the one-way missions of the past in which "missionaries felt the pressing need to bring (!) salvation to non-Christians"; and "the motives that urged missionaries to sacrifice themselves for the salvation of non-Christians." The weakening of these motives by "recent theological opinion on non-Christian religions" is lamented. References to "other religions," to the "great ancient religions" are, as a rule respectful, though the phrase "non-Christian" is frequent, and "theories which exalt the role of other religions" are resented. Tomko's talk concludes with a passage from <u>Evangelii nuntiandi</u> with which he concurs. In brief, then, the Cardinal is saying that God wills to save all peoples through Jesus Christ, the only Mediator: salvation may not be reduced to liberation, justice, love and peace; the Church's mission, proclaiming the Gospel and planting the Church, is necessary and mandated: and the traditional mission is in essence valid. Ideas about the saving role of other religions need to be clarified and critically matured. A fair-enough demand of which the sincerity and seriousness are transparent.

It seems to me that the conservative point of view from which Tomko's challenges and questions proceed also need clarification and critical examination. How is it that it is only "in the last two decades" that the Church reached a "balanced position" in the understanding of salvation, mission and other religions? Admittedly, then, there was a long period of imbalance in the Church's conception of salvation and its practice of mission. How is it that it was only in 1949, as Tomko recalls, that the axiomatic "No salvation outside the Church," which had fuelled nearly all the missions of the past, was found to be erroneous? To admit now that God's grace, guidance and salvation are offered to all even outside the Church and before its birth, is to speak from within a frame of thought very different from the one used by traditional mission. The way the old frame of mind jarred with the Faith and yet persisted for centuries need careful probing. To be similarly probed is a history of reluctance to admit the full, positive and independent role of religion in God's plan of salvation; the narrowness of exclusivism; the imperialism of inclusivism; and the many intellectual gymnastics to come to terms with the fact of religions and with God's will to save everyone while clinging to a theology of the Man Christ Jesus as absolutely sole mediator of salvation.

2. "GRASP THE BREADTH, LENGTH, HEIGHT AND DEPTH"

Our faith in the Creator God includes faith in everyone's call to share in God's life, and everyone's openness to God's friendship. We cannot hold the first article of the creed without sensing at once that the call to friendship and filiation is constitutive of women and men; it is not extrinsic and accidental, not an addition or afterthought. It is woven into the fabric of our being. Creation is a first grace, the beginning of salvation, the covenant and promise of final fulfillment. God therefore accompanies human history, walking with every person and every community, enlightening and guiding, urging justice and compassion, enabling, liberating, forgiving, and leading to wholeness. Revelation and experience of the Creator God is at the same time revelation and experience of God our Savior. (See Rom 1 and 2.) The original blessing is the dawn of the Eschaton. We are not forgetting that this truth has been evaded by a tragic psyche which chooses to concentrate on (original) sin rather than on (original) grace; the same psyche that chooses to dominate rather than liberate, to amass rather than share, and spend enormous resources on weapons and death rather than on children and life. The Western Church has concentrated on the middle portion of the creed and elaborated a christomonistic theology, but failed to develop reflection on the Creator God and on the Holy Spirit, Lord or Lady and Life-giver and Father-Mother of the poor.

Faith in the Creator God sees the many religions of humankind as so many concrete historical-cultural expressions of the saving presence and activity of the Mystery in their hearts, their communities and their respective histories. The religions are at once God's gift and people's responses--in the Holy Spirit. They are marked by differences and limitations. They are different: because God's dealings with each person or group or epoch is different and distinct; because God's truth is unspeakably rich and inexhaustible; because all God-experience is refracted through the prism of diverse cultural contexts; and because history keeps unfolding and disclosing fresh possibilities and promises of the human and of the human-divine encounter.

They are limited because they are realities of time and space, relative and relational, and marred by human sin. Each religion has its own face and voice, its own distinctive personality and concrete history. As responses to the Mystery, the religions relate to each other within the Mystery and within our shared yet distinctly realized humanity, and within the complexity of our common history. To ignore the richness and promise of this diversity or to seek to reduce the religions to their least common denominator, or to judge one by the criterion of another would be great impoverishment, an act of aggression and a methodological mistake. Our faith educates us to respect God's gifts present in every tradition, meant for sharing, meant as a place of meeting and mutual enriching. The distinctive spiritual wealth of each tradition is to be the pride and the heritage of all. The religions are sister traditions representing some of the infinite facets of the Mystery. It is by being open to each other and letting ourselves be influenced, challenged, nourished and completed by the others that all can grow together and blossom into a many-splendored Lotus. Working together for liberation and for a community of justice, equality and peace, the religions enter a process of self-discovery and inter-fecundation. All spiritual traditions are on a mission to one another, and there is, or is to be, a glad history of mutual evangelization. A case of Deep calling to Deep in the voice of God's cataracts. The cataracts are many.

Every religious reality is experienced as unique, like flowers in a garden, like children in a family. A sense of uniqueness is part of faith. Uniqueness is the language of love, worship and doxology. It is not a subjective sentiment, but a factor in all personal/interpersonal relationship and commitment. For me, for all Christians, Jesus Christ is unique, incomparable and irreplaceable. All significant experiences and visions of reality and all great hopes and endeavors of many years or of a life-time have been, for so many of us, mediated by Jesus and his Gospel. We therefore wish to tell others about him, to share him and his story and the hope he creates. We would have others love and follow him, not in our way or the manner we prescribe, but in their own way, the way the Spirit leads them. And we are aware of similar hopes and experiences being historically mediated to others, before Jesus' birth and after, not through Jesus but other Symbols which to them are as significant, sacred and vital. Our faith-experience of Jesus' uniqueness educates our hearts to a spiritual sensitivity capable of recognizing and respecting similar religious experiences of our Hindu, Muslim, Buddhist, Sikh, Jain, Shintoist, Taoist brothers and sisters. Any deficiency in sensitivity will mean my faith is flawed. In mutual reverence all want each to be faithful to the gift of God that has come to each, as well as be open to fresh gifts that are being offered through the neighbor.

Such is the world of the Spirit who bursts upon us in many tongues, diverse accents and endless resonances; and who scatters varieties of gifts in great profusion; who is free and unorganizable like the wind; who breaks through clear and precise theological formulations and gives birth to polyvalent symbols which alone can bear and image forth the realities we are here concerned with. It is significant, then, that Cardinal Tomko's difficulties with the pluralist theological thesis and his anxious search for "the greatest precision," clarity, certainty and security go together with a total absence of mention of the Holy Spirit. Significant, but also strange because there can be no mission, no Church, no Lord Jesus apart from the Spirit. Or perhaps not strange but understandable, since the speaker's concern is not so much with spiritual life or Christ-like existence the world over, or the Reign of God and its justice, as with Christianity, its clear and precise doctrines and the Church as an institution.

3. KNOW THEM BY THEIR FRUITS"

The unique role Christ plays in God's saving plan is central to Tomko's concerns, as it is to ours. But the speaker goes farther when he reduces "the focal centre" of the question in hand to two poles: Christ and non-Christian religions. "Jesus Christ is the best Revealer of God; He is man's only Savior and the only mediator." "Does not the fact that Jesus Christ is the Son of God . . . have some impact on the quality of his message?" "Can He be put next to or together with other founders? Is he not a Savior also for them?" "Can the revelation brought by Him be put on the same level as the "revelations" contained in other religions?"

Is the sense of superiority and exclusiveness implied in such questions integral to faith in Christ? Superiority claims seem more political and partisan than religious, spiritual and Christlike. Does the fact that the God who reveals Self savingly in creation and in conscience (Rom 1 and 2; Acts 14:17) is the God and Father of Jesus Christ qualify Tomko's questions and call for a new outlook on God's self-communications in the spiritual experience of peoples throughout history? Are we sure that in placing God's saving acts on various, higher and lower, levels, we are moved by Christ's interests and not by our own (political, economic, racist, imperialist) interests and prejudices? Is one saving touch of God superior to another saving touch of God? One forgiveness better than another? I submit that what matters is not disputes about higher levels and first places; what matters is hearing and heeding. Faiths are not for comparison like commodities; they are graces to be lived. Not that knowing Jesus is not a privilege, but that the One who privileges me this wise privileges others otherwise.

That Christ's uniqueness has been transmuted into Christian superiority and exclusivism is evident from the, often a priori, devaluation of other religions and from Christian collusion in imperialist projects of world domination. Christians have viewed other religions as human strivings against God, as human gropings for salvation, as natural, as imperfect etc. What was it that led to the eclipse of the common courtesy of acknowledging another's face as a face? When in the early 18th century the Danish Bartholomew Ziegenbalg made a study of the religious beliefs of South India and sent the results of his researches to Europe, "he received the tart reply that his business was to root out Hinduism in India, and not to propagate heathen superstition in Europe" (Stephen Neil, A History of Christian Missions, p. 196). In the early 15th century popes (Martin V, Eugene IV) encouraged the Christian conquest of Africa. In 1452 Nicolas V used his "apostolic authority" to empower Alphonsus of Portugal to "invade, conquer, overthrow, and subjugate" all Saracens, pagans, infidels and enemies of Christ," to grab their lands, goods and possessions, and "to force their persons into perpetual slavery" provided the king's idea was "to bring them with a powerful hand to the Christian faith." In 1493 Alexander VI wrote to Ferdinand and Isabella of Spain, praising as God's work their effort to subdue and dominate "barbarous nations" and bring them to the faith. He used "the authority of God" and his own power as Vicar of Christ to "donate to the king and his successors all the lands and islands discovered [read: invaded] by Columbus and inhabited by peaceful people who believed there was one God creator of all in heaven."

Underlying all this and subsequent world conquest, under the pretext, often, of the need of evangelization and the right of Truth, is a peculiar conception of Christ's uniqueness, which we find unacceptable. Imperialist missions have projected Christ as a new, religious, Julius Caesar, out to conquer. We therefore have other questions to raise than those raised by Tomko. We ask about the subterranean connection between the Western conception of Christ's uniqueness and authority on the one hand and the Western project of world domination on the other. Tomko surely will not want to identify with this tradition. But it is up to him to spell out the difference between colonial missions which destroyed the credibility of the Christian name for decades to come in our land and the new mission he advocates which however is reluctant to affirm "human promotion" as the historical phase and sacramental presence of integral salvation.

4. BAPTISM AND DISCIPLESHIP

It is easy verbally to claim uniqueness and universality. Authentic confession, however, of Christ's uniqueness can only be made and mediated in confessing communities' life-styles that are unique and surpriseful. The question cannot be settled merely on the basis of faith-statements and doxologies from the scriptures. The convincing basis is praxis which images forth Christ's uniqueness by embodying it in concrete social and historical realities and relationships. The question to ask is, Where is the Christian community that reflects Christ's uniqueness and thus "verifies" its confessional claim, redeeming it from being mere vocables which project nothing but our collective ego? The question is whether we as communities are prepared to continue the praxis of Jesus, appropriate his vision of authority, his rejection of throned foxes and owners of wars, his interventions on behalf of the broken and the downtrodden. It is finer faith and witness to live and act from the Spirit of Christ than to announce stray phrases from early Christian writings. How is "the quality of Jesus' message" duly discerned except in the culture and the community which that message shapes and nurtures?

Use of scripture texts is risky, involving as it does complex problems of exegesis and hermeneutics. Much use is made in Tomko's speech of Acts 4.12, the No Other Name passage. The entire context shows that this is a word spoken to Jews (see Acts 2:5,14,22,29,31,36,38,46; 3:1,12,13,17,18,22,23; 4:1,12). It means that "we (Israel) can be saved" only in this man; our (Israel's) history can be fulfilled only in this man, our Messiah. The message is the same as in Acts 3:23, the one who does not listen to that foretold, expected and coming prophet shall be cut off from the people. Acts 10 is referred to, but the story means to teach Peter and us (i) that no person is unclean or profane; (ii) that all who fear God are acceptable to God; (iii) that there are God-fearing, devout people outside the Jewish and Christian circle; (iv) that the Spirit and Gifts are given to people before and independently of baptism to the surprise of Jews and (v) that Jesus is Lord and Judge of all.

The text does not seem to imply that all the God-fearing are called like Cornelius to baptism and the institutional church. The story also makes clear that till the vision came to him Peter had no idea of a world mission (to Gentiles) enjoined by Jesus. Hence Mt 28:18-20 calls for far more nuanced handling than Tomko allows for it. Even granting that this late text interprets the mind of Jesus, we must observe that making disciples is not the same as planting the hierarchical church. Does the phrase "all the nations" refer to more than the Jews of the Diaspora? (cf. Mt 10:5-6; 15:24; also Lk 24:44-47, scripture-based call to Israel of all nations to repent). The sending is not linked to salvation except in the Markan appendix, 16:15-16, which also Tomko cites with no critical comment. Nor is baptism. Earlier, Matthew relates salvation not to baptism and church but to doing God's will and to justice and compassion (Mt 7:21-27; 25:31-46; also Lk 19:1-10). The baptism which defines discipleship is not the one Jesus or the Church gives but the one they receive, namely, the costly, painful, immersion in and commitment to God's cause in the world, which is one with the cause of the oppressed, the cause of justice and freedom (Mk 10:35-40; Mt retains only one of Mark's two metaphors).

In the same vein the rich man seeking eternal life is referred back to his own traditional religion and its commandments, and not to the person and project of Jesus. The reference to Jesus comes in the end in view of something "more" than possessing eternal life. That "more" is, I suggest Jesus' project of the Reign of God on our earth. If Tomko's question whether "the Reign of God is the centre of Christ's mission" is in order at this time of the day after all the researches on the point, then still more in order would be the question whether Jesus had any interest at all in an institutionalized church. And yet that question is muted. (See Mt 10:1, 5-8; Lk 9:1, 60; Acts 1:3 with note in the Jerusalem Bible).

Another conspicuously used text is 1 Tim 2:4-6: there is one God who wants everyone to be saved and reach the knowledge of the truth, and one mediator, the man Jesus who sacrificed himself as a ransom for all. The passage occurs in a context dealing with intercessory prayer. The mediator idea is a difficult one though common in worship contexts; and the ransom concept is problematic, burdened as it is with bizarre interpretations. For Christians at worship Jesus is the only medium of encounter with God. This is rightly affirmed against the capricious chain of mediation in Gnosticism. Our context today is different, and our knowledge of the world of religious experience is larger and profounder. The passage cited needs reinterpretation. If God wills everyone to be saved and to come to know the truth, the possibility and offer of salvation and knowledge has been there for the people from the time God willed it and people needed it. If not, did God really and seriously want the salvation of everyone? And the truth God wants everyone to know includes (i) the saving revelation made in creation, Rom 1:18-32; (ii) the Torah inscribed in every heart, Rom 2:14-16; (iii) the view implied in Rom 2:12 that to know the truth is to embrace and live and experience it (Mt 7:21-27); (iv) the fact that God has never been left without witness, Acts 14:17; (v) the theology of Acts 17:16, 22-31, that people can already be worshipping the living God without knowing it; and (vi) the teaching of Hebrews 11:6, 13 that the faith without which it is impossible to please God has existed from the beginning among all kinds of people, and its core is that God exists and rewards those who try to find God. Salvation is a larger divine project than is envisioned by an exclusivist Christian interpretation. The suggestion that God provides for peoples' salvation only with the life and death of Jesus of Nazareth is unfair to God, too narrow for biblical perspectives, and too inept for a Spirit-led history of over two million years.

5. ALTERNATIVE

We have had experience of mission based on such texts as Tomko cites, and we are not impressed. If we must build on scripture, we would use other texts, and project a different perspective on mission. Go and do likewise (Lk 10:37); love one another (Jn 13:34); wash one another's feet (Jn 13:14): these are great mission mandates. Luke 4:18, the Spirit of the Lord is given to me, he has sent me to bring good news to the poor, to proclaim liberty to captives and new sight to the blind, and to set the downtrodden free, is a description of Jesus' mission, by continuing which people become church. We are commissioned to pray that the Father's Reign may come, his will may be done on earth, and that everyone may have everyday the food and resources required to live as God's daughter or son (Mt 6:9-12). We are sent to be light to the world, salt to the earth, and Christ's aroma and a "sweet smell of life that leads to life" (Mt 5:13-16; 2 Cor 2:14-16). "Not those who say to me, Lord, Lord, belong in the Kingdom, but those who do the father's will" (Mt 7:21-27). "What I want is mercy, not sacrifice"; justice and mercy and good faith are the weightier matters of the Torah (Mt 9:13; 12:7; 23:23). "Go and be reconciled with your brother first, and then come back and present your offering" (Mt 5:23-24). "Seek first the reign of God and its justice" (Mt 6:33).

Thus, then, salvation and mission and service of the Reign consist in and grow through compassion and responsibility for the downtrodden, siding with the dispossessed and marginalized, commitment to the liberation of the oppressed striving to do God's will in the economics and politics of daily life, and becoming, through such praxis, a bit of flavoring salt, a little transforming leaven, a small light in God's great world, and a perfume that sweetens its atmosphere and attracts. We recall Gandhiji's advice to missionaries to consider the gospel of the rose which draws people without many words. We would develop mission on lines such as these instead of others with a penchant for uniformity and global control. We would base mission on I Cor 13: we may have mountain-moving faith and angel-eloquence, but if we have no love, we are nothing, and our proclamation is no more than the booming of a gong signifying nothing.

6. "THINK OF THE FLOWERS GROWING IN THE FIELDS"

Salvation-liberation goes beyond repetition of correct religious words and ritual performances. Evangelizing mission transcends proclamation (Matthew and Mark) to become witness (Luke and John) through life and work (Matthew, John, James). Mission is witness which embodies in dim, distant, symbolic ways the Mystery we call God or Brahman or Allah, Reality greater than our heart, greater than our religions, churches, scriptures and theologies, whose truth and beauty no spiritual tradition, no symbol system can exhaust. Mystery expressible only in a thousand historical mediations. The religions are some of these symbolic mediations, joint creations of the Spirit and the Spirit-experience of human groups. Each group seeks to affirm its faith-experience through symbols within its culture and world view; to live it, tell it, share it, without wanting to impose it on anyone, without pretending that it alone is privileged and that for others God cares less. What each is and has is meant for all, for the correction, support, enrichment and completion of each. Each needs the other; each is a dimension of the other.

We are clear in our minds that missions of the past four centuries, vitiated as they are by association with Mammon and Moloch, greed and cruelty, cannot be the ideal and the norm. We let the Spirit lead our history further forward. We need not stop to answer all the questions coming from the academy and the world of the powerful who control world wealth, control world economy, control the life of the poor, possess enormous killer power and threaten the earth with annihilation. The questions which mater are those that emerge from the victims of the powerful. The victims ask: what bearing do your anxieties, questions and challenges have on the exploitation, oppression and dehumanization we are subjected to? Could your questions be genuinely human and profoundly theological if they concern mainly not with what troubled Jesus but with clear and precise ideas, formulations and orthodoxies, and insufficiently with the sufferings, torture and privations forced upon us? If their link to our wretchedness and humiliation is weak and tenuous, their relation to Jesus and his mission will be thin or none. The real question is whether the religions can now muster their resources to act together with the oppressed to struggle for the liberation of all and for new-creative pro-existence. In the process of a liberating, whole-making collaboration with God and neighbor, the different spiritualities will progressively discover one another, discover themselves with their weaknesses and strengths, and encounter more intimately the Mystery they bear, symbolize and convey.

MISSION AND INTERRELIGIOUS DIALOGUE: WHAT IS AT STAKE?[1]

Hans Waldenfels

In recent decades dialogue has been spoken of more loudly, and consequently mission more softly. The relationship between mission and dialogue, however, has thereby been no whit clarified. For not a few, dialogue appears to have taken the place of mission. For others dialogue is nothing other than a new tactic of mission. Finally there are those who wish to accord to both mission and dialogue their rightful place because for them the two are not congruent.

Here of course we are concerned with <u>interreligious</u> dialogue, and not dialogue in general. For Christianity there exists today a situation of competition with other religious proclamations which has not been known for a long time. In other words, Christianity, and its message, finds itself in a pluralism of religions.

Facing these conditions, several theses resulting from the new situation are here offered for discussion. They concern: 1) the changed

---

[1] An earlier, shorter version of this essay was in *Zeitschrift für Missionswissenschaft und Religionswissenschaft*, 73, 3 (July, 1989), pp. 182-194. Here I extend my earlier reflections, calling attention to: "Von der Weltmission zur Kirche in allen Kulturen," P. Gordan, ed., *Die Kirche Christi--Enttäuschung und Hoffnung* (Graz, 1982), pp. 305-350, reprinted in: *Theologisches Jahrbuch 1987* (Leipzig, 1987), pp. 447-480; "Theologie im Kontext der Weltgeschichte," *Lebendiges Zeugnis* 32/4 (1977), pp. 5-18; *Kontextuelle Fundamentaltheologie* (= KF) (Paderborn, 1985), pp. 76-80, 397f. "Das Christentum im Pluralismus heutiger Zeit," *Stimmen der Zeit*, 206 (1988), pp. 579-590; "Buddhismus und Christentum im Gespräch," *Internationale katholische Zeitschrift COMMUNIO*, 17 (1988), pp. 317-326.

conditions of mission and dialogue, or the dissolving mission structure and interreligious dialogue; 2) the structures of interreligious dialogue; 3) dialogue as a challenge to Christianity; and 4) the question of the normativity of Christianity.

I. MISSION AND DIALOGUE

1) Mission

When we speak of mission we usually mean the mission as it has been customarily been understood in the history of mission since the discovery of the new continents, after the Reformation, or after Francis Xavier. We mean thus mission as it is understood in the modern sense. That does not imply that the fundamental aim of mission is not supported in the origins of Christianity. The mission command in its various forms--Mt 28: 18 ff. par.; Acts 1: 8--makes of Christianity, as distinct from Judaism, e.g., a "world Religion" which promises salvation to all human beings, to all peoples and to all times, and fundamentally excludes no one from this promise of salvation.

Of course the realization of salvation appeared to be uniquely bound up with the figure of the crucified and risen Jesus of Nazareth, the only mediator between God and humanity (see 1 Tim 2: 5), in whose name alone there is salvation (see Acts 4: 12). The message of the Gospel was carried from Jesus Christ into a godless, unsaved, salvationless world. The modern practice of mission was essentially dominated by the conviction that the lack of the spread of the message of Christ meant the lack of salvation for the world.

The shock of learning that there were countries outside the Holy Roman Empire of the German Nation resulted in the tremendous effort both to transform those countries into a Western shape and to Christianize them. The Western-European conquest of the world and the Christian world mission were one and the same. Since in the sense of this mission unsaved men and women as such were seen as likewise retarded in the development of the possibilities of their being human, for the missionary the Christianization of the peoples meant at the same time their humanization. Only those who were baptized, and thereby became Christian, were likewise full human beings. One of the terrible discoveries made in the literature on the mission work of Latin America today, five hundred years after its beginning, is that often enough in this mission process the humanity of the Latin Americans was denied because they were not Europeans and Christians and their human dignity was trampled upon.[2]

2) Dialogue

Where dialogue, other than in a general sense, is discussed the following notion is stressed: Women and men of the most diverse ways of thinking, cultures, races, worldviews and religions encounter each other with the desire of taking each other seriously in their otherness. The presupposition for such encounters is that the different human groupings in the world no longer simply shut each other out, but rather live together. That, however, at no time in the history of the world has so decidedly been the case as it is today.

In fact the consciousness of the present-day pluralism is on the one hand the result of the still ongoing migration and mixing of peoples and national groups. In my own land, Germany, not only are the borders between the Christian denominations broken up, but today, as in North

---

[2] Concerning this see the various works by M. Sievernich, including "'Theologie der Befreiung' im interkulturellen Gespräch" *Theologie und Philosphie*, 61 (1986), pp. 336-358, and. H. Sievernich, ed., *Impulse der Befreiungstheologie für Europa* (Munich/Mainz, 1988), pp. 15-43.

America, Great Britain, France and the majority of European countries, the most various national and religious groupings are living side by side. Even if the non-Christian groups among us still form only minorities, they nevertheless represent in a tangible way the pluralism of religions.

The consciousness of pluralism is then further increased through the encounters resulting from modern mobility, tourism, international politics and economic relations, and also because of modern news reporting, and especially audio-visual technologies. Never before has the knowledge of the Other and the Alien been so wide-spread as today. Such a knowledge may be general and superficial, but it increasingly prevents once-and-for-all decisions and the holding of prior choices as being unrevisable. Whoever here--as, for example, the Church-expects or demands something else, engenders skepticism rather than trust. When religions in a hawking-like manner promise all-encompassing possibilities of salvation, they fall into the disrepute of present-day commercialism and advertising.

The experience of pluralism, however, leads to a positive result only then when for me (that is, for the modern Western subjective "I") the alien you becomes an equally significant subject. From a liberation theology perspective we can say: Where in the place of the modern "I" the "poor Other" so intensely becomes the focal point that s/he is taken seriously in her/his subjectivity, there intersubjectivity, dialogue and solidarity will arise.[3] In other words, the "poor Other" must be for me more than the necessary object of my concern. Only there does a double liberation--his/hers and mine--take place, that is, where the encounter with the alien releases her/him and me, each in our own subjectivity.

---

[3] See Sievernich, *Impulse*, pp. 18-23; J. B. Libanio, "Europäische und lateinamerikanische Theologie. Unterschiedliche Perspektiven," ibid., pp. 139-158, esp. 149 ff.

Dialogue as it is used here means three things: a) I share in the view of another; b) the Other shares in my (and others') views; c) mutual sharing with one another by different subjects does not end merely in a joint "We" of the actual partners, but rather in the openness to all who in principle could participate in this process of communications. Said in other words: The human dialogue ends in the openness of sharing, the sharing of one's self, of giving and receiving, of communication and participation, or however one wishes to name the self- forgetting, selfless exchange between humans.

II. LEVELS OF INTERRELIGIOUS DIALOGUE

The description of the fundamental structure of dialogue already makes it clear that in the encounter between different subjects who take each other seriously, there are different levels. In interreligious encounter I had earlier distinguished roughly four levels:[4] a) the social-political, b) intellectual-scholarly, c) "philosophical"-"theological," d) ascetic-spiritual. These levels cannot be completely separated, but they nevertheless demarcate certain emphases in the encounter.

1) Social-Political

On the social-political level the religions encounter each other through their representatives in order to address the social challenges of the times and--in the sense of the demand made of the Church in Nostra aetate 1--"foster unity and charity among individuals, and even among nations." What here comes to the fore is what binds humans together. In a certain sense the religions themselves become almost faceless. For the most part

---

[4] In the following I use the formulations from my essay in *COMMUNIO* listed in note one.

the concern is with practical steps and assistance. The questions about each religious understanding of peace, justice, and freedom, about the world, humanity and human history, its beginning and its fulfillment arise only when the religious grounding and motivation for the practical assistance to the world are asked about.

2) Intellectual-Scholarly

On the intellectual-scholarly level the effort is directed toward learning to know the alien better by means of a phenomenological grasp and the employment of other scholarly techniques, e.g., historical, sociological, psychological. This level is like the first steps which are taken in a scholarly manner in comparative religion. They are characterized by an attitude of "independence from normative restrictions," which came from the comparative religionists who extensively influenced this level.[5] Even if this attitude has in the meantime become ever more questionable for many scholars themselves--because the essence of "religion" cannot be grasped without recourse to norm-communicating disciplines--it has nonetheless gained in influence in the non-scholarly area. The scientific "how" of practical comparative religion has largely neutralized the normative claims of the religions.

3) "Philosophical"-"Theological"

I designate the third level "philosophical"-"theological" in order to call attention to the fact that the division between philosophy and theology which is customary in the West appears to be largely useless in a dialogue with the religions of Asia. One can hardly speak of theology within the context of

---

[5] H.-J. Klimkeit, "Religionsschaft," in: Hans Waldenfels, ed., *Lexikon der Religionen* (= LR) (Freiburg, 2nd. ed., 1988), pp. 560 ff.

Buddhism in face of the fact that God-talk is either absent or only reluctantly entered into. On the other hand, Asian philosophers often range more widely than do Western. Aloysius Pieris, along with other Asian theologians, have pointed out that in Asia culture and religions are overlapping facets of an indivisible soteriology, wherein simultaneously philosophy is a religious worldview and religion is a philosophy of life.[6]

4) Ascetic-Spiritual

We experience the fourth level of encounter in our encounters with Jews, but also with Buddhists. The mutual spiritual exchange which has already taken place between Benedictine communities and Buddhist monasteries and centers should be recalled, as well as widespread renewal of meditation which has been influenced by Asian methods. As an example which "stands out"--because it has not yet been assimilated and therefore is intensely disputed--is the Prayer for Peace which was initiated by John Paul II in Assisi in October, 1986.[7] Opposition to the pope on this point came not only from Marcel Lefebvre and his followers, but also vigorously from conservative Catholic missiologists like the German J. Dörmann.[8]

The fact that developments have cropped up outside Europe which deserve attention is evidenced most recently by the documentation of the challenging Research Seminar on "Sharing Worship" (Latin, communicatio

---

[6] See Aloysius Pieris *Theologie der Befreiung in Asien. Christentum im Kontext der Armut und der Religionen* (Freiburg: Herder Verlag, 1986), pp. 80f., 155f. and elsewhere. English, *An Asian Theology of Liberation* (Maryknoll, NY: Orbis Books, 1988).

[7] See *Die Friedensgebete von Assisi*, introduction by Cardinal Franz König and commentary by Hans Waldenfels (Freiburg, 1987), reprinted later in *Theologische Quartalschrift*, 169 (1989), p. 1.

[8] See the interview with F. Schmidberger, in *Herder-Korrespondenz*, 42 (1988), pp. 417–424, esp. p. 421; J. Dörmann, "Der theologische Weg des Papstes zum Weltgebetstag in Assisi," *Theologisches*, 18 (1988), pp. 323–332, 376–388, 453–464; already before then in *Die eine Wahrheit und die vielen Religionen* (Abensberg, 1988).

in sacris) January 20-25, 1988 in Bangalore, India.[9] The fundamental thesis which was worked out there I would like to express in the following formula: Whoever is convinced that s/he knows and has the best that there is, may not hold it for her/himself, but must share it with all. Not exclusion and excommunication is trump, but inclusion and community--in short, sharing.

III. INTERRELIGIOUS DIALOGUE AS A CHALLENGE TO CHRISTIANITY

From the survey of the various levels of interreligious dialogue it can be easily seen that the future decisions will occur mainly on the third and fourth levels. Here, however, all the participants in the dialogue are challenged in the identity of their own fundamental commitment. For Christians that means they will become aware of the challenge which participation in interreligious dialogue, which they have demanded, carries with it.

1) The Everyday Dialogue

In this, dialogue is far from any longer being a matter for specialists alone. It occurs much more expressly, or inclusively, everywhere, overtly or covertly, where human beings live together on a daily basis with those who have another religious or worldview orientation. One may avoid dealing with the issue directly out of indifference, but in everyday life one unavoidably must behave one way or another in ethical-practical matters, and consequently cannot avoid every taking of a position. The indifference itself, however, is already a first, negative rather than positive, result of a life in a pluralistic society. In a positive sense, it is largely covered over by talk of religious tolerance, which today by no means pertains only to those persons

---

[9] See P. Puthanangady, SDB, ed., *Sharing Worship. Communicatio in Sacris* (Bangalore, 1988).

who think and believe differently from us, but also to the alien views and convictions themselves which are in competition with our own views and convictions.[10] Public pluralism makes the religious convictions, and the accompanying religious life, a private matter.

This attitude toward religion, however, which also characterizes central Europe, has consequences for the understanding of Christian teaching and the Christian proclamation itself. The new questionableness of Christianity can easily be explained in terms of the collapse of what in the post-Hegelian era would be described as the Christian claim to absoluteness.

2) The Renunciation of the Christian Claim to Absoluteness

The following is not an attempt at a history of the concept of the Christian claim to absoluteness, which has already been extensively dealt with.[11] Rather, I wish to pursue the history of this claim in praxis. There we see a development from ecclesiocentrism to christocentrism to theocentrism and finally to soteriocentrism.

a. Ecclesiocentrism: "Outside the Church No Salvation"

Until the Second Vatican Council the statement from the time of the Fathers of the Church, Extra Ecclesiam nulla salus was held to be valid.[12] With a reference to the necessity of faith and baptism for salvation the

---

[10] On this see Hans Waldenfels, "Wahrheit - Toleranz - Indifferenz," *Lebendiges Zeugnis*, 38/2 (1980), pp. 5-18.

[11] See the lexikon articles relevant to the topic, e.g., Walter Kasper, ed., *Absolutheit des Christentums* (Freiburg, 1977). I myself have dealt with the question a number of times, as for example, "Der Absolutheitsanspruch und die grossen Weltreligionen," in J. Beutler/O. Semmelroth, eds., *Theologische Akademie*, 11 (Frankfurt, 1975), pp. 38-64, and K F, pp. 193-199.

[12] On this see Johannes Ratzinger, *Das neue Volk Gottes* (Düsseldorf, 1969), pp. 339-375; Waldenfels, K F, p. 394.

Constitution on the Church Lumen gentium 14 insists on the necessity of the Church: "Hence they could not be saved who, knowing that the Catholic Church was founded as necessary by God through Christ, would refuse either to enter it, or to remain in it."

Clear as the central idea may be, its margins are equally unclear. In practice it turns out that the dividing line does not run between those who belong to the organization of the Church and those who do not. For the thrust of the statement presumes two things: 1) the clear knowledge of the saving function of the Church and 2) the defective will of the individual to follow her/his insight. A clear insight, however, can escape those who do not belong to the Church, just as it can escape those who have received baptism. The additional phrase "or refuse to remain in it" in any case points up the insight that has been growing in the Church itself that there is obviously a leaving of the Church which cannot be interpreted simply as bad will.

Whoever insists on outside the Church no salvation must, however, take into consideration that about the same time as this statement turned up in the texts of the proclamation--not those of systematic theological reflection--reference was likewise first made to ways which are wrapped in the mystery of God. Talk of the baptism of desire should also be recalled, and of the various kinds of desire (Latin, votum), which in its turn, along with the Extra Ecclesiam nulla salus, found its way into the systematic reflections on ecclesiology.

b. Christocentrism: "In No Other Name Is There Salvation"

Even when the necessity of a visible belonging to the Church for salvation has long been relativized, nonetheless eschatological salvation remains christocentrically anchored to the present. In other words: it was bound to Jesus, the incarnated Son of God, crucified and risen. Theology was correspondingly concerned to highlight the connection between the history of humanity and the saving deed of Christ. That was done in this century in the reflection on history as "saving history," Heilsgeschichte, in talk of "anonymous Christians," etc.

Christocentrism clearly dominated the texts of Vatican II. That is the case where in the Constitution on Revelation, Dei verbum 4, the saving work of Christ is presented as the fulfillment of the history of salvation from its beginning. Christocentrism manifests itself where in Lumen gentium 14 before any reflection on the various grades of being near Christ and the Church (ibid., 15/16), "Christ alone," is declared as the "mediator and way to salvation," and where the same thing is repeated in the Decree on Missions, Ad gentes 7, before it incidentally remarks that, "although in ways known to himself God can lead those who, through no fault of their own, are ignorant of the Gospel to that faith without which it is impossible to please him." It is found in the Declaration on the Relation of the Church to Non-Christian Religions, Nostra aetate 2, where it says that the Church must proclaim Christ, "who is 'the way, the truth and the life' (Jn 14:6). In him, in whom God reconciled all things to himself (2 Cor 5: 18-19), men find the fullness of their religious life," and in the Pastoral Constitution Gaudium et spes, where Christ is presented as the Alpha and Omega of human history.

Since then this form of Christocentrism has likewise been placed in question. There are, for example, works such as, Raimundo Panikkar, The Unknown Christ of Hinduism,[13] John Hick, God Has Many Names,[14] and

---

[13] Raimundo Panikkar, *The Unknown Christ of Hinduism* (Maryknoll, NY: Orbis, rev. and enlarged, 1981); *Der unbekannte Christus im Hinduismus* (Mainz, 2. ed, 1986).

[14] John Hick, *God Has Many Names* (Philadelphia: Westminster, 1982; *Gott und seine vielen Namen* (Altenberg, 1985).

Paul Knitter, No Other Name?[15] Theologians of this orientation, despite
their differences in details, agree in their rejection of Jesus of Nazareth as
the universal mediator of salvation; in any case, the Christian "Jesus alone"
or "only Jesus" is seen as rhetoric and hyperbole. In contrast, they refer to
the always greater God. In the place of christocentrism there appears
theocentrism.

c. Theocentrism: "God Has Many Names"

In all the places where Vatican II speaks of the ways by which those
who do not know the Gospel of Christ and his Church can be saved
reference is made to the always greater God. The classic biblical text for
the universal salvific will of God, 1 Tim 2: 4-6, bases this on the universal
mediation of salvation by Jesus: "God . . . desires all humans to be saved
and to come to the knowledge of the truth. For there is one God, and
there is one mediator between God and humanity, the human being Christ
Jesus, who gave himself as a ransom for all, the testimony to which was
borne at the proper time."

This view of things, however, in the new attempt is cut in half. More
precisely said, the first sentence in the cited scriptural text, which speaks of
the universal salvific will of God, is separated from its grounding--that there
is one God and one mediator of salvation--and is taken alone. The basis for
this is that God's salvation also finds expression in other religions. If the
one God in the many religions is in fact one, the adherents of the various
religions indeed meet at the one God of salvation, but they do not need the
name of Jesus to attain this salvation.

---

[15] Paul Knitter, *No Other Name? A Critical Survey of Christian Attitudes Toward
the World Religions* (Maryknoll, NY: Orbis, 1985); *Ein Gott--viele Religionen*
(Munich, 1988).

Christianity must face up to this challenge, which comes not only from representatives of non-Christian religions but also from Christian theologians, above all of English-American origin, but also from Asia as well, especially India. It is not adequately dealt with simply --in view of the Asiatic images of God in India or "godless" Buddhism--by referring to the aporia, mystery, of a theocentrism ultimately conceived within the Jewish-Christian thought world. Paul Knitter seeks to avoid the difficulties which he has obviously subsequently recognized by proceeding from theocentrism to soteriocentrism.

d. Soteriocentrism: Religions as Soteriologies

The substitution for talk about God--theology--by talk of salvation-- soteriology--has the advantage in the Asian area that even where there is no talk of God, as in Buddhism, a common denominator can also be found, namely, the search for salvation. The questionable distinction between philosophy and religion, which is evident in the West, but not in non-European cultures, can be easily gotten around here. All human beings can be united in the common striving toward a comprehensive salvation.

This view of things, incidentally, can also call upon Vatican II. In both the beginning section of Nostra aetate 1 and in Gaudium et spes 10 reference is made to the fact that individual human beings as well as religions see themselves facing the same fundamental questions: The meaning and purpose of life--the way to happiness--death, judgment, reward/punishment--the mystery of our existence. In both instances the questions are formulated without God being expressly referred to; for those who have ears to hear and eyes to see, however, God appears simultaneously on the horizon of the human questions.

The journey from ecclesiocentrism, through christocentrism to theocentrism and soteriocentrism marks for Christians a process of growing speechlessness as the vision of the specifically Christian is lost. Neither mission in its old sense nor the call for dialogue have a chance, however, if Christians have nothing more to say. Thus in my final section the question of the enduring message of Christianity is raised: What do Christians really have to say yet?

IV. CHRISTIAN NORMATIVITY

In the course of the rest of my reflections I am not going to restrict myself to speaking of the properly or uniquely Christian because such talk does not automatically carry a generally valid obligatory character. I will speak of Christian normativity. That means: What I am asking is how from the Christian side the proclamation as an obligatory call to the world is to be brought into the dialogue with the religions?

Now the thrust of disputing the Christian claim to absoluteness must not be seen only in its negative aspect vis-à-vis Christianity. Ultimately along with the disputing there is likewise the attempt to stress what is common to all the religions, in contrast to what is special and different in them. Where the enduring normativity of the Christian claim is sought, precisely the opposite path, however, must be taken. Consequently, at the starting point I will set out the concrete question directed to Christianity, and then, in reversal of the direction taken up until now, test the enduring Christian normativity.

1) A Double Starting Point

The reference to Vatican II points up within the field of tension between "the signs of the times" and "the light of the Gospel" (Gaudium et spes) two starting points.

a. First Starting Point: The Human Questions

The disorders and dangers in the world, the uncertainty of the future, the questions of the origin and goal, the sense and purpose of life, the yearning for peace, salvation, happiness and fulfillment--all these, each in its own way, bind together the men and women of all times and peoples. Even if we could ask these questions abstracted from their time and space contexts, they would clearly contain a component extending beyond their time and space limitations. These questions belong together with humanity, perhaps even with being human, but in any case with the concrete history of the world as far back as we can follow it as the history of humankind. Philosophers call humans question-raising beings. Whoever asks a question, however, is not yet at the goal. In this sense all human beings are "on the way." In the history of religion "way" has long been another name for "religion."[16] The characteristic of human life as being on the way can then also serve as a starting point of religious consciousness common to all religions.

b) Second Starting Point: Connection with Jesus Christ

For Christians--analogous to corresponding starting points in other religions--there is added as a second starting point the connection of the human way of life with Jesus Christ as the way (Jn 14: 6). The understanding of the way of Jesus--that Jesus paradigmatically has gone, as a way in its life existence which endures--again admits of various adaptations and degrees of penetration. Contemporary theology, but also interreligious dialogue which includes Christianity, can easily be described under the

---

[16] On this see Hans Waldenfels, "Heil/Heilsweg I, pp. 243f., and "Weg," p. 698, as well as further discussion of mine on pp. 349-354, in *Lexikon der Religionen*.

heading of a new discovering of Jesus.[17] Thus all the more are Christians called upon in living their lives to turn to Jesus and respond to the question: "But who do you say that I am?" (Mk 8: 29 par.)

2) The Enduring Answer of Christianity

From a Christian perspective there is no answer to the question of women and men about their salvation which bypasses Jesus Christ. Starting points one and two as the human questions and the question concerning Jesus Christ must consequently meet in an answer which will be given in the view of Jesus of Nazareth.

a. Religion as an Element of Culture?

Here, however, there first of all needs to be a warning about an interpretation of the historical religions which at first glance appears to be well-intended and is to be found today even in post-Marxist theories of religion.[18] The idea is that the concrete forms of religions are to be seen as necessary elements or moments of the culture. To be sure, a religion always attains its concrete form under the influence of one or more cultures--just as conversely religions leave their mark on cultures--and becomes an element of cultures. The essence of a concrete religion, however, will be missed if the concreteness is ultimately presented as a product of a particular culture and the religion itself is reduced to a cultural product. Correspondingly, a religion would likewise not be taken seriously in its claims if the individual founding figures (where there is one) were dismissed with the help of a historical-cultural localization and a similar

---

[17] See ibid., pp. 205-228, where there is also further bibliography.

[18] As an example see the impressive study by the Chinese X. Zhuo, *Theorien über Religion im heutigen China und ihre Bezugnahme zu Religionstheorien des Westens* (Frankfurt, 1988).

explanation of their authoritativeness, and its universal claim were a priori relativized. The much-discussed question in Christian theology about the grounding of the historical Jesus-figure as a concretum universale is a contribution to the rational penetration of this thematic. Of course it cannot be discussed in detail here. The discussion, however, is a religious-theological issue of the greatest significance not only for Christianity, but for all religions which make the claim to be world religions, that is, which proffer a trans-cultural contribution to the solution to the previously addressed fundamental questions.

With this I return to the question of Christian normativity. I will handle the question in three steps.

b. There Is Salvation for Everyone

It pertains to the essence of world religions that they proclaim salvation fundamentally for all human beings. This claim first of all is not concerned with whether or not men and women accept this promise for themselves, but rather with the fact of a promise which has all humanity, indeed, the entire world, as its addressee. Now this is true for Christianity. It is undeniable that it proclaims God's salvation for all human beings and the entire creation. Today, however, it finds alliance partners for this pledge of universal salvation in other religions which from their side are also convinced of a possibility of salvation which is fundamentally open to all humankind. Regardless of how irritating it was to Christian preachers over a long period, the fact that other religions also were convinced of the same matter--the possibility of salvation for everyone--does not in principle disavow the Christian message. Instead, Christians should much rather rejoice that fundamental conviction is effective beyond the borders of the Christian community of believers.

c. A Universal Mediator of Salvation

It is also undisputed that Christianity sees the universal salvific will of God bound up in its effectiveness with the figure of Jesus Christ as the universal mediator of salvation. The linking of universal salvation with the figure of the crucified Lord can be expressed positively: In principle no one is excluded from the salvation of the world that has been effected in Jesus Christ; it concerns all humanity. There remains a question that is still discussed, namely, whether the mysterium iniquitatis, the mystery of evil, can be and remain so effective that in the end there will still be some human beings outside of salvation. In other words: There remains the question of whether talk of the eternity of hell is meant as a possibility or a reality. However this question is answered, it remains true that in the intention of God the salvific deed of Jesus Christ is universal; it pertains to all men and women of all times and in all places without exception.

From this beginning point it is obvious that Christian theology has always been concerned to make the salvific effectiveness of the redeeming deed of Christ understandable for every time, place and group of women and men for whom an explicit acceptance of Jesus as the mediator of salvation was and is de facto impossible. For our own time the already referred to talk of "anonymous Christians" by Karl Rahner is just such an outstanding interpretative attempt. It does not need to be discussed here, however. The limitations of this attempt of course become apparent where the "being an anonymous Christian" is neutralized by "being an anonymous Buddhist" and the like. We can also say: It will become apparent there where the universal salvific mediatorship of Jesus is likewise neutralized through other universal promises of salvation. The alternating talk of the presence of an anonymous structure is, however, at once an indication that the history of humanity in its greatest depth is marked by a process of intercommunication which cannot be absorbed in reflection but which binds together all human beings.

What, however, does the uniqueness of Jesus mean in this process of intercommunication? Is he--thus will it be asked today in view of the other religions and their offer of salvation--really the only mediator, or should Christianity now reject this claim as an expression of an as yet not overcome false domineering thinking?

d. "The One Mediator and the Many Mediations"

The question which is posed today in interreligious dialogue is not as new as it appears at first glance. Within the context of Catholic theology there have long been discussions about the one mediator of salvation and the many mediations under the heading of ecumenism. From the Protestant side the accusation has been leveled, not least in view of the mother of God as the mediatrix of grace and the Catholic veneration of the saints, that Catholics would in this manner detract from the uniqueness of the mediation of Jesus. What Karl Rahner had stated in a lecture from 1966 on the theme "The One Mediator and the Many Mediations"[19] attains new pertinence today in a world religious framework.

According to Rahner, four things are to be noted:

1) Talk of a universal mediation of salvation presumes as a horizon of understanding "the inter-communicative existence of the human being as experienced, which is set before us, that is, our freedom, for either acceptance or rejection" (p. 226).

---

[19] See Karl Rahner, *Schriften zur Theologie*, vol. VIII, pp. 218-235. The following citations in the text are from this article.

2) Talk of a universal mediation of salvation includes the notion "that such an intercommunicative existence always takes place before God, comes from and flows toward God, unthematically and anonymously as that may happen" (p. 228).

3) Whoever speaks of other mediations of salvation "in competition" with the mediation of salvation of Jesus must do so in full awareness of what the Christian radical and total free self-communication or self-emptying of God in the incarnation of Jesus Christ means. Precisely because what is Christian is not about a model of thinking or a speculative reflection, but rather about the historical figure of Jesus of Nazareth, his teaching and his life, his death and his resurrection, the historical beginning point of the Christian faith cannot be blocked out in the dialogue of the religions. Hence, what Rahner said concerning the question of the Christ- principle also applies.

4) "If Jesus Christ is not to become an abstract idea, a Christ-principle, and thereby a mythologem unworthy of belief, then Jesus of Nazareth, the concrete historical figure, must be able to be loved; he may not, then, be just another term for the unfathomable sovereignty of the grace of the transcendent God. How shall I receive him, however, as a concrete human and really be able to love him (and not merely accept a theological word from him), and how should this love for this concrete human being be my salvation, if I could not love other human beings who concretely are my neighbors, and be loved by them in a mutual love (in God's Spirit, naturally, and toward God), which is not just a commandment, but is salvation itself?" (p. 233).

It is doubtless striking how with Rahner, after a long involved argumentation, his thought in the end shifts in an extraordinary way. Argumentation turns into testifying, the demand for insight now calls for love. For our topic we can assert: Out of dialogue there will come again the largely stammering and silent fulfillment of the mission in the loving witness of a life in the following of Jesus. From this life the Christian must of course be prepared to speak and answer to all who ask about the hope which fills her/him (see 1 Peter 3: 15).

To be sure, in his time Jesus placed himself among the sinners of Israel and let himself be baptized by John. In interreligious dialogue today he may again become one of many mediators of salvation. Only who sees how the heavens open over Jesus can testify with John: "Behold, the lamb of God who takes away the sins of the world" (see Jn 1: 29-34). The new word then, however, stems from the silent-seeing worship.

Translated by
Leonard Swidler

PROTESTANT RESPONSES

SPEAKING THE TRUTH IN LOVE: AN EVANGELICAL RESPONSE

Gerald H. Anderson

Cardinal Tomko has raised some fundamental theological issues that trouble the Christian mission today. The issues focus on a Christian theology of religions, that is, our understanding of the relation between God's redemptive activity in Jesus Christ and people of other faiths, as well as those faiths themselves. This understanding determines our attitude and approach to people of other faiths, in terms of mission, evangelism, dialogue, service, and other modes of Christian witness.

Cardinal Tomko's analysis and critique primarily express Catholic perspectives, but the issues are ecumenical. Protestants face the same tensions in missiology. The virus of theological relativism is non-denominational! As an evangelical Protestant, I am grateful to His Eminence for this address and the concerns he has raised. They are crucial issues that require prayerful reflection and response. So my first word to Cardinal Tomko is one of appreciation, as I share many of his concerns.

Secondly, however, I am surprised that the head of the Vatican's Congregation for the Evangelization of Peoples has not mentioned the most significant doctrinal statement of the Catholic Church for mission theology--in my judgement--since Vatican Council II. I refer to the first encyclical of John Paul II, <u>Redemptor hominis</u>, issued in march 1979. In this encyclical the pope says:

> The human person--every person without any exception whatever--has been redeemed by Christ; because . . . Christ is in a way united to the human person--every person without any exception whatever--even if the individual is unaware of it. (par. 14)

I have always been intrigued that John Paul II, at the beginning of his papal ministry, chose this topic for his first formal doctrinal statement, with the specific emphasis that "every person without any exception whatever--has been redeemed by Christ," that Christ is united to "every person without any exception whatever--even if the individual is unaware of it." Shortly after the encyclical was issued I wrote, "While this view is grounded in biblical and patristic testimony, and has never been entirely absent from Catholic doctrine, it has seldom--if ever--been singled out in the official teaching of the church with such clarity and visibility for the kind of unqualified emphasis that is given to it here by Pope John Paul II."[1] Ten years later I would suggest that this one-sided emphasis has contributed to the dilemma in mission theology the Cardinal described. While the corporate and cosmic character of Christ's redemptive work--as witnessed in Ephesians and Colossians--is fundamental, it is balanced and related in biblical teaching with judgement and the need for personal faith in Jesus Christ. Cardinal Tomko has rightly emphasized the need for "clarity in the missionary motivation of the Church and of the missionaries themselves." But if everyone without any exception is already redeemed by Christ and united with Christ, even when they are unaware of it, why is there any urgency or need for persons of other faiths to hear the Gospel, to have faith in Jesus Christ, to be baptized into the visible church, to partake of the sacraments? What is the difference between a Christian and a non-Christian in terms of what happened at Calvary? Is redemption synonymous with salvation?

---

[1]Gerald H. Anderson and Thomas F. Stransky, eds. Christ's Lordship and Religious Pluralism (Maryknoll, N.Y.: Orbis Books, 1981), p. 111.

These issues are, at best, unclear in Redemptor hominis. So what has Redemptor hominis done "for clarity in the missionary motivation of the Church and of the missionaries themselves?"

Before discussing what others are saying about a theology of religions in mission today it is important to recognize that there is some ambiguity in official statements of the Catholic Church in these matters. One Catholic missiologist has observed that "the magisterium itself wishes to opt for the absolute supernaturality of the Christ-event and its de facto import for human salvation, but the 'modernizing' agenda felt acutely by many Catholics leads them to exploit a certain ambiguity in the formulation of the conciliar magisterium."[2]

Having said this, however, I want to go on to affirm the main thrust of what Cardinal Tomko has said. There are, indeed, certain trends in the theology of religions today that seem quite contrary to biblical teaching and historic Christian affirmations of faith about the person and work of Jesus Christ. As such, these trends call into question the need to be a Christian and to belong to the church, and thereby they undermine the missionary vocation for evangelization.[3]

1. THE GOSPEL AND THE JEWISH PEOPLE

In addition to what Cardinal Tomko has said, the problems are evident at two points that are especially important. First, the Gospel and the Jewish people. This is where the Christian mission began. Initially Jesus saw himself as "sent only to . . . the house of Israel" (Mt. 15:24) and

---

[2] Emphasis added; William R. Burrows, "Tension in the Catholic Magisterium about Mission and Other Religions," *International Bulletin of Missionary Research*, 9, 1 (January 1985), p. 3.

[3] See Roger D. Haight, S.J., "Mission: The Symbol for Understanding the Church Today," *Theological Studies*, 37, 4 (December 1976), p. 629.

he forbade his disciples from going among the Gentiles or even entering a
Samaritan town (Mt. 10:5-6). For St. Paul the pattern of mission was "to
the Jew first" (Rom. 1:16), and it was his custom "to begin his work in every
city at the local synagogue."[4] All the Apostles were Jews, the first church,
in Jerusalem, probably consisted entirely of Jews, and all the churches
mentioned in Acts presumably had Jewish members. The first major
controversy in the primitive church was whether anyone other than Jews
should be discipled. Today--quite the opposite--the debate is over whether
Jews themselves should be discipled.

There has been a trend among some Protestant and Catholic
theologians in recent years to suggest that the Jewish people do not need
to acknowledge Jesus as the Messiah. In this view the Jewish people have
their own covenant with God through Abraham which renders faith in Jesus
unnecessary.[5] Some theologians have gone so far as to say that not only do
Jews not need to profess faith in Jesus as the Messiah, but that, "By no
stretch of the imagination can Jesus be understood as the 'Messiah of the
Jews,' despite Christian belief. The most that can be claimed is that Jesus
was a failed messiah, as was bar Kokba."[6] If this be true, we pity the poor
Apostles and other Jewish disciples who apparently misplaced their faith in
Jesus, and were led astray!

---

[4] L. Harold DeWolf, "The Interpenetration of Christianity and the Non-Christian
Religions," Gerald H. Anderson, ed., *The Theology of the Christian Mission* (New
York: McGraw-Hill, 1961), p. 199.

[5] Evangelical Protestants opposed this theological trend in "The Willowbank
Declaration on the Christian Gospel and the Jewish People," *International Bulletin of
Missionary Research*, 13, 4 (October 1989), p. 161-64, and in "The Manila Manifesto"
of the Second Lausanne Congress on World Evangelization (July 1989), ibid., pp. 164-
66.

[6] Allan R. Brockway, "Learning Christology Through Dialogue with Jews," *Journal
of Ecumenical Studies*, 25, 3 (Summer 1988), p. 351.

In 1988 a study by four North American and European Protestant members of the WCC's Consultation on the Church and the Jewish People (CCJP) was published, with an analysis of statements about Jews and Judaism by the World Council of Churches (WCC) and by some member churches of the Council. The authors concluded that, "Though a number of churches have denounced coercive proselytism, the next step may be to proscribe all proselytism of Jews on the theological ground that it is rejection of Israel's valid covenant with God."[7] One has the feeling that the authors are engaging in wistful prescription, rather than objective prognosis.

Of course, both the WCC and the Roman Catholic Church long ago proscribed proselytism of any people of any faith, because proselytism is defined and understood as "whatever violates the right of the human person, Christian or non-Christian, to be free from external coercion in religious matters, or whatever, in the proclamation of the Gospel, does not conform to the ways God draws free men to himself in response to his calls to serve in spirit and in truth."[8] It is puzzling and unfortunate that a study sponsored by the WCC with reference to the church and the Jewish people would introduce this confusion of terminology. It seems clear, however, that

---

[7] *The Theology of the Churches and the Jewish People: Statements by the World Council of Churches and its Member Churches*. With a commentary by Allan Brockway, Paul van Buren, Rolf Rendtorff, Simon Schoon (Geneva: World Council of Churches, 1988), p. 186.

[8] Joint Working Group Between the Roman Catholic Church and the WCC, "Common Witness and Proselytism," *The Ecumenical Review*, 23, 1 (January 1971), p. 11. See also the authoritative document prepared by Dr. Tommaso Federici of the Urban University in Rome for the Vatican's Commission for the Religious Relations with the Jews, "Study Outline on the Mission and Witness of the Church," in which he defines proselytism as "anything that forces and violates the right of every person or human continuity to be free from external and internal constrictions in matters of religion" (II, A, 12). The revised and authorized English translation of the study paper by Professor Federici was published in the English edition of *SIDIC*: Journal of the Service International de Documentation Judéo-Chrétienne (Rome), 11, 3, 1978).

what the authors tend to say is that they hope the next step may be to proscribe all missionary witness to Jews.

After reading this volume, one has the distinct feeling that, if Jesus returned tomorrow and asked one of these theologians for directions to the nearest synagogue, they would be try to dissuade him from going. It seems that they do not believe he is the Messiah of the Jews, and it might be embarrassing to them if he made some awkward statements in the synagogue. Perhaps one reason for their attitude is that none of them comes from a Jewish background. Neither do I, but I have learned to listen and appreciate the testimony of a great many Jewish friends who have come to faith in Jesus as the Messiah. And one part of their testimony--without exception--is that they have a new pride in their Jewishness; their being Jewish means more to them after they came to faith in the Messiah. Therefore they have a special desire and sense of responsibility to share their experience with fellow Jews.[9]

I find it astonishing that often in books and meetings dealing with the Gospel and the Jewish people, the testimony and experience of those Jews who have come to faith in Jesus as Messiah is unwelcome or ignored. I once asked an American Protestant member of the CCJP how she would feel about a Jew who became a Christian. She said, "It would make me angry." This peculiar attitude of wanting to deny the Gospel to Jewish people is, in my judgement, a virulent form of antisemitism. Either everyone needs the Gospel, or no one needs it. Or, as Arthur F. Glasser

---

[9] This was also the finding of Donald R. LaMagdeleine in his unpublished Master of Arts thesis, "Jews for Jesus: Organizational Structure and Supporters" (Berkeley: Graduate Theological Union, 1977).

puts it, "If Judaism can manage without Christ, do the churches really need him?"[10]

It should be noted that after defining proselytism, the landmark document "Common Witness and Proselytism" by the Joint Working Group Between the Roman Catholic Church and the WCC goes on to state that the basis and source for common witness "is given in Christ. He is sent into the world by the Father for the salvation of mankind. There is no other Name in which men may find salvation and life (Acts 4:12). Christian churches confess Christ as God and the only Savior according to the Scriptures. . . . The central task of the churches is to proclaim the saving deeds of God. . . . Indeed all forms of common witness are signs of the churches' commitment to proclaim the Gospel to everyone."[11]

Nowhere in the New Testament or in official statements of the World Council of Churches or of the Roman Catholic Church have I found any exemption of the Jews, or anyone else, from the universal claims of the Gospel. To the contrary, Jesus sends his disciples--then and now--to all nations and peoples, to proclaim the Gospel, to make disciples, to baptize them, and teach them all that he commanded us. Obviously, this must be done with sensitivity, respect, humility, and repentance for sins of omission and commission. We go also expecting to learn in the encounter with Jews and people of other faiths about what God has done and is doing among them, while seeking to give our witness and testimony in proclaiming the Gospel through word and deed, in dialogue and mission.

There is a biblical balance, in regard to our understanding of the Gospel, between continuity and discontinuity, promise and fulfillment,

---

[10] Arthur F. Glasser, "Response" [to "The Churches and the Jewish People: Towards a New Understanding"], *International Bulletin of Missionary Research*, 13, 4 (October 1989), p. 159.

[11] Emphasis added; "Common Witness and Proselytism," pars. 10, 17, 19.

preparation and completion. Pope John Paul II, in his visit to the synagogue in Rome on April 13, 1986, affirmed the "'common spiritual patrimony' that exists between Jews and Christians," as it was expressed in par. 4 of Nostra aetate at Vatican Council II, and in subsequent guidelines published in 1974 and 1985 by the Holy See's Commission for Religious Relations with Judaism.[12] On another occasion, in reflections on Pentecost (August 2, 1989), the pope reminded his audience that "Pentecost is the solemn public manifestation of the New Covenant made between God and man 'in the blood' of Christ. . . . . This is a new definitive and eternal Covenant, prepared by previous covenants spoken of in the Old Testament." With the coming of the Holy Spirit at Pentecost, he said, the new covenant is "fully fulfilled in Christ . . . in his Gospel which renews, completes and vivifies the Law; and in the Holy Spirit . . . thus fully confirming what God had already announced through the prophets in the Old Covenant."[13]

The main point here is theological. The relation of the Gospel to the Jewish people is foundational for a theology of religions. If mission to the Jews is removed, then mission to people of other faiths soon follows (as is happening), and we end up with a radical relativism and rejection of the Christian mission to all people of other faiths. For while the relation of the church to the Jewish people is distinctive, it is not totally different or separate from the relation of the church to people of other faiths.

This "domino effect" in a theology of religions occurs when central affirmations about the person and work of Jesus are disavowed--beginning with a denial that Jesus was the Messiah. The same author who says "the

---

[12] *Information Service of the Secretariat for Promoting Christian Unity*, Vatican City, no. 60 (1986), pp. 27f. See also Eugene L. Fisher, "Interpreting *Nostra Aetate* through Postconciliar Teaching," *International Bulletin of Missionary Research*, 9, 4 (October 1985), pp. 158-65.

[13] The text is published in *L'Osservatore Romano*, August 7, 1989, pp. 1, 12.

most that can be claimed is that Jesus was a failed messiah," also raises "questions about Christology, about mission, about soteriology, exegesis, doctrines of God, and all the rest."[14]

I think it can be demonstrated that the trend toward radical relativism in the theology of religions since the 1960's, developed in the wake of theological views espousing that Jews do not need the Gospel, starting in the United States about 1958.[15] Today if a Christian theologian says the Jewish people do not need the Gospel, it is very likely the same theologian will also deny that people of other faiths need the Gospel.

I realize that the position taken here is not popular in many circles today, especially in North America and Europe. As would be expected, there were strong critical reactions from the Jewish leaders--and from some Christians--to the message of the pope on Pentecost cited above, and also to the Willowbank Declaration of the World Evangelical Fellowship in April 1989, on "The Christian Gospel and the Jewish People."[16] In this milieu, I appreciate the firmness of the Roman Church, especially the Holy Father, in maintaining a solid theological foundation for a theology of religions. With St. Paul, we can say that the Gospel is still "a stumbling block to Jews and folly to Gentiles" (1 Cor 1:23).

---

[14] Allan R. Brockway, "Vancouver and the Future of Interfaith Dialogue in the Programme of the World Council of Churches," *Current Dialogue,* 6 (Spring 1984), p. 7.

[15] Reinhold Niebuhr gave impetus and legitimacy to this view among American mainline liberal Protestants with his address in 1958, "The Relations of Christians and Jews in Western Civilization," to a joint faculty meeting of Jewish Theological Seminary and Union Theological Seminary in New York. See the discussion of this by John Murray Cuddihy, *No Offense: Civil Religion and Protestant Taste* (New York: Seabury Press, 1978), pp. 38 ff.

[16] *International Bulletin of Missionary Research*, 13, 4 (October 1989), pp. 161-64.

2. DIALOGUE AND MISSION

More briefly, I wish to stress the concern expressed by Cardinal Tomko about current theological trends in some programs of interreligious dialogue. I am especially concerned about the polarization between mission and dialogue created by advocates of dialogue who deny the validity of mission. This anti-mission attitude is ironic, because the genesis and impetus for interreligious dialogue came from the missionary movement.

Recently a secretary for dialogue in the World Council of Churches said, "Dialogue does indeed call into question the missionary enterprise and . . . dialogue may be seen as striking at the foundations of long-cherished Christian beliefs."[17] This unfortunate statement tends to confirm the suspicions of those who contend that dialogue undermines the mission of the church, and leads to theological compromise and religious syncretism. I think it should be pointed out that the statement does not represent the WCC (and the speaker, Alan Brockway, is no longer a member of the WCC staff).

Dialogue can and should have its own validity as a mode of Christian witness. The WCC "Guidelines on Dialogue" affirm that "Dialogue has a distinctive and rightful place within Christian life, in manner comparable to other forms of service. . . . We do not see dialogue and the giving of witness as standing in any contradiction to one another. . . . We feel able with integrity to commend the way of dialogue as one in which Jesus Christ can be confessed in the world today."[18]

I would be hesitant, however, to speak--as Cardinal Tomko seems to suggest--of dialogue as part of evangelization, if we understand evangelization as Christian witness with the motive or intention of conversion (see Ad

---

[17] Allan R. Brockway, "Vancouver and the Future of Interfaith Dialogue," p. 6.

[18] *Guidelines on Dialogue with People of Living Faiths and Ideologies* (Geneva: World Council of Churches, 1979), par. 19.

gentes, 13; CIC 787, no. 2). People of other faiths are already wary that dialogue may be the new name for evangelism, so we must take care not to confuse or misuse dialogue for evangelistic purposes. The 1983 Vancouver Assembly of the WCC, in a report on "Witnessing in a Divided World," pointed to this problem when it said, "We see the need to distinguish between witness and dialogue, whilst at the same time affirming their interrelatedness. . . . Dialogue is not a device for nor a denial of Christian witness. It is rather a mutual venture to bear witness to each other and the world, in relation to different perceptions of ultimate reality."[19] The World Conference on Mission and Evangelism at San Antonio, Texas, in 1989, made a similar point: "We affirm that dialogue does not preclude witness but extends and deepens it. Dialogue has its own place and integrity and is neither opposed to nor incompatible with witness or proclamation."[20]

Pope John Paul has commended efforts for interreligious dialogue. At the same time, he reminds us that the church's commitment to dialogue with people of other faiths in no way alters its "essential mission of evangelization," and that Christian witness "must always be accompanied by the proclamation of Christ."[21] The reminder is terribly important at a time when some are suggesting that dialogue is the mission of the church, as they judge evangelization to be theologically passé.

So dialogue is not to be used for evangelization, and mission is more than dialogue.

---

[19] David Gill, ed., *Gathered For Life: Official Report, VI Assembly, World Council of Churches, Vancouver, Canada, 24 July-10 August, 1983* (Geneva: WCC, 1983), p. 40.

[20] "Section 1: Turning to the Living God," *International Review of Mission* 78, 311/312 (July/October 1989), p. 352.

[21] *The Tablet*, July 15, 1989, p. 822.

CONCLUSION

In the face of a "creeping acceptance of religious relativism among Catholics,"[22] Cardinal Tomko has raised the right questions. What is at stake is nothing less than the soul of the church.

---

[22] William R. Burrows, "Tensions in the Catholic Magisterium," p. 4.

HOLDING FAITH AND CONCEDING PLURALISM:
A CHRISTIAN POSITION

Kenneth Cragg

Cardinal Jozef Tomko writes as theologian and cardinal, and it was appropriate to do so. I read his paper with alert sympathy and with admiration for its will to "good faith" in the issues painstakingly commended to his hearers. If we could have this will to be "inter" from "within" all faiths it would be a benediction in our common situation. But he "writes as theologian" not merely in the obvious sense that he is concerned for doctrine: he is also inside a universe of discourse about God. The careful and exacting exposition of the resulting problems makes the reader ask whether pluralism has really been "conceded."

Topically, of course, the paper derives from the fact of pluralism and its demands on Christian conscience. But, essentially, it retains a "singular" perspective. It sets the discussion in the framework of "salvation"--a term which brings with it a strong Christian implication about God and humanity, meaning and destiny, which are not shared and cannot well be made to serve as the "premise" from which, and round which, discussion has to move. "Salvation" begs too many questions, in its ambivalence and "direction," to provide the context in which answers are to belong. To start in this way incurs the charge that we have not yet begun to live and think "plurally."

Is not this borne out by the complexity in which the paper is involved in trying to bring contraries together around it? One might wonder whether the exercise is not like trying to square the circle. Enquiry about things "salvific" as Christianly understood in relation to religious diversity becomes speculative about "invincible ignorance," or "intention," or "anonymity belief," or versions of what is intra ecclesiam and extra ecclesiam. We can even imply the conclusion that it would be better not to affirm the Gospel in order not to terminate the anonymity of ignorance. "The practical disruptive consequences . . . in the field of mission" are, indeed, crucial for Christians and, with them, a right alignment of dialogue and mission. (To this point we will return.) But that preoccupation is precisely what motivates the anxiety that attempts the resolution of a dilemma which stems from having "salvation" as the point of departure.

It may be argued that a "stance" of doctrine is mandatory and inevitable. Unless we are honestly bringing ourselves, and all that "makes us," how are we meeting? Sincerity demands that faith, in the venture of "meeting," be authentically itself. That is required, further, by structures of authority such as cardinals represent. Yet, in "holding faith," there is an obligation to "concede" pluralism, not only de facto but also somehow de jure--in terms, that is, of the right of others not to start where we start, nor to conclude where we conclude. If we can do so we shall be divested of the need to "engineer" subtle, and unconvincing, theories of how our denominators--theistic, christological, salvific, eschatological--can be applied to other "universes of belief." Letting other faiths be de jure "there" in the human whole will not obviate "mission" on our part among them. Nor will such mission be less articulate or loyal because it does not first require its own prescripts about "salvation." Indeed, it may well minister more convincingly by encountering others within their own answers rather than through our questions.

Our instinct to domesticate the deep issues belonging to <u>de facto, de jure</u>, plurality of religions might be perversely illustrated by a revealing comment of Chaim Weizmann about his role in the 1920s in the running of the Zionist executive: "If I want to take a decision, I stand in front of a mirror and hold a conference with my reflection and that is how the organisation is run."[1] A perverse illustration indeed, since the Congress in Rome in October, 1988, was so valiantly striving to transcend particularity. Yet, if perversely, it makes the point. For the effort has to go further. We shall still be "looking in our own mirror" if we talk "soteriocentrism" rather than "theocentrism" (assuming we--and others--know what we mean.) For, then, having commended the former, as Paul Knitter does, we shall find ourselves denying that "the salvation business" is "the primary mission of the Church." In the denial there has been a shift in the meaning of "salvation" (from "heaven" to "the Reign of God"). But neither are within the purview, for example, of the Buddhist who disowns the personhood which can anticipate "heaven" and disallows to history the meaning that "the Reign" entails. And, if we talk at large of "the well-being of humanity," we are still at odds about what is "being" and what is "well." Are we not somehow in a sort of Kantian situation in which "there is nothing in the dialogue which is not first in the faith," analogous to: "There is nothing in the mind which is not first in the sense, except the mind itself." Is this situation insuperable, in that faith cannot relate without its "givens" of conviction? The Christian criterion of "salvation" then (to press the Kantian terms) "phenomenalises" all that--could we "reach" them--are the <u>noumena</u> of other faiths? We apprehend them only by our categories.

To put the situation that way captures how far we are liable to require--even when not suspecting it--or own criteria. But to think it

---

[1] Ed. B. Litvinoff, *The Essential Chaim Weizmann* (New York, 1982), p. 211.

inevitably so would be a counsel of despair and, as such, a falsehood. For one thing, all religions belong to humanness, not necessarily in Wilfred Cantwell Smith's sense of "the humane science" (for that may ignore how perverse they can be, and damnable), but as having to do with the same, mortal wistfulness and finitude which belong to "this world which is the world of all of us." Religions, as we know, cluster around crises of existence and purport to order and interpret them. There are "rites of passage" everywhere because temporality is common. Humans interrogate themselves comparably, despite being massively induced by tradition, dogma or culture, in the answers they adopt. Also it is well to remember, when we are daunted by great disparity, that all major religions enclose the kind of wide inner diversity which relates them to each other in spite of themselves. Many of the issues between them are seen to be tensions within each of them. And none have a monopoly of saints, or villains, or hypocrites, or mystics. We need a robust faith in the mutual factors within the bewildering plurality. And are there not reassuring limits to the reach of metaphor, language and analogy available to faiths? Symbols, too, must be drawn from a common, and not inexhaustible, quarry of sensuous experience of a shared universe.

Such thoughts should fortify us to look for criteria of appeal on which to ground the vocation, and the task, of mission--criteria on which we can offer to proceed which do not begin from the dogma which disengages us from the instinct, or the need, to seek them. They will be criteria within the orbit of the other tradition of religion. They will not first assume, still less impose, "the salvific," nor "the necessity of the Church," nor the "means of grace," as our specifics require. Nor will they require us to phrase that embarrassing--and surely odd--question (in its condescension) about "what God is doing (trying to do?) in other religions?" For that question can only be formulated if it anticipates an answer conformable to our demands. It is a question which betrays our complete self-enclosure. It only has to arise because we are predisposed to ask it. Foregoing it will, therefore, be part of our readiness for unscripted (which may mean also "unscripted") terms of commendation.

Indeed, in this context, "commendation" is exactly the right word--a very biblical one. When Paul writes about "God commending" and "apostles commending" (Romans 5:8, 2 Corinthians 4:2) the word is <u>sunisteme</u>, to set together, to constitute by aligning. There is no "commendation" which is not engaging with consent. The "commender" holds himself liable to recruit that which, elsewhere, can "acknowledge what he offers." Is not this the idea within that emerging credal phrase in the New Testament: "worthy of all acceptance?" (1 Timothy 1:15) and the "worthiness" can only be externally adjudged.

This, emphatically, returns us to "mission." It also commits us to a Christian "distinctiveness" which deserves to be the theme and warrant of "commendation." But as such it belongs within a realized pluralism in which it is present, not as requiring a theory by which first to mitigate the plural implications, but as a witness ready for their fascinating actuality. As so often in things Christian, it is not an explanation we pursue but a vocation. "Commendation" of "God in Christ" respects the autonomy of other faiths simply by addressing them in the integrity of its own conviction that there is that vitally and authentically within them to which that Gospel is eminently "addressable." It does not need, or require, further to have its own criterion negotiate with their validity. This can be left to the good faith in which, and to which, they are "commended." Commendation is not, then, preoccupied with theory about others but with them as they are. The seriousness of the faith within us shares the seriousness of the others' faith. Otherwise--either way--there would be no "commendation." Witness has learned to submit its "worth" to criteria not its own. That it does so is its tribute to plurality: it is its way of belonging plurally de jure.

Would it be unfair, then, to suggest that the "Introductory Discourse" is perhaps too abstract, too concerned for the rational, too problem-minded? Is this why it gets involved in an effort to explicate (for itself) what has just to be "let be" as the diversity is? To suspect so is not to abdicate a theological vocation. For a world-theology, "theology on full alert,"[2] is urgent in our time and neglect of it quite culpable. It is, rather, that seeking and finding such theology can only be in the concreteness of "'commendation." Mission, through all the Christian centuries, has been the setting of theology. It was so, manifestly, with Paul and in the Fourth Gospel. A faith which is not proceeding hospitably is not proceeding "in the Holy Spirit." Only in "finding" the world does it define itself. So it is in letting other faiths be what they are (rather than seeking to subsume them to its own canons of scrutiny) that it can hope, as neighbor and perhaps as catalyst, to articulate itself in "commendation."

This sense of things has the advantage of letting the contraries and antipathies between faiths be the realities they are. We do not have to seek ingeniously to reconcile what is opposed or pretend to be sanguine about what should only disturb. We shall be exempt from seeming to "disbelieve beliefs" and the liberty will be mutual. Is not "dialogue" at times liable to enervate itself by easy complacence? Realism knows that when Buddhist meets Christian they are not in blindfold identifying the contours of a parabolic elephant whose legs might be a tree and its flank a wall. Nor are

---

[2] To borrow a phrase from the British Council of Churches' Committee for Relations with People of Other Faiths, in its liaison with theological colleges in Britain.

Hindu and Jew climbing in mist towards an unseen summit about which they are agreed. Sinai is not the Himalayas.

Yet it is precisely within--and because of--these understood and acknowledged disparities that "commendation" belongs at once in trust with witness and responsible for credentials that obtain as only disparity can exact them. If such is the "faithful" way of truly conceding pluralism then it deserves some detailed illustration in response to the careful question-posing of Cardinal Tomko. Let us venture this with particular reference to Buddhism as being, perhaps, at the furthest removed among the great faiths from Christianity. (Not ignoring how close it is qua technique of spirituality despite remoteness of convictions.) All, however, will bear strongly on multi-directional Christian "commendation."

Can we begin, without dogmatic fanfare, from the human end where we all participate in fact, however we diversify interpretation of that experience? We shall at least then be starting where we all are. To be sure, we have conflicting appeals to "revelation" in this context. But this must not be initially our ground, since "revelation" is like "salvation" in being itself at issue. We shall be involved in it, nevertheless, but not as the criterion we will upon the other. For we have determined that criteria shall be accountable to them, in their "otherness" from our premises but in the common-ness of our being human. We may also suspend purely methodological debate about the relative roles of "reason," the psyche, emotion, etc. We are seeking simply to be within the way all these operate for the other.

The paramount criterion for the Buddhist is that of dukkha, the pain of impermanence. Christian "commendation" has no quarrel with the fact of finitude. Do we not sing: "Change and decay in all around I see"? But the pain of time's frustration of "desire" need not be read as "commending" desire's abandonment. Indeed, <u>dukkha</u> lies precisely in desire's (potential) legitimacy. For only so does the pain of impermanence become significant. If time <u>per se</u> makes all aspiration illegitimate then it cannot well be read as teasing us with hope. It is only the propriety, the appropriateness, of desire that suffers <u>dukkha</u>, or--indeed--admits it into con- sciousness. The meaning of <u>dukkha</u>--so we "commend"--may well proceed within, if not actually necessitate, the positive significance of time. Can life-span be fraught with frustration if not also with opportunity? That it is "critical" none will deny. But there cannot be "crisis" if there is no option. Life cannot suggest "renunciation" if it has no quality as "annunciation." So we "commend."

That will for the positive can, of course, enlist the question: How if <u>dukkha</u> is definitive for all else, everything supervened that way in the first place? But that would be purely argumentative. More sympathetically to Buddhism, which makes "desire" central in the case for "undesiring," why not allow it a centrality over all? This would be the instinct of the Semitic doctrine of creation. This means an "intendedness" behind all things, a cosmic will that they should be. Such a conviction--we commend--implies a "wantedness" as the clue to being as we know it. Such a conviction can ride readily with variant--and forever scientifically expanding--explorations of <u>how</u> the wantedness proceeded. Faith in it is about the <u>why</u>. Creation need not, as a doctrine, be concerned with when and "a start": it has to do with <u>whether</u> and an initiative. It encourages us to take our mortality as an invitation, not an enigma, and to find it enclosing a manifold of experience that suggests a "guesthood," a receiving of hospitality to which a courtesy, a gratitude, a wonder, are the due response. That reading of personhood has of course, to defy the hints of despair, the scruples of illusion, the counsels of conceit, with which it is beset. But if its premise is sound, these are the tests of its fidelity and, fidelity apart, they could have no point.

Being is, then, in a kind of becoming. Creation, Creator and creaturehood have between them something of the reciprocity which exists in music and in art. Drama, dramatized and dramatist have something of the same relation. There is a self-relatedness in being which takes care of the besetting philosophical problem of "origination." The questions "whether so?" and "how so?" are taken up into that which is "let be." Proof, in some laboratory sense, cannot be had: nor yet can disproof. Either way it remains an option of response or voidance. Faith is only in the business of "commendation," not of imposition or a tyranny of dogma. As with music, so with meaning. In the phrase of Walt Whitman it is: "What awakens in me when I am reminded by the instruments."

But the more we accept (if we do) this "wantedness" about all that is and about ourselves, the more we proceed upon this "intendedness" about this world and history and life within them, the more the perplexities of evil confront and daunt us--as, indeed, they only do on that hypothesis. For if we assume a mere mechanism, or a futility, or a pointless riddle about all that is, the less we incur any real "problem of evil." We have, of course, the events, the situations, the occasions, but they remain only that if we unhallow the world. For then their 'meaning' is forfeit. They merely happen. Indeed, the 'theism' so often 'accused' by the problem of evil is the only conviction that really incurs it--a paradox which may have ironical place on our 'commendation.'

We are thinking here of 'evil' in its most ultimate sense as required by faith in 'creation,' the evil in human to human as history writes it large, and as structures of society generate and devise it in the working of their purposes. This evil is more than incidental, more than accidental: it has a dynamism, a perversity, what the Qur'an, in its concept of <u>Zulm,</u> knows as a chronic 'wronging,' a violation of the right and the good which is willful and defiant of order.

Taken in its full measure of satan's 'evil be thou my good,' as Milton has it, and read as the ultimate flouting of the creation's 'intendedness,' it constitutes the crucial challenge to a divine order. It is other than that 'evil' which belongs simply with transitories, the evil that vetoes desire and dismays the will confesses its own illusions. This other Semitic 'evil' (shall we call it?) is aggrandizing, reproductive, violent. It masquerades as good. It is a pride that disguises humility: it is capable of what Kierkegaard called 'an infinite regression.' It can betray even penitence. There is no limit to its subtlety and prevarication.

As the tragic crisis of creaturehood it has to be the vital issue for any confidence in creation. Manifestly it 'involves' the Creator, if all is not illusory. But--if illusion is all--how then the tragedy? Significance has to be retrieved by its very anguish. That is the 'commendation' to which the Christian is witness. What, then, can we say of the theist to the realist in this context? How are they one and the same? If we see the question of evil as big enough for God, the answer has also to be big enough for God, the answer has also to be big enough for God. Law will plainly be part of the answer, for it is necessarily part of the question. 'By the law is the knowledge of sin.' 'I have sinned,' 'we have sinned,' cannot be said except in the hearing of: 'Thou shalt,' 'thou shalt not.'

But will law suffice? Will prophethood avail, given the evident competence of evil to deny the command and defy the constraint? Is it not precisely its defiance which nerves it, its malice which impels it? Are not both somehow excited by the very fact of law? Will-power among us is 'won't-power,' and for one and the same reason. Exhortation may well be futile, while sheer retribution is defeated. It is here, of course, that Christian 'commendation' has such relevance to Islam. The very dignity of prophethood conceals the question (of God) whether prophethood can be all. Yet, by the sending of prophets, the divine is clearly, and vitally, 'associated' with the human, ruling out that 'dissociation' which Islam (very rightly) out of its intense concern with idolatry seems--mystics apart--to make total.

It is in this whole context that we reach Christian Christology and its reverent, patient 'commendation' to all. What we are commending--if not the option (it can be no more though it is to us a necessity) to identify in the fact, the ministry and the cross of Jesus an event-symbol where we can the interplay of a just and good creation and the reality of human wrong within it. We have there, manifestly, a climax of an expression of evil arising in and from a context of encounter in which a teaching undergoes rejection and, so doing, may be said, truly, to bear the evil, but is seen to bear it in such fashion as to 'bear it away.' That reading quickly became a gospel to, and about, 'the sin of the world.' The assurance--and speed--with which it did so must be part of its credential. The teaching finds it epitome in the action. The whole may be seen and read as the action of God within the action of Christ.

The concept of 'sending' and 'being sent' is Judaic, Islamic, and Christian. The question for each is how far it 'entails' God. 'Sending' means a stake in the response. Humans are not puppets but addressees. It is characteristic of all three theisms that prophethood is full of hazard. By its very nature it becomes the butt, or center-point, of the obduracy that will not abide the summons--away from wrong and unto good--which the prophet brings. Without him, the issue might be dormant: because of him it is fully joined. What this comes to mean for prophets (remember

Jeremiah), it comes to mean on behalf of God. The suffering is not privately theirs, except in its pain. They would not have incurred it had they not been God's messengers. They are in it for him: is He in it with them? Sheer omnipotence is of no avail here. For if its exercise could obtain, there need be no issue in the first place. What, then, does human freedom cost God? The Christian answer is: 'His being "In Christ" reconciling a world.' Prophethood has deepened into biography, 'the Word is made flesh.' The divine/human relation is defined in terms of the love that suffers. This love is the shape of omnipotence in its mode of relation with the creaturehood once for all willed into freedom and so only restored from evil by the bearing of that which the cross epitomizes as, concurrently, the deed of men, the way of the Christ and the self-expression of God.

Perhaps, with Jewry in mind, we should say, could 'epitomise' all these. For there is that in Jewry which reads Jesus' death in a sense that disallows its Christian dimensions. It emerges then as a regrettable, perhaps preventable, tragedy, a mere miscarriage, a sad misadventure. Jesus' teaching was not so confrontational as the Gospels suggest. There was no essential enmity between Jesus and the Pharisees. Alright, history has its interpreters. But the Christian interpretation became 'history' and that has to have its point, and came from a theological necessity with which historicism has to reckon. The symbol remains, even if--for 'historians' --it can be no more than symbol.

But it is 'over-loaded' as many feel? Can you have 'the sin of the world' in any one focus? And what of wrongs vastly more horrendous? Yet, qualitatively, what it takes to 'answer' evil may be gathered at and into one point and God be discovered there, consistently with all those other intimations of our 'wantedness' which we may everywhere discern. If so, then--to use appalling jargon --Christocentrism and theocentrism are one and the same. Or, more happily stated: 'God was in Christ.' We can 'hold these truths' Christ-evident, with the 'Christ-evidence' apposite for, and commendable to, every religious reckoning with our humanness and with the plural interpretations round which we wait, wonder and are wistful.

We are back, to be sure, with a Christian theme of 'salvation.' But, instead of somehow striving to fit them into it, we have studied--if highly selectively--how we might introduce them to it by deferring to their otherness and believing to find there that to which our credentials are accountable they are. Is not this how genuine participation and open mission meet? The tests of a mission's relevance are set, not first by what it brings, but by where it goes. If 'salvation' is to be recognized, it will need to come as an open question. For a Gospel only becomes one in the receiving. With the careful solicitude which the Introductory Discourse exemplified to the Congress let us sustain witness with a lively will for credentials it was to offer to criteria not its own. Such is the vocation into pluralism on which we are embarked. And, as Noah said, according to the Qur'an: 'With God be the mooring.'

A LARGER ROOM FOR CONVERSATION

Robert W. Huston

The connection or relationship between Christian evangelism and Christian neighborliness is a contemporary "hot issue," but it is not a new dilemma for theologians, pastors, administrators, and laity. The primary opposites of choice were lined out in the 1930's in the debates between Professor Ernest Hocking and missionary Hendrik Kraemer and the discussions in missionary conferences, speeches, and books that ensued. The "either/or" options of radical displacement or of "honoring, for Christ's sake, other responses to God's creativity and work" have from time to time surfaced ever since. Current lexicon usage pits "evangelism-witness" and "dialogue" as the supposed opposites.

Cardinal Tomko has outlined thoroughly most of the current loci and foci of the contemporary delicate and turbulent issues. His extensive list of questions for the daring follow his list of the "practical disruptive consequences in mission fields." Matching those areas of the Cardinal's concerns (that seem possibly anachronistic in an era of missions on six continents of mutual witness) are the often disruptive and unseemly absolutistic arguments at "home." The editors are to be commended for providing for diverse responses to his work to encourage more persons to grapple with the core issues.

This response will focus on several of Cardinal Tomko's questions but not attempt to address them all. Some of the questions on which I shall touch are the relationship between Christian witness and other forms and purposes of dialogue, the uniqueness of Christianity, the purposes of missions, the nature of "truth" and the limits of revelation, God's grace within other religions and practicing persons, and, most important of all, in my view, the relationship between dialogue and announcement. This response brings together reflections of early experience with some persons of other faiths prior to my own conversions and call to the ordained ministry, nineteen years as a pastor and nearly a quarter-century as the ecumenical staff officer in the denomination of my ordination. It will articulate the position of The United Methodist Church as expressed in a statement adopted by our General Conference in 1980, but the illustrative hints of theological, hermeneutical, social, ethical, and practical influences are completely my own. The United Methodist General Conference statement, published as Called to Be Neighbors and Witnesses, clearly rejects the "either/or" flavor of the debates of the 1930's. It reflects the conviction that there are biblical texts supporting the "both/and" stance and that these seem akin to the spirit of the Christ. It says: "Dialogue creates relationships of mutual understanding, openness and respect. Witness presses dialogue to the deepest convictions about life, death, and hope. The command to love one's neighbors and the call to witness to Jesus Christ to all people are inseparably linked." It is, therefore, not a simple task either in biblical, theological, or epistemological frameworks. As Albert Einstein once noted: "Keep things as simple as possible but not simpler!"

The way sensitive thinkers change their minds encourages us to avoid dogmatic stances. I studied with Dr. Kraemer in 1953-54 when he was the director of the World Council of Churches Ecumenical Institute near Geneva. He was moderating his "radical displacement" view even then, and, by 1956, in Religion and the Christian Faith (p. 321), he asserted that in all religions there is a dialectical response to what God is trying to reveal of himself (sic). But the simpler view always appeals to some people.

1. AN EXCLUSIVIST MODEL

A shipmate during World War II (Robert Whitlock) took so seriously the admonition of 2 Cor. 6:14-18 that he refused to eat meals with not only Jews and Buddhists and Mormons but also with other Christians, because their beliefs were not precisely and absolutely the same as his. He had bought into an insensitive Christology and then used it to sin against Christians and those of other faiths. He was my first experience with those who easily, rigidly, and fearfully take God's power into their own hands and decree an exclusivist position with a vengeance. Other persons are simply objects of conversion to their view. Such Christian chauvinist prooftexting ignores Acts 15 and the judgment that circumcision was not to be required of new Christians because to so insist would be a contradiction of the work of the Creator. Such prooftexting takes Christian uniqueness to mean an automatic disparagement of other religions and their adherents. It misses other uniquenesses such as assessment of moral concern for the oppressed, the sick, those with handicapping conditions. It misses the revelation that there are two Jerusalems coming down to earth. As James Efird points out in Revelation for Today (Abingdon, 1989) the "new" Jerusalem (Rev. 21:10-14) includes apostles, Israel, Jesus, and multitudes entering heaven through the holy cities of Judaism--a mild yet important counter to the rigidly interpreted Great Commission! Mr. Whitlock's evangelistic style, espoused and practiced, led him finally to abstain from our weekly prayer group, shouting with considerable arrogance and panic that we needed to be saved. But this mode denies the spirit of the One to whom we all would testify. Such a style did not and could not build a relationship with persons of other religions because no dialogue, no interchange, was allowed. Indeed, in 1942-43 and since, it has seemed to me that such a mood and mode of absolute certainty (even more than his vehemence) might be an expression of basic insecurity in faith. To proclaim the Gospel is a clear mandate. It is simple to say it. But what that Gospel includes and how one proclaims it best often seem elusive. Exclusivism confines us in a very small room where the intriguing question of why other religions exist, being founded before or after Christianity, is excluded from God's creative grace. Fortunately, there are mysteries that entice us to live in a larger room. In a new book, Michael Barnes of Heythrop College, the University of London, declares a theology for dialogue, not merely a theology of dialogue.

Are all other religions the creation of the devil? If there is room for doubt about that, then there is genuine excitement and grace in conversation with those of other faiths of God, without the presence of a selfish or unselfish "end" called conversion. The issues are not simple. The reminder by Dr. James Sanders that scripture itself is theocentric should give us pause. The work of and existence of Jesus Christ is to point to God. Trinitarian theology need not eventuate in tritheism. As United Methodist Bishop Roy Sano reminds us, God is one: the work of the Savior cannot violate the work of the Creator. One does not have to "agree" with the sociocentrist position or define salvation as the "well-being of humanity" to perceive that the Reign of God is a center of the mission of Jesus Christ. The Reign of God thus is not separate from nor set against the mandate to teach and make disciples of all nations; but the prime meaning of the Matthew reference is trivialized if we interpret it that we must "make" Christians rather than that we teach all commandments. We dare not settle for something less than what the whole Gospel demands of us. "Witnessing" in a salvation-emphasis style may well be easier than full-orbed witnessing to the message of the

Reign of God in ways that challenge the secularization of societies. Witnessing even means challenging those "members" of churches who actually worship other gods than Yahweh, but the real target for Christian witness in word and deed might well be those for whom God makes no difference. As someone quipped years ago, "Indifference is our greatest problem, but who cares?"

2. ANOTHER MODEL

How did Jesus share the Good News? Setting up apparently mutually exclusive shibboleths in defense of one "side" or the other misses that point, I feel. When Jesus met the woman at the well, for example (John 4:7 ff.), he made a simple request and then quietly related to her by listening to her questions empathetically. Then he quietly shared the Good News in a way that evoked from the Samaritan woman the deep request for the water that would quench thirst. There is both love and mission embedded here. Can love for the Gospel be commanded effectively? Can zeal for the mission be more than something given to those who are already part of Christ? For the woman at the well, the news was not so much in the words as in an experience of recognition. It was witnessing, not in arrogance, but in love. Loving only those of an absolutely like mind rejects the grace-filled elements outside the Christian revelation.

Understanding of the historical and social influences at work in the development of Christianity as well as in the development of other religions is an essential tool. It is astounding and moving to grasp that in widely scattered geographical areas, without known contact among humans then alive and within a relatively short span of history, similar religious experience developed. Finally, every experience, every reception of what seems to be revelation is tested through inevitable epistemological filters and logical judgments. "Biblical realism" that is used to judge everything else is not holistic. All possible data have not been placed in as coherent a whole as possible. Numerous revelations abound, and reasoned evaluation is necessary lest we be slaves to errant revelation. Our deepest convictions are mediated and organized by all our personal and group cultural and experiential foundations. Someone has written that John Wesley, a founder of Methodism, was a "dialogian" of the faith because he perceived the fallibility of all human thinking. Even these words about important issues may be in error! On balance, THE biblical understanding of evangelism/mission/dialogue has not yet been plumbed. THE theological perception of God's ultimate will for all creation is not yet written. Does anyone believe that God can be pictured in a definitive snapshot of human words? A sense of humor about all our disputations may be a saving grace, even as we pursue the search for more truth than we now can articulate. Thus, it is humanly impossible to conclude that any religion, including my own, can claim exclusive right to the truth. My personal testimony is and can be to the nature of Jesus Christ as the most complete revelation of God I know, but that does not require dogmatic brittleness.

Absolutism fails both theological and practical tests, in my experience. Given the fragmentary nature of our understanding of God's will and nature, fixed ideas, fixed institutions, and fixed theologies are inadequate for the future or, according to John Oman (Honest Religion), they may be symptoms of spiritual sickness.

There are a variety of criteria by which we evaluate all religions, but a caution is needed, particularly for "Western" theologians. Dr. J. Deotis Roberts, in Christ's Lordship and Religious Pluralism (Orbis, 1983), wrote cogently about the European-American standards of progress that are no longer tenable in "rating" other religions. We are reminded that our first responsibility is to let the sacred "show itself" before we think of applying traditional Western interpretations, many of which are culturally bound. At the Vancouver World Council of Churches Assembly in 1983 we were reminded that "our" bread and grape agriculture is not universal. The meat and milk of the coconut make a more meaningful eucharistic substance in some parts of the world! Though for Christians the incarnation is the supreme instance of revelation, God's Self is revealed in creation and history.

Hendrik Kraemer and Ernst Troeltsch were in agreement that religions are cultural totalities and make sense in particular cultures. This suggests that religions are not the only locus of God's revelatory activity. One Barthian view is that Jesus is humanity, and thus the distinction between Christian and "non- Christian" becomes blurred. It may be that, contrary to our precious sanctified-by-habit institutionalism, anyone or everyone is saved, not through the works of religion, but simply by the grace of God! The role of Christ in revealing God's redemptive activity is primary for me, but truth is greater than any of our "truths," and the "finished nature" of all theological claims is more than questioned--it smacks of the immoral. Precisely because of our still imperfect understanding, Christians are not expected to leave their Christology outside the room for dialogue. Without our practice based on convictions, there would be little beyond academic interest to encourage dialogue, whether impromptu, informal, or formal. My personal testimony to the nature of Jesus Christ as the most complete revelation of God I know does not lead to a comparative religion relativism, nor does it require dogmatic brittleness.

God's grace in the midst of "non-Christians" does not release the church or church-persons from the announcement of the Gospel, else why the commandments (see below) and the commission? God's grace, operating on every human person, does not preclude our personal and corporate announcement of our experience of that grace through Jesus Christ. Arrogance about the faith is unseemly, however. In the John 20 account of the resurrection, Mary first confused the Lord with a gardener. Private faith-experience is both possible and necessary, but it is an expression of a larger experience of salvation. The larger experience of salvation is not an expression of the private experience, I think. The private experience is not to be had at the expense of the more universal reception of God's grace. The universality of revelation may indeed explain why religions are closer in practice than they seem to be in theological formulations.

My sabbatical period in 1975 was invested in concentrated reading of the writings of the mystics of the major faiths while developing personal practices of meditation (a crucial element in my survival as a bureaucrat). The radical similarity in the practical methods of approaching Ultimate Reality was startling, despite easily identified theological and ethical differences. When religions are observed to be closer in practice than one supposed from a distance, the broader experience of revelation is more fully received. When the theological formulations (i.e., the religions) are put foremost, then the broader experience of revelation can be lost. To insist that other religions be defined from our perspectives is not only to denigrate their faith, worship, spirituality, religious experience, and witness, but it is also to keep the religious room of our own lives limited. If we are secure, truly, in our Christian faith, we are free to live in a larger religious room in which Christianity will not be part of the problem, a block to rapport and relationship. We are free to contribute its spiritual treasure and resources as we receive from the experience of others. Dialogue thus is based not on a "lowest common denominator" relativism but on commitment to God's overarching providence for all persons and our own experience of revelation through Jesus Christ.

3. COMMISSION AND COMMANDMENTS

In the great commission we are mandated to teach all things commanded of us. Which takes precedence? We are commanded to love God and our neighbor as ourselves. We are commanded to pray for God's Reign on earth as in heaven. This puts the issues of dialogue and "evangelical witness" above the level of debating points. The key is in knowing what forms of service God intends for all the people of Creation and toward God's Reign. Witnessing is not abrogated, but the command to love our neighbor takes precedence, among other reasons, because the mode of witnessing is thus determined. Whenever our "witness" denies or inhibits the fullest possible understanding and reception of who Christ is and what the message of the way is, we have created a skandalon. Such method blocks our full witness. Irrational triumphalism is such a barrier. Indeed, our failure as Christians to manifest more fully the oneness we have been given by God through our Lord Jesus Christ is such a barrier. We are deluded, if we suppose that persons of no faith or of other faiths will believe our witness as long as we are so obviously divided in spirit and intention. The absence of love divides us and saps our power. Who has the capacity, the ability, or the authority to set limits to the saving power of God? The Manila Manifesto of the Lausanne II Conference during the summer of 1989 suggests that because the world is "under the control of the evil one" (that is, not Christian?) there is no salvation outside Christ. This statement is moot, but can we not be faithful witnesses to Jesus Christ--in word and deed--and leave the result in God's hands? In the Book of Romans, Paul does not name Jesus Christ in the image of the grafting process, and the final doxology is in God-language--that all comes from God; all lives through God; all finds its goal in God. Emulation of Jesus' practice of preaching the Reign of God, rather than preaching Jesus, is biblically defensible and in relationships with other religions and persons of other faiths may be a more concrete expression of love.

4. RELATIONSHIP IS THE KEY

Dr. L. Harold Dewolf reminded students that the Christian church is the one institution that one may enter only by confessing one's unworthiness to be a member. Once accepted by God in our unworthiness, we need no longer carry the burden of defending our supposed righteousness. Are any Christians worthy and righteous? Then is the process of dialogue not better understood to be redemptive, not retributive? As Bishop Lesslie Newbigin suggests, "It is not up to the testifier to judge." God finally is the judge about the redemption of all persons.

So, how and to what shall we witness? This selective response to the questions raised by Cardinal Tomko is not a systematic, comprehensive presentation, but a few capsule comments may be illustrative. The testimony can be simple expressions about what God has done and is doing and will yet do for me. I can express the substantially repeated experience in my life that nothing can come to us that is beyond God's power to utilize toward the best intended in creation. I must testify to the personal and intense crucial role of Jesus Christ in this faith-experience and to the best evidence of the role of the Christian church to announce and to embody the Reign of God. I can testify to my experience that the best witnesses who are involved in liberation theology have a vibrant, personal experience of Jesus Christ as Lord and Savior. I can testify to the several kinds of salvation experienced: the sense of wholeness and peace; hope instead of despair and helplessness; the renewing liberation, the constant infusion of emancipation from sin's power permanently to dominate; the heuristic vision of a future in which God reigns in every heart and the systems of society reflect that love and care.

How to witness? Not, in my experience, in the zealous mode. The testimony must not contradict the message of the One whom God chose as messenger. So, witness is made through worship of Word and Table, a combination of act and material symbols that John Wesley understood as a potential conversion ordinance. It is made in our concern and concentrated attention to the social systems that denigrate or manipulate or oppress individuals. It is made through relationships anywhere-- at the bank, in the school, in the factory, in the professions, in the way we drive a car. As Col. 3:15-16 puts it, "Let the word of Christ dwell in you richly." We may witness when our congregation offers the use of its building to Jews or Muslims if they are in need of space. We may witness, if we keep foremost the commandment to love, when we converse with those of other faiths or of none. The church, and we in it, then has greater promise of being a community of reconciliation (2 Cor. 5: 18-19) in which barrier walls are broken down again and children of God's creation are no longer divided from one another and from God.

5. CONVERSE!

Can we honestly think that the reality of Jesus Christ as Savior and Lord is put in jeopardy when we converse with those of other religions? That seems absurd on the face of it. And to what purpose? The word "conversation," which has etymological connections with the word "conversion," may be a better code-word for contemporary times. Are we afraid of being "converted" to another faith? Or are we aggressively proud

and arrogant in our profession? In either case we deny the exemplary faith
of the One we profess.

So we are called to converse: a meeting of persons, not a debating
discussion about objects for which there are no real counterparts in words.
To converse in love, not grudgingly to allow that there is "some beauty,
some truth in another's faith," even if we do not know enough about it to
mean our statement. To get inside--einfülen --the faith of another, not
judging an external shell. To converse. To make sure that we do not
disobey the commandment not to bear false witness against another. We do
bear false witness when we compare the "best" in our religion with the
"worst" in another. To converse in love. Making sure that the neighbor's
right to define her or his faith is as sacrosanct as is our right to define ours.
To converse in love that will learn from others and will most favorably invite
others to learn from us.

Relationship is the key to demonstration of that uniqueness that God
through Christ has revealed ultimately to all persons. Conversation that
allows for the possibility of conversion will have to be done in a mode and
mood that reflects our deepest respect for another's faith. If its aim is the
avoidance of bearing false witness, it will have a validity all its own. That
will be understood. Most importantly, conversation as an expression of love
of neighbor will lead us to reconciling acts in the name of and for the sake
of Jesus Christ. Acts of healing mercy and active concern for God's people
wherever they are oppressed are in the Gospel too. Converse--for the sake
of a future in an already interdependent world that is not yet interrelated.

The Roman Catholic Archbishop Pantin in the Caribbean, in a
sermon for an Assembly of the Caribbean Council of Churches, pungently
reminded us that, while it may be true that nothing happens before its time,
nothing will happen at its time unless some people are prepared to try to

make it happen before its time. Communion with all peoples and with everything that is made holy by the work of God is urgent. Conversation in love with those of other faiths, I believe, is an essential ingredient for the future of humankind.

THE IMPORTANCE OF THE SECOND ARTICLE
FOR LUTHERAN THEOLOGY

Thomas F. Livernois

What is striking in the address by Cardinal Tomko is that we are dealing with a crisis that originates within the Christian community: the challenge comes from missionaries, traditional emissaries of the Gospel. From within the church, people are raising questions of the role of the church and the status of the church's message. Does the church alone have the means of grace which lead to salvation, or are there other means that God makes available to those who do not know Christ?

The answer one gives to that question leads to another one, equally fundamental: In what way then does the church best remain faithful to its mission? When, in the name of the Gospel, it seeks to convert people to the way of Christ and eschatological salvation; or when, without seeking to convert others, it seeks to correct and construct the structures of the world in light of the coming Reign of God.

The problems raised by Cardinal Tomko are serious, central to our faith, and certainly complex. Increasing awareness of other faiths and interaction with other cultures require the Christian community to go beyond stereotypes, to enter into dialogue with representatives of other religions, and to take seriously the teachings of other religious traditions. The mutual questioning, which such dialogue develops, has meant that basic doctrines concerning the uniqueness of Christ and the church have been brought out of the security of textbooks and the sanctuary onto the proving grounds of missionary encounter.

No one should be surprised that the "missionary challenge" provokes vigorous discussion and vehement debate within the church. More than twenty-five years ago, Paul Tillich remarked that continuing tension within the Christian community between its universalist intentions and its particularist claims had produced "the unsettled and contradictory attitude of present-day Christianity towards the world religions."[1] This writer doubts that we have come far beyond that state of affairs. In fact, Paul Knitter has carefully described the conflicting and even contradictory theological positions which mark a community that is painfully aware "of religious pluralism and of the many different ultimate answers."[2]

We are constantly learning more about the great religious traditions, both in terms of expanding scholarly research and increased popular encounter through travel, education, the workplace, the media, marriage, and family life. But, if the debates of scholars can get heated, how much more will the everyday experiences on the popular level cause problems for the faithful? For if the general sentiment has been that we should be more sensitive to other religious traditions, that feeling coexists with a host of existential fears and doubts provoked by the rapidly changing world of religion and culture.

Tensions in the Middle East increase our public skepticism about the religions there, about the Islamic faith certainly, but strong reactions against the Jewish and Christian communities have also been registered. Interest in the Hindu tradition was gaining momentum in this country, only to be

---

[1] Paul Tillich, *Christianity and the Encounter of the World Religions* (New York: Columbia University Press, 1963), p. 78.

[2] Paul F. Knitter, *No Other Name?* (Maryknoll, NY: Orbis Press, 1985), p. 1.

undercut by the proliferation of gurus, not all of them above reproach. The Confucian tradition was seen as a fruitful source of ethical principles and political reform until events in China raised doubts about that tradition's ability to extend ethical reflection beyond familial and regional loyalties.

In short, no religion has been left unscathed. Perhaps the "kairos" for our time is to capitalize on these "falls from grace"--not in a triumphalist sense--that we can move beyond both stereotypes and naivete. Chastised by our own history and more understanding of the problems faced by others, we may be better equipped now to reflect upon religious pluralism and to do so with both critical scrutiny, scriptural fidelity, and ecumenical openness. Perhaps it is the moment when Christian theologians should attempt to develop a balanced and systematic theology of the world's religions.[3]

In the midst of these debates and doubts, the church is once again called to reflect upon the nature of its mission. How are we to reconcile the biblical command to proclaim the Gospel to all nations with the equally biblical injunction to love and respect the neighbor? At one time there seemed to be no problem with that mandate. There was nothing to reconcile. Conversion and service, Gospel and development went hand in glove.

Today we are not so sure. The relation between faith and culture is seen to be much more complex, much more ambiguous. The problem admits to no quick solution but it is important to state the problem accurately. The statement of the World Council of Churches, "Mission and Evangelism: An Ecumenical Affirmation," puts the matter best when it declares:

> Christians owe the message of God's salvation in Jesus Christ
> to every person and every people. . . . True witness follows

---

[3] Cf. Paul V. Martinson, *A Theology of World Religions: Interpreting God, Self and World in Semitic, Indian, and Chinese Thought* (Minneapolis: Augsburg, 1987).

Jesus Christ in respecting and affirming the uniqueness and freedom of others. We confess as Christians that we have often looked for the worst in others and have passed negative judgement upon other religions. We hope as Christians to be learning to witness to our neighbors in a humble, repentant and joyful spirit.[4]

We have no need to be defensive in wanting to proclaim the message, the "Good News," that has come to us in Jesus Christ. To react in that fashion would be to deny the rich, if not altogether innocent, history of missionary involvement. The fact that the missionary heritage has been responsible for more than the salvation of souls evokes untold stories of Christian love and unselfish sacrifice.

Any one who would develop a theology of world religions and an ecumenical understanding of salvation cannot dismiss the tradition of Christian mission and the theological principles which interpreted and sustained the missionary effort; but neither can that person ignore the current intensification of religious pluralism and of all the questions related to that phenomenon. A recent publication of the Lutheran World Federation affirms:

> (I)n our situation of religious pluralism all our traditional theological formulations and categories of understanding cannot be assumed to be adequate responses to the challenge before us. . . . Being faithful to our inherited principles does not necessarily mean that we repeat the language of those principles; rather we should evolve principles that continue to represent the grammar of that faith, the reasons for which these principles were evolved.[5]

---

[4] "Mission and Evangelism--An Ecumenical Affirmation," Geneva World Council of Churches, 1983.

[5] J. Paul Rajashekar, "The Challenge of Religious Pluralism to Christian Theological Reflection," *Religious Pluralism and Lutheran Theology* (*LWF Report* 23/24, January 1988), pp. 20f.

It is common today that mission societies, conciliar bodies, and Christian communions are calling for dialogue with the world religions. The Evangelical Lutheran Church in America is no exception. The Statement on Ecumenism recently approved by the Churchwide Assembly makes explicit the desire of that church to pursue the task of dialogue among Christians and commits that church to the development of a similar document which will cover the interfaith conversations that are or will be taking place.[6]

On the level of international discussion, the Lutheran World Federation, at its 8th General Assembly in Curitiba, Brazil in 1990, will take up the challenge of other faiths under the rubric "I have heard the cry of my people for salvation." The Study Book, prepared for the Assembly, gives an indication of the far-reaching consequences of the proposed dialogue with people of other faiths when it states: "In a world of religious pluralism, encounters with people of different faiths do indeed raise profound theological questions, especially about the role of other faiths in God's plan of salvation."[7]

What will this new dialogue look like in the Lutheran Church? What biblical themes, confessional principles, and theological rubrics can we look for in this discussion? One element that will certainly remain constant will be the centrality of Christ in the salvation of the world. Professor James Scherer, a leading Lutheran missiologist writes:

> With regard to other living faiths and ideologies making salvific claims, Lutherans hold much the same view. . . . In the final analysis, other religions are no more than systems of self-

---

[6] "Ecumenism: The Vision of the Evangelical Lutheran Church in America." Copies of this statement are available through the office of the Secretary, ELCA, 8765 W. Higgins Road, Chicago, IL 60631.

[7] *I Have Heard the Cry of My People* . . ., Eighth Assembly Study Booklet (Geneva: The Lutheran World Federation, 150 rue de Ferney, 1989), p. 22.

salvation. Everything depends, said Luther, on the Second Article![8]

Is it the same thing to say that "other religions are not salvific" and "only Christians will be saved?" Here Lutherans are very subtle but equally emphatic. Everything may depend on the Second Article, but the Second Article does not tell the whole story. The scope of God's saving activity must be seen in the full sweep of Trinitarian theology. The full view of the history of salvation lends a dynamism and openness to the Lutheran concern for the Reformation principle of "Christ alone." Two theological principles tend to be invoked in this discussion: the mystery of the transcendent God and the eschatological Reign of God.

In the Lutheran tradition one finds a willingness to admit that God's full reality exceeds our doctrinal formulations. There is always a residue of mystery, a "cloud of unknowing," an eschatological proviso in our understanding of God. One Lutheran theologian, Theodore Ludwig, sees the encounter with people of other faiths as an occasion for recovering our appreciation of the divine mystery:

> This is perhaps the key to all the rest, for retrieving this principle changes our way of looking at things, realizing that we do not know as much as we sometimes think we do about God and his ways. This is nothing new, of course. Luther talked about the Deus absconditus, recognizing that we only have clear knowledge of God as he reveals himself, and all the rest is hidden.[9]

This appeal to the mystery of God is not only fundamental for developing the Lutheran position on religious pluralism; insofar as it is a biblical concept, it will serve as a bridge linking the approach of other

---

[8] James A. Scherer, *Gospel, Church, & Kingdom: Comparative Studies in World Mission Theology* (Minneapolis: Augsburg, 1987), p. 87.

[9] Theodore M. Ludwig, "Some Lutheran Theological Reflections," *LWF Report* 23/24, p. 150.

Christian communions to this issue. But for Lutherans, whose strongly christocentric confessional writings, such as the Augsburg Confession of 1530, were forged in the arena of intra-Christian debates and even intra-Lutheran polemics, the doctrine of the transcendent mystery of God seems the most logical, important place to start.

It may be "the key to all the rest," as Ludwig says, but, to be successful in developing the tradition, this key will have to open many doors in the Lutheran fortress. The traditional Lutheran emphasis on Word and Sacrament contributes to the solid confessional and communion theology of this tradition. The conviction that "faith comes by hearing" has developed a strong emphasis on preaching and doctrine. The commitment to the "external word" has meant that a visible, worshipping community of faith is the most celebrated locus of grace. But a reaffirmation of the enduring mystery of God, together with a renewed understanding of the full scope of divine presence and Trinitarian activity from Creation to the Reign, can be powerful forces for stimulating theological reflection.

Joseph Sittler has suggested that the Christology of Irenaeus may be helpful in that search. He writes that in the teaching of Irenaeus:

> The Son is revealed in Jesus Christ but does not originate in Jesus Christ. Therefore it is not correct to argue that belief in him could only come from the Incarnation. "The Word was in the beginning with God." He is (for us) in the Incarnation; there we see him. But he is before the creation of the world.[10]

Sittler makes it clear that he is speaking about creation seen in the light of the Incarnation, not of a natural theology leading from creation to the Father. He calls attention to the cosmic scope of God's redemptive activity in Christ. Christ is the embodiment and the fulfillment of God's

---

[10] Joseph Sittler, *Essays on Nature and Grace* (Philadelphia: Fortress Press, 1972), p. 57.

universal presence. From the Christian perspective a relationship develops between Christ and the creation: Christ fulfills what precedes and anticipates what follows. If that be the case, can what precedes and follows Christ be devoid of grace and salvation?

Sittler further notes that "Irenaeus regards all life, man's life in solitude and fellowship, in history, and in the life of nature, as in the hands of God."[11] At the very least, this perspective suggests that within the Christian community the possibility exists of assessing world religions in terms of a more inclusive christological context. The Second Article would remain decisive, but its sense would not be exclusive.

We find a confirmation of this perspective at the very end of the confessional documents of the Lutheran Church, specifically in the Eleventh Article of the Solid Declaration (1577). Again, no affirmation of salvation outside Christ is found, but the text strongly indicates that, if the Father draws all things to himself, in Christ, there can be room to explore the means--ordinary and extraordinary--of salvation. The Declaration states:

> It is indeed correct and true what Scripture states, that no one comes to Christ unless the Father draw him. But the Father will not do this without means, and he has ordained Word and sacraments as the ordinary means or instruments to accomplish this end.[12]

The notion that the Father may find means other than the "ordinary," is entirely consistent with an earlier section of the same document which argues, quoting Luther, that "the right hand of God is everywhere," and that the body of Christ, in its "divine, heavenly mode" is able to be "present in

---

[11] Ibid., p. 58.

[12] Theodore Tappert, ed., *Book of Concord*, p. 628.

all creatures . . . where they cannot measure or comprehend him, but where he has them present to himself, measures and comprehends them."[13]

Yet another confirmation of this "expanded" understanding of the Second Article can be found in the liturgical prayers of the Evangelical Lutheran Church in America. The Lutheran Book of Worship contains several invocations which reflect a positive evaluation of those who respond to the presence of God in their lives. In the "Prayer of the Church" we can read:

> We thank you for the lives of all faithful and good people. . . .
> Comfort with the grace of your Holy Spirit all who are in
> sorrow or need, sickness or adversity. . . . And to all grant a
> measure of your love, taking them into your tender care.[14]

In the "Prayer of the Day" for the Fourteenth Sunday After Pentecost Lutherans pray together:

> God of all creation, you reach out to call people of all nations
> to your Kingdom. As you gather disciples from near and far,
> count us also among those who boldly confess your Son Jesus
> Christ.[15]

The church and its missionaries will remain the primary emissaries of the grace of God, but there may be many ways, and there must be other means, in which this Creator God reaches out to all, even if the ideal remains to confess explicitly and even boldly that Jesus is the Son.

Such examples could be multiplied, but the essential point is clear: For Lutherans the Second Article, the grade of redemption revealed in Jesus Christ, is central. All else depends upon it. But, in a very real sense, all else is included in it because the power of his Holy Spirit, the One God and

---

[13] Ibid., pp. 586f.

[14] *Lutheran Book of Worship* (Minneapolis/Philadelphia: Augsburg/Board of Publication, Lutheran Church in America, 1978), p. 52.

[15] Ibid., p. 27.

Father of Jesus Christ, actively pursues the whole of creation and unites that creation in one single bond of love.

The Lutheran approach to other religions seems firmly rooted in an attitude combining the conviction that salvation occurs in Christ alone, but that the Father and the Holy Spirit are able to call all nations to salvation in ways that remain hidden and mysterious, extending the love of Christ to many. In preparation for the Eighth General Assembly of the Lutheran World Federation, Lutherans are invited to consider this preparatory text:

> We affirm that God's own mission is larger than the mission of the church and that God also chooses other instruments than the church to further his purposes. We acknowledge that the church's mission is carried out by justified sinners who are themselves in constant need of hearing the gospel. Humility and servanthood therefore mark the basic posture of the church's mission in the world.[16]

The text, symbolic of the Lutheran tradition, makes room here for celebration, but not for arrogance; for critical understanding, but not for total suspicion. What we can look for in the Lutheran tradition will be a development of this dialectic.

---

[16] *I Have Heard the Cry of My People*, p. 21.

WHAT'S THERE TO WORRY ABOUT?

Paul Varo Martinson

One result of the ease of global communication with its mix of cultures and worldviews is an intense sense of incommensurables--some call it pluralism. This is joined by the moral summons, fostered by the UN Declaration on Human Rights, to toleration. Fact (e.g., pluralism) and value (e.g., toleration)--this twin confronts Christian mission. And Cardinal Tomko begins to worry.

His worry list is really quite short. The many lesser worries all individually recede into the single large worry--what significance Jesus Christ? In his words, "a common tendency to eclipse or reduce the role of Christ" is afoot. All other issues, whether God, Church, Reign, Mission revolve around this one. "Obviously," Tomko remarks, "what divine revelation understands as 'salvation' desired by God for all must be established. <u>Jesus Christ is humanity's only Savior and the only Mediator between God and humanity</u>." The worry is a christological one.

The source of the worry is not so much that Jesus Christ as such is by the standards of other religious persuasions not the final criterion of truth; rather, the source of the worry is that persons who profess to speak from within the Christian fold disagree on that issue. For some Jesus Christ is "the" final criterion, for others "a" criterion. The worry is not so much with the pluralism that is outside, but the pluralism inside that the impact of other religious claims generates within the Christian community. How one will respond to external pluralism depends in the first place on how one responds to internal pluralism.

In the context of mission and the encounter with other religions the reason for the internal uncertainty seems clear. Two incommensurable world views encounter each other, one Christian and one Buddhist, let us say. Both have a rich and deep history, both are convincing for large human populations having shown a long term staying power, and both provide noble insights into the human condition and yield amongst their practitioners persons of impressive integrity. This readily raises the question of the relative merits of each worldview. Outright rejection of either viewpoint does not seem in order. Thus, the external question raises an internal query. Is one's own concrete reference adequate? The solution then is either to relativize one's own point of departure, step aside from it without entirely rejecting it, and seek a broader basis for compatibility, or to accept the given of one's own point of departure and on that basis explore to the full its possibilities and limits as well as that of the alternative religious worldview. Both solutions present problems.

The problem with the first solution is that one must choose an alternative starting point that is neither of the first two. This in fact constitutes in nuce a third worldview which will prove its incommensurability with the two prior worldviews. Now one has only compounded the problem. This seems to be what Cardinal Tomko sees taking place. The problem with the second solution is that one does not have a neutral point of reference whereby to make a judgment between alternatives, and so one is locked into one's original worldview. The hermeneutical circle threatens to become vicious.

In fact, neither solution escapes the problem to which the second solution leads. The first solution simply adds a new problem (three instead of two alternatives) to the interpretive question. For this reason alone it seems that the second way to a solution is the more rational. That is to say, the problem of incommensurability with which plural religious views present us cannot be short-circuited by appeal to a third alternative or presumed neutral stance.

The difficulty of finding a neutral or universalist stance from which to proceed is graphically illustrated in John Hick's chimeral quest for such a stance. Forsaking his earlier christocentric focus because he finds it too narrowly constraining he moves to a theocentric focus. But this proves also to be too narrowly constraining since it filters out a radically non-theocentric view, such a Buddhism. Thus he moves to a reality-centric focus. But this too proves to be inadequate because, being vacuous, all possible criteria evaporate. Thus, he moves to a soteriocentric approach to recover the possibility of having criteria.[1] Knitter makes a parallel set of moves.[2] Now, however, it proves difficult to define of whose morality one speaks. Alasdair MacIntyre's recent book poses precisely the question this soteriocentric stance now faces: Whose Justice? Which Rationality?[3] Either this quest for a neutral, comprehensive criterion will come to an end, and then a new

---

[1] See Gavin D'Costa's thorough and perceptive analysis of Hick in *John Hick's Theology of Religions: A Critical Evaluation* (Lanham, MD: University Press of America, 1987), especially chapter 5, "An Examination of John Hick's Copernican Epicycle." John Hick's recent book bears this analysis out. See *An Interpretation of Religion* (New Haven: Yale University Press, 1989).

[2] See for instance Paul F. Knitter, *No Other Name?* (Maryknoll: Orbis Press, 1985), especially the last three chapters where he moves from theocentrism to an early formulation of soteriocentrism, and then to a fuller statement of the latter in "Toward a Liberation Theology of Religions," in *The Myth of Christian Uniqueness*, ed. by John Hick and Paul F. Knitter (Maryknoll: Orbis Press, 1987), pp. 178-200. John Cobb notes that Knitter skips the reality-centric move and "is wise to move instead to soteriology." John B. Cobb, Jr. "Response to S. Mark Heim," *Journal of Ecumenical Studies*, 24,1 (Winter 1987), p. 23.

[3] Alasdair MacIntyre, *Whose Justice? Which Rationality?* (Notre Dame: University of Notre Dame Press, 1988).

incommensurable arises, or it will continue indefinitely. But one can hardly converse with a "moving target."[4] The view that spoke critically of epicycles is itself now epicyclic.[5]

All of this is not intended to say that it is not legitimate for one to argue for pluralism on religious grounds. Indeed it is. In fact, there are many ways to argue for pluralism. But to argue for such on non-normative grounds,[6] is to argue from a different base line then one whose base line is the Christ event as testified to in the apostolic witness. Here the over-whelming evidence is that Jesus Christ in his life, death and resurrection was so identified with God, the final source of all life, that henceforth to speak of God was to speak of Jesus Christ and to speak of Jesus Christ was to speak of God.[7] The early "world" mission of the church indicated the comprehensive conclusion it drew from this. It is entirely possible that, as the Arian and Nicaean views proved incommensurable once upon a time, that normative and non-normative appropriations of Jesus Christ will prove as incommensurable today. Surely there is no harm in naming difference where there is difference. What may be confusing, if not harmful, is for one or the other to pose as a commensurable form of the other when or if in fact that is not so. Doubtless Cardinal Tomko is calling for this clarification. This is necessary, for, as we have already said, the answer to the external question is dependent upon the answer to the internal one.

---

[4] Cobb, "Response to S. Mark Heim," p. 22.

[5] For John Hick's charges of epicyclic Ptolemaic theology and his proposal for a Copernican revolution see *God and the Universe of Faiths* (London: Macmillan, 1973).

[6] Knitter, No Other Name?, p. 172.

[7] The argument from love language by Krister Stendahl hardly applies to this situation. See his "Notes for Three Bible Studies," in *Christ's Lordship and Religious Pluralism*, Gerald Anderson and Thomas Stransky, eds. (New York: Paulist Press, 1974), p. 14.

One typology of possible positions on religious truth--exclusivist, inclusivist, pluralist--has become a near cliche and is beginning to work its own mischief by being taken too seriously.[8] These three quickly become mutually exclusive positions. In fact, it is probably closer to the truth to say that a Christian stance will include elements of all three without becoming one or the other. The very logic of incommensurability would suggest as much. There is a base line from which a particular religious faith proceeds (this exclusive, since it is not another base line); this faith is convinced that it speaks of something that characterizes the way reality is in fact (thus inclusive); yet is clear that it has not said everything that is to be said (thus pluralist). It is within this logic that we shall proceed to the external question.

If in Cardinal Tomko's address the overriding internal issue is a theoretical one--Christology, the overriding external issue is a practical one--mission. Let us state that question more fully.

The worry has a context, as already indicated. That context is the seeming clash between the apostolic destiny of the Church and the pluralism/tolerance ethos of the day. The summons to tolerance comes, not because tolerance as such is the goal, but because tolerance is the presupposition for mutual collaboration so as to achieve, among other things, liberation for people in an unjust and troubled world.

But just what is tolerance? Tolerance is a virtue. It is a passive virtue--it allows something. Its original meaning, it "to bear" to "to endure." In political discourse toleration means to allow rival proposals and practices to have the same rights and freedom as one's own. It does not mean to agree with other viewpoints, for then toleration is no longer necessary.

---

[8] For this typology many refer back to Alan Race, *Christians and Religious Pluralism: Patterns in the Christian Theology of Religions* (Maryknoll: Orbis Books, 1983).

Neither does it mean to discard all limits, for that would be tantamount to anarchy. It implies a notion of reciprocity in which the one who tolerates and the one who is tolerated play interchangeable roles and bear corresponding responsibilities towards each other. If it becomes indifference, then it fails, for it is essentially a communal notion. It is a notion that seeks to make it possible for groups with divergent viewpoints to share in a common life. It is part of a cluster of concepts that spell out our contemporary democratic assumptions--freedom, equality, rights, etc.

Do mission and tolerance collide? No one ought to deny the historical evidence that they in fact have. Indeed, the intolerance practiced by the Church in the past and into the present is one of the main pragmatic arguments for a "pluralist" stance that sets aside the christological norm.[9] No one dare be uninstructed by that.[10] Past failure invites judgment by norms external to that behavior. Of that the Gospel does speak.

But should they collide? Taking a clue from the Christ event we can define the <u>missio Dei</u> as "God's movement in love towards the world," a movement in which, the Christian confesses, God is identified in the life, death and resurrection of Jesus. The mission of the Church, then, is participation in that movement.

What characterizes that divine movement? There is no time to develop a full blown theology of mission here, but some possible directions can be indicated. It is, for instance, world-oriented. This means that "the

---

[9] See, for instance, Hick and Knitter, eds., *The Myth of Christian Uniqueness*. Nearly every article raises this issue as a major point and some treat it as an inherent in traditional Christology and its resultant mission orientation.

[10] Of course the history of Christian mission is more complex than this one issue may indicate. One who has not been hesitant to criticize Christian missionary behavior of the past also provides a theoretical model for a much more complex and critical/affirmative analysis. See Lamin Sanneh, *Mission as Translation: The Missionary Impact on Culture* (Maryknoll: Orbis Books, 1989). For the implications of this method for pluralism see his "Pluralism and Christian Commitment," *Theology Today*, 45,1 (April 1988), pp. 21-33.

other," in this case that which is not God, is taken with utter, even in a sense, absolute seriousness--so serious that would will have consequence for God. It is an activity of love. That is to say, it risks relationship, rather than coercing sameness. What is risked is pain if that relationship is rejected, or if accepted, the consequences of the claim the invited has upon the invitor. It is, further, mediated. That is to say, this movement takes place in concrete, historical form. The story of Israel and the story of Jesus are the two concrete forms this movement takes through biblical narrative. As an extension of that it takes place through the Church. Beyond that, that movement is concretely evident throughout all the vast reaches of human history. It is, finally, final. That is to say, arguing from the Christian base line, only in the life, death and resurrection of Jesus is that which love intends confirmed and guaranteed. Israel, the Church and the Nations, if they mediate that love, do so in a way congruent with that sign and guarantee. A Christian pattern for interpreting the world emerges.[11]

Are the statements of the above paragraph commensurable with other religious worldviews? Hardly. The Muslim would take exception to language about consequence and risk in connection with God. The Buddhist would take exception to the language about God and relationship. The Jew would find it hard to accept the particular death of Jesus and yet name him Christ (Messiah). And so it goes.

We have characterized the divine movement. What ought then to characterize Christian participation in that movement? There are many modalities of mission. We shall mention three.

Mission is a public offer--evangelism; mission is a public reasoning--dialogue; mission is a public action--discipleship. Remove one and the integrity of the other collapses.

---

[11] See, for instance, the argument in William C. Placher, Unapologetic Theology: A Christian Voice in a Pluralistic Conversation (Louisville: Westminster/John Knox Press, 1989).

Were there time here to explore each of these separately and together we would surely find that if implemented in a way congruent with the divine movement itself pluralism will be both honored and engaged in the process. An offer implies the freedom for contrary offers being made. Reasoning implies accountability both to one's own claims as well as to the claims pressed by others, and a willingness not merely to make but also to heed a convincing witness whatever its source.

Action, if it takes its cue from the divine movement, is action that gets to the center of things by the discovery of peripheries, boundaries, zones of ambiguity,[12] places of oppression, rejection and suffering, bringing to these the transforming possibility that love makes possible. Here may well be a move beyond theoretical tolerance to the creative possibilities of practical intolerance where such is called for. This intolerance for the dark underside of human culture does not cancel out the healthy theoretical tolerance outlined above but works in conformity with it--as collaboration with all who are also intolerant of these oppressions and injustices.

Pluralism implies incommensurable worldviews. Can they really converse? If tolerance as defined above prevails, then no preconditions are required to begin to find out other than "being conversant--that is, being well versed on one's own tradition and on speaking terms with others."[13] Can they really collaborate? One needs no fancy theory for this. Wherever, in a world of ill-will and ill-deeds there are people of good will the conditions are sufficient for collaboration to begin.

---

[12] See Kosuke Koyama, *Mt. Fuji and Mt. Sinai* (Maryknoll: Orbis Books, 1984), p. 255 and the whole chapter on "Theology of the Cross." Victor Turner's notion of liminality is also useful to characterize this situation. See Victor Turner, "Passages, Margins, and Poverty: Religious Symbols of Communitas," in *Worship*, 46,7 (August-September 1972), pp. 390-412 and 46.8 (October 1972), pp. 482-494 as well as *The Ritual Process* (Chicago: Aldine Pub. Co., 1969).

[13] Paul Nelson, "An Unapologetic Middle Ground," in *The Christian Century*, 106,28 (October 4, 1989), p. 883.

We have in this response identified an internal issue (Christology) and an external issue (mission) that are the matters about which Cardinal Tomko publicly worries. Both were generated initially by the problems that Christian claim and missional action encounter in a pluralistic world. Addressing the first issue we rejected the way to a solution that argues for a neutral mediating ground in preference for way that takes incommensurability and the fact that every rationality works within a tradition[14] seriously. This means that as Christians we can only truly engage a plural reality by beginning where in fact we are, as one of those plurals. Addressing the second issue we have argued for an understanding of mission that requires tolerance and that engages pluralism fully and creatively in a variety of ways.

What this response has not done, cannot now be done here. That is, to demonstrate how in fact it is that incommensurable worldviews can converse. That they can converse we have assumed. Incommensurability does not mean incommunicability. But how that can be so is another discussion.

---

[14] MacIntyre, *Whose Justice? Which Rationality?*

A FREE CHURCH RESPONSE TO
"MISSIONARY CHALLENGES TO THE THEOLOGY OF SALVATION"

Melanie A. May

Cardinal Tomko has appropriately asked Christians to address again the heart of the Gospel: salvation in and through Jesus Christ. Too many contemporary Christians--at least in the United States--are too preoccupied with shrinking statistics and sagging structures. In this context, Tomko's call to be mindful of the "missio Dei" is timely and true to the faith we confess.

But, in the context of the wider world, Tomko's call has an ambiguous ring. His concern for the centrality of the Gospel seems tangled with concern for the continuity of the Christian church now challenged by growing recognition of religious diversity. This undertone in Tomko's call leads me in response to reflect first of all on the nature of the church, turning on this foundation to reflection on the purpose of the church's mission.

Contemporary circumstances call us to recover earlier understandings of the nature of the church. This is to say, in fact if not in theory, our thoughts about the church are increasingly focused on institutional continuity. Orders and offices, hierarchies and bureaucracies, are often the churches most obvious characteristics. Tomko's remarks themselves remind us that the church, by its very constitution, is meant for mission. The church was not created to establish and maintain itself. Indeed, the early church even condemned the community of faith from which it was increasingly distanced precisely for the predisposition to self-preservation. The church arose around a particular people to proclaim God's promise for all people and for the whole creation. The church was and is called to move out beyond its own boundaries into the world God so loves.

The central challenge for the missionary church today is the recognition and respect of diversity. Here I recall a comment made by professors teaching ecumenical studies at various Roman Catholic universities in Rome to the National Council of the Churches of Christ in the USA delegation to the Vatican during the spring of 1989. Their greatest challenge, they said, was not the confessional as much as the cultural diversity embodied by their students coming from around the world.

We Christians in the West, particularly we Protestants in the United States, have hardly begun to deal with this cultural diversity. We are blind to the cultural baggage we carry, for we still simply assume what is ours is normative. But our sisters and brothers in African, Asian, Caribbean, Latin America, and Pacific contexts are acutely aware of the cultural burden we have imposed on their customs and climes. And our Western predisposition to presuppose a distinction, indeed a dichotomy, between culture and Gospel, as between husk and kernel, form and content, even as in encoded in our word "inculturation," will ever violate the integrity of other cultures seeking authentic articulation of the Christian faith.

This predisposition to dichotomy also underpins the ecclesiological heresy that the church of Jesus Christ becomes incarnate as African or Asian or Caribbean or Latin American or Pacific when white Western faces are replaced by the colors of God's rainbow. The church of Jesus Christ will be truly incarnate as African or Asian or Caribbean or Latin American or Pacific churches as these local churches are baptized with their unique cultural heritages. Since in many settings, culture and religion coinhere, interfaith dialogue will be part of this engagement with cultural heritage.

As we Christians come out of the Western cultural closet into the wider world of God's good creation, we will challenge other Western philosophical assumptions. We Westerners have too long assumed that Christian identity truly exists as an a priori always already given. Accordingly, we Westerners have too long assumed that identity--whether Christian or any other--is established and maintained by separation from what is other. We are called to consider that as we enter into risky relationship with what is culturally and religiously other, Christian identity will truly be consecrated. For we will thereby be turning to our Lord who enunciated the way of losing one's life to find one's life anew.

Of course, as we Christians entertain diverse peoples and places, extending ecclesial boundaries, persistent questions about the limits of diversity will press us anew. The Christian church has lived with these questions for the nearly two millennia of Christian history. Earlier this century, against the backdrop of the German church struggle, German theologian Edmund Schlink stated the concern clearly and concisely:

> The most important and decisive reason for the various limitations of the diversity possible within the unity is the concern to maintain the distinction between truth and error, between the Church and the pseudo-church, i.e., the concern about the danger of apostasy.[1]

But I am convinced that the discernment of the limits of diversity calls for contextual sensitivity and for love. For God did not speak a word from on high, but because of love for us and for the world humbly became one of us here on earth: frail and finite flesh. As Christians, therefore, we are called not to make judgments about the limits of diversity by transcending but by being transported into contexts where the diversity of confessions and

---

[1] Cited by Michael Kinnamon, *Truth and Community: Diversity and Its Limits in the Ecumenical Movement* (Grand Rapids: Eerdmans/Geneva: World Council of Churches, 1988), p. 13.

cultures, religions and races, is recognized, respected, indeed, received as a gift for upbuilding a fuller, richer common life.

This call for contextual sensitivity and love moves me in my reflection to the purpose of the missionary church. Here, hewn from the quarry of my own Church of the Brethren heritage, I offer an understanding of the sacramentality of life able to save us from limited understandings of salvation. The Church of the Brethren does not understand sacrament or sacramentality in a classical sense, but as based on the belief that human beings are created to live as a community characterized by mutual giving and receiving with others in response to God's grace. From this perspective, the great mystery of the Christian faith, Christ's real presence, is recast. Christ's real presence is not perceived as predominately communicated in the bread and the cup by the ordained one recognized to be Christ's representative, but in the believing community who bears witness to and participates in God's work of redeeming the whole creation. Christ not only died for us, but rose to live in us for the sake of the world God loves.

The church as the body of Christ, in short, is sacrament; it is called into being through baptism as a sign of its commitment to live as the believing community of Christ. The daily life of the members of Christ's body is suffused with sacramental significance. For us, the ordinary as well as the odd stuff of life is sacramental.

From this perspective, the purpose of mission is the preservation of life as sacrament rather than the preservation of souls still outside the church. This perspective is by no means unique to the Church of the Brethren. St. John Chrysostom articulated a similar spirit:

> Do you wish to honor the body of Christ? Do not despise [it] when [it] is naked. Do not honour [it] here in the church building with silks, only to neglect [it] outside, when [it] is suffering from cold and from nakedness. For [the one] who said, "This is my body," is the same one who said, "You saw

a hungry one and you did not give to eat!" Of what use is it to load the table of Christ? Feed the hungry and then come to decorate the table. You are making a golden chalice and you do not give a cup of cold water? The temple of your afflicted brother's body is more precious than this Temple. The Body of Christ becomes for you an altar. It is more holy than the altar of stone on which you celebrate the holy sacrifice. You are able to contemplate this altar everywhere, in the street and in the open squares.[2]

These words of St. John Chrysostom point to the permeability of the missionary church's boundaries, boundaries beyond which it is perpetually called for the sake of the whole creation.

Indeed, from this perspective, it is clear that the missionary church is called, precisely <u>not</u> to be the preserver of structures or of souls, but to be a partner with God for the sake of renewing creation. Hewn from the quarry of my heritage comes a critical perspective on the call to be a partner in new creation. The Church of the Brethren has given birth to fruitful projects through the years in proportions beyond what our size would suggest: Heifer Project International; Civilian Public Service; Christian Rural Overseas Program (C.R.O.P.), International Christian Youth Exchange (I.C.Y.E.). I name these projects, not primarily to point to the Church of the Brethren's creativity, but to point to the way in which the Church of the Brethren did not control that which it created. Each of these projects initiated by one church is now an international and ecumenical project. Precisely because the Church of the Brethren was willing not to retain control of these projects they have had a life far more abundant than we could have sustained. They have been a blessing to many more of the least of God's people.

---

[2] Cited by Tissa Balasuriya, *The Eucharist and Human Liberation* (Maryknoll, NY: Orbis Books, 1979), pp. 26-27.

There is, therefore, a critical moment in the creative process without which it would not come to fruition: the moment of relinquishment. By relinquishment I do not mean simply subordination or subjugation or surrender. Relinquishment is more profound than passivity and more substantial than sheer obedience to God's will. Relinquishment is more a matter of the spirit than the will; it is rooted in compassion that does not control any more than it protects or preserves or possesses. The loss relinquishment endures is chosen for the sake of life. Accordingly, Eastern Orthodox Christians view the context for theological reflection on relinquishment not as the event of crucifixion, but as God's act of creation. Relinquishment is the moment in the creative process that leads to the life abundant about which Jesus spoke. Relinquishment is participation in God's very life.

The missionary challenge to us Western Christians today is the challenge of receiving diversity as God's gift for fuller life. It we so choose, this challenge may be a chance for us to come into a new identity as bearers of God's image: an identity characterized by relinquishment that offers ourselves and our traditions to one another as blessing rather than authority over one another. Identity in God's image is characterized by commitment to live so the whole of God's good creation may be transfigured as unceasing praise to God.

THE WITNESS-DIALOGUE DIALECTIC

Norman E. Thomas

Four major international interfaith organizations jointly will observe 1993 as a Year of Interreligious Understanding and Cooperation.[1] That year will mark the centenary of the World Parliament of Religions (Chicago, 1893) which heralded the start of the interfaith movement.

Our starting point must be the incontrovertible fact of religious pluralism. No longer are peoples and cultures insulated with competing truth claims. With the migrations of peoples pluralism is both a global and a local phenomenon. Today there are more Muslims than Methodists in Great Britain, and Islam is the fastest growing religion in North America. All claims to universality have to be evaluated in the light of the fact that for the foreseeable future no particular religion will be the sole religion of humankind.[2]

---

[1] The International Association of Religious Freedom, the Temple of Understanding, the World Congress of Faiths, and the World Congress on Religion and Peace. *Current Dialogue* 17 (Dec. 1989), p. 4.

[2] Donald G. Dawe, "Christian Faith in a Religiously Plural World," in Donald G. Dawe and John B. Carman, eds., *Christian Faith in a Religiously Plural World* (Maryknoll, NY: Orbis Books, 1978), p. 15; M. M. Thomas, *Risking Christ for Christ's Sake: Towards an Ecumenical Theology of Pluralism* (Geneva: WCC Publications, 1987), p. 2.

But while acknowledging the fact of religious pluralism, Christians believe, in the words of the World Council of Churches' mission statement, in the "decisive presence of God in Christ"--"in him is our salvation."[3]

A third starting point for most Christians is a mandate for witness including persons of other faiths. Again the WCC expressed it succinctly: "Christians owe the message of God's salvation in Jesus Christ to every person and to every people."[4]

Pluralism--uniqueness--witness--can Christians hold to all three? Cardinal Tomko in his stimulating essay expresses concern lest new theocentric theologies of salvation reject the uniqueness of Christ and blunt the church's witness and evangelization.

In this response I shall present an alternative position that pluralism, uniqueness, and witness can all be affirmed by Christians engaging in inter-religious dialogue. I agree with Gerald H. Anderson that "spiritual integrity and faithful affirmation of historical Christian doctrine are not antithetical to dialogue with people of other faiths."[5] Instead, they can be understood to be the raison d'etre for Christian participation in interfaith encounters.

Much of the argument that follows comes from the deep well of ecumenical thought (World Council of Churches and its participants) from which I have received nourishment. It shall include an outline of ecumenical debate on how pluralism, uniqueness and witness are to be related, and theological understandings of missio Dei, the Reign of God, and of holistic salvation.

---

[3] *Mission and Evangelism: An Ecumenical Affirmation* (Geneva: WCC Publications, 1983), par. 42.

[4] Ibid., par. 41.

[5] "Christian Mission and Human Transformation: Toward Century 21," *Mission Studies*, vol. 2, no. 1 (1985), p. 59.

1. THE ECUMENICAL DEBATE

Cardinal Tomko's questions concerning witness and dialogue sound familiar notes for those who have participated in World Council of Churches' conferences and consultations concerning these issues. They are heirs of the vigorous Hocking/Kraemer debate of the 1920s and 1930s concerning Christian approaches to persons of other faiths. Rejecting dialogue as sharing of similar points of context between faiths in "preparation for world unity in civilization," Kraemer argued that the Christian Gospel is unique and in radical discontinuity with other religious aspirations.[6]

Such exclusivist attitudes towards other faiths prevailed in ecumenical circles until the WCC's Third Assembly (New Delhi, 1961). There ecumenists recognized that a living dialogue with people of other faiths would provide helpful theological insights. By 1971 the WCC would found a sub-unit of "Dialogue with Men of Other Faiths and Ideologies" to foster such encounters, with Stanley Samartha of India as its first director.[7]

At the WCC's Fifth Assembly (Nairobi, 1975) guests of other faiths (Jewish, Hindu, Buddhist, Muslim and Sikh) were present for the first time. While many delegates reacted positively to this paradigm of dialogue in interreligious community, others feared that the WCC was moving away from belief in the "uniqueness" and "finality" of Christ, flirting with syncretism, and

---

[6] See Carl F. Hallencreutz, *Kraener Towards Tambaram: A Study in Hendrik Kraemer's Missionary Approach* (Uppsala: Gleerup, 1966); Thomas, op. cit., pp. 45-105. For primary sources see William Ernest Hocking, Chairman, the Commission of Appraisal, <u>Rethinking Missions: A Laymen's Inquiry after One Hundred Years</u> (New York: Harper & Bros., 1932); Hendrik Kraemer, *The Christian Message in a Non-Christian World* (London: Edinburgh House Press, 1938); and International Missionary Council, *Tambaram Madras Series*, 7 vols. (Oxford and London: Oxford University Press, 1939).

[7] See Paul Knitter, *No Other Name? A Critical Survey of Christian Attitudes Toward the World Religions* (Maryknoll, NY: Orbis Books, 1985), pp. 138-139; and S. J. Samartha, *Courage for Dialogue* (Maryknoll, NY: Orbis Books, 1982), pp. 35-48.

veering from its mission mandate. To assuage such fears the assembly reaffirmed that the Great Commission to make disciples of all nations and baptize them "should not be abandoned or betrayed, disobeyed or compromised."[8]

At the next WCC assembly (Vancouver, 1983) issues of witness and dialogue reached sharpest focus. Raymond Fung, the WCC's Evangelism Secretary, judged the report on "Witnessing in a Divided World" to be "the most theologically polemic issue" at the Assembly.[9] The key issue concerned conflicting faith-claims. All drafts were rejected that implied that God's truth can be found through other faiths. The amended paragraph, as approved by the WCC's Central Committee after the assembly, read:

> While affirming the uniqueness of the birth, life, death and resurrection of Jesus, to which we bear witness, we recognize God's creative work in the seeking for religious truth among people of other faiths [italics added].[10]

Fifty years after Tambaram 1938, at which mission and dialogue had been so vigorously discussed, an international team of scholars updated the debate at the same location.[11] Stanley Samartha, former director of the WCC dialogue program, called for a breakthrough in the present "confusion" over the relation between mission and dialogue. He would have based it upon two premises--the acceptance of the plurality of religions and

---

[8] David M. Paton, ed., *Breaking Barriers: Nairobi 1975* (London: SPCK; Grand Rapids, MI: Eerdmans, 1975), p. 73. See also Samartha, op. cit., pp. 49-62, for an interpretation of the Nairobi debate.

[9] *A Monthly Letter on Evangelism*, November 1983, p. 1.

[10] David Gill, ed., *Gathered for Life: Official Report, VI Assembly, World Council of Churches, Vancouver, Canada, 24 July-10 August, 1983* (Geneva: WCC; Grand Rapids, MI: Wm. B. Eerdmans, 1983), p. 40.

[11] See *International Review of Mission*, vol. 78, no. 307 (July 1988) for the papers of Tambaram II.

reexamination of all exclusivist claims.[12] But the outcome was thirty-five questions on seven issues for further study, with no suggested answers. They included:

> In what ways is plurality, including religious plurality, within God's purpose?

> What do we say about the saving work of God through other religious traditions?

> How do the confessions in other religious traditions of decisiveness/uniqueness/universality challenge and clarify Christian convictions about the uniqueness of Jesus Christ?[13]

Creative answers to those questions, I believe, are to be found in the documents of the subsequent World Conference on Mission and Evangelism (San Antonio, 1989). There for the first time the WCC invited persons of other faiths to a major conference as consultants and active discussion participants. The desire was to avoid polarization and to achieve a new synthesis between witness/proclamation/mission and dialogue concerns. The evangelization mandate was reaffirmed--that "the proclamation of the gospel includes an invitation to recognize and accept in a personal decision the saving lordship of Christ" (ME 41), that "Christians owe the message of God's salvation in Jesus Christ to every person and to every people" (ME 10), and that Christians "cannot point to any other way of salvation than Jesus Christ." But then follows the statement: "at the same time we cannot set limits to the saving power of God" (Par. 26). The statement continues: "in dialogue we are invited to listen in openness to the possibility that the God we know in Jesus Christ may encounter us also in the lives of our neighbours of other faiths" par. 28). With confidence the delegates affirmed

---

[12] "Mission in a Religiously Plural World," ibid., p. 320.

[13] Ibid., p. 449.

"that witness does not preclude dialogue with people of other living faiths, but that dialogue extends and deepens our witness." [14]

I agree with Wesley Ariarajah, the WCC's secretary for dialogue, that San Antonio may have opened some windows through which we can see beyond the witness-dialogue dialectic. He concludes:

> Dialogue theology is rooted in our commitment to Jesus Christ. . . . Yes, we know God in Christ . . . But that should in no way exclude the possibility that we take our neighbours seriously when they witness to having been touched by the gracious love of God. . . . that God is savingly present among others."[15]

2. THEOLOGICAL GROUNDING

In his section on "salvation and the specific purpose of mission" Cardinal Tomko analyzes three themes in theology: the missio Dei, the centrality of God's Reign, and salvation and human promotion. He believes that they have been used to weaken missionary motivations for witness and evangelization among persons of other faiths.[16] In contrast, I believe that these themes, as used by prominent conciliar Protestant theologians, undergird an emerging consensus that both witness and dialogue can be affirmed.

---

[14] Paragraph 39. Frederick R. Wilson, ed., *The San Antonio Report: Your Will Be Done: Mission in Christ's Way* (Geneva: WCC Publications, 1990), pp. 31-32, 36. See Raymond Fung, *A Monthly Letter on Evangelism* 6-7 (June-July 1989), pp. 1-7, for an evaluation by the WCC's secretary for evangelism; and S. Wesley Ariarajah, "San Antonio and Other Faiths," *Current Dialogue* 16 (August 1989), pp. 3-8, for that by the WCC's secretary for dialogue.

[15] "San Antonio and Other Faiths," p. 8.

[16] Op. cit., pp. 546-549.

Missio Dei: How shall we understand the particularity of God's revelation in Jesus Christ in the larger framework of God's universal love?[17] A focus on the mission of God, rather than upon the mission of the church or of Christ, can provide a trinitarian--not a unitarian--theology of mission.

Mission is not "the apostolic road from Church to Church," but the triune God moving into the world. It was Karl Hartenstein who made this contribution at the Willingen (1952) conference on mission and evangelism, thus introducing the missio Dei concept into the ecumenical debate. It is the mission of the Creator seeking the restoration of the integrity of all that had been made and judged to be good (Gen. 2:3). It is the mission of God who took the world seriously and judged it, yet on the Cross reconciled it to Godself. It is the mission of God the Spirit at work both through Christ's disciples in the world (Acts 1:8). It is also the Spirit that blows freely (John 3:8) and calls even those who do not know the divine name (e.g., Cyrus) into God's mission (Isaiah 44:28-45:7).[18]

Cardinal Tomko's concerns over the "radical derivations of the theory of the missio Dei" are justified. During the 1960s Johannes Hoekendijk, the WCC's Secretary for Evangelism, led in studies using missio Dei to signify exclusively God's hidden activities in the world independent of the church and its mission. Such usage is contrary to biblical understandings. Nevertheless, the issue of the relation between "history" and "salva-tion

---

[17] See Stanley J. Samartha, "The Lordship of Jesus Christ and Religious Pluralism," in Gerald Anderson and Thomas Stransky, eds., *Christ's Lordship and Religious Pluralism* (Maryknoll, NY: Orbis Books, 1980), pp. 19-36. Also published in Samartha, op. cit., pp. 88-104.

[18] See David J. Bosch, *Witness to the World: The Christian Mission in Theological Perspective* (London: Marshall, Morgan & Scott; Atlanta: John Knox, 1980), pp. 239-248; and Christopher Duraisingh, "Issues in Mission and Evangelism: Some Reflections," *IRM* 77, no. 307 (July 1988), pp. 404-405.

history" remains.[19] Christians who would avoid the temptation to equate their religion with God by making it absolute and final, who desire to be open to sings of the working of God's Spirit among others without denying their own mandate to mission, will find the missio Dei concept of continuing value.[20]

Reign of God: If missio Dei was a dominant theme in mission theology in the 1960s, the kingdom of God replaced it in the 1980s. "Your Kingdom Come" was the theme of the World Conference on Mission and Evangelism (Melbourne, 1980).[21] In the decade that followed key ecumenical mission leaders, including Mortimer Arias and Emilio Castro, the WCC's General Secretary, plumbed its meaning.[22]

This was a recovery of the biblical perspective of the Reign of God as a mandate for mission. The affirmation of the poor as having God's preferential option became the missionary yardstick of faithfulness in mission. Evangelical and conciliar Protestants came to share a common concern, recognizing that the "poor" of the former and the "unreached" of the latter were the same. Emilio Castro expressed well the convergence after Melbourne as he wrote:

> This preferential option for the poor is not an elimination of the invitation to faith, to conversion, to discipleship. The poor are not only the recipients, the objects of God's love; they are

[19] Bosch, op. cit., pp. 179-180. For primary sources see J. C. Hoekendijk, *The Church Inside Out* (Philadelphia, PA: Westminster Press, 1964), and Department on Studies in Evangelism, *The Church for Others* (Geneva: WCC, 1968).

[20] See Ans J. van der Bent, "Dialogue with People of Living Faiths," *Current Dialogue* 16 (August 1989), p. 35.

[21] See *Your Kingdom Come* (Geneva: WCC, 1980).

[22] Mortimer Arias, *Announcing the Reign of God* (Philadelphia: Fortress Press, 1984); Emilio Castro, *Freedom in Mission: The Perspective of the Kingdom of God* (Geneva: WCC Publications, 1985).

also called to grow into faith, into community, into discipleship.[23]

It is significant, however, that Castro and Arias, attuned to liberation thought in Latin America, mute the implication of the Reign of God theme for mission amidst the plurality of religions. Stanley Samartha expressed disappointment that Melbourne gave little attention to the Kingdom of God in a religiously plural world.[24] Christopher Duraisingh, the WCC's new secretary for mission and evangelism, prefers the goal of a "world embracing shalom" rather than a "world embracing church," and would prefer that the "shalom of the kingdom of God" be the goal of mission.[25]

The Kingdom/Reign of God can remain a creative Christian contribution in interreligious dialogue if grounded in its biblical meanings. It need not be used as a pretext for replacing orthodoxy with orthopraxis, as Paul Knitter has proposed.[26]

Salvation and human promotion: Cardinal Tomko's third theological concern is that religious salvation will be replaced by an exclusive concern for human development (or liberation, or justice, or peace).

The corrective, I believe, will be found in a rediscovery of biblical understandings of liberation. This will shift the focus from a preoccupation with individual salvation to that of how persons in community can glorify

---

[23] "Editorial," *IRM* 69, nos. 276-277 (♦1980), p. 381. See also Castro, *Freedom in Mission*, pp. 31-34.

[24] Stanley Samartha, "The Kingdom of God in a Religiously Plural World," in *Courage for Dialogue*, pp. 105-120.

[25] Duraisingh, op. cit., p. 406.

[26] See "Toward a Liberation Theology of Religions," in John Hick and Paul F. Knitter, eds., *The Myth of Christian Uniqueness* (Maryknoll, NY: Orbis Books, 1987), pp. 178-200.

God.[27] After all at the final judgment the righteous among all nations, even those not conscious of having served the Lord, will be welcome (Mt. 25:31-46). It also implies a change from a narrow concern for contemporary acts of justice to a broader search for their relevance in the divine plan of redemption. The whole creation groans in the pangs of childbirth (Rom. 8:22). God's action is calling persons from the East and the West to sit at table in the eschatological Reignof God without first becoming "Christians" (Mt. 8:11).[28]

Christians need not fear that dialogue replaces witness. Instead, they can participate with integrity only by presenting in word and deed their central Christian convictions. Between faiths Christians must "make themselves guests," as Kenneth Cragg aptly puts it, "and learn thus to be hosts."[29] Genuine dialogue thus becomes an open, honest sharing in which trust deepens so that teach partner can witness to the reality of the divine encounter as each has experienced it.[30]

---

[27] See Lesslie Newbigin, "Religious Pluralism and the Uniqueness of Jesus Christ," *International Bulletin of Missionary Research* 13, no. 2 (April, 1989), p. 54.

[28] Van der Bent, op. cit., pp. 36-37.

[29] *The Christ and the Faiths* (Philadelphia: Westminster Press, 1987), p. 326.

[30] See Duraisingh, op. cit., p. 407.

A REPLY TO THE RESPONSES

CHRISTIAN MISSION TODAY

Jozef Cardinal Tomko

1. INTRODUCTION

During a congress on Missiology held in Rome in 1988, I had raised some key issues in contemporary Mission Theology and praxis. They centered around the meaning of Jesus Christ for human salvation and the radical pluralism of world religions which now are being considered as independent ways to salvation by some theologians. I also pointed out the serious dangers to the understanding and praxis of Christian mission today posed by some of the emergent Christian theologies of the world religions.

My article was widely circulated by the international religious press and media and commented upon [and reproduced at the beginning of this volume]. It has generated positive and negative reactions and further theological discussion. A number of theologians have been invited to make a written response to my paper to the Rome Congress on Missiology. The organizers of this theological response have given me an opportunity to make my considered reply to their reactions. I am glad to make this response, and I want to express my gratitude to the theologians who have taken time out to make written responses.

I do this as the head of the Catholic Church's Congregation for the Evangelization of Peoples, with a sense of responsibility to the Church, to the peoples of the world and in fidelity to the Gospel entrusted by Jesus Christ to his disciples.

Obviously the fifteen or so replies of the theologians deal with mission theology from various angles. Their value too is varied. Some of the replies deal with the central problems of Christian mission today from a denominational point of view; others deal with a particular situation and are descriptive. But they all contribute to the mission debate that is going on within all the Christian Churches today. I can only wish that my response to them, though collective, will be of some service to all concerned.

2. CONTEMPORARY SITUATION OF THE WORLD, RELIGIONS AND THE CHURCH

a) A Growing Awareness of Interdependence and Need for Collaboration

We are living in a world that is becoming more and more interdependent economically, culturally and even religiously. Animosities, hostilities and suspicions that kept peoples and nations divided are gradually crumbling. Many ideological divisions of the past decades and centuries are also being levelled by new perceptions of interdependence and complementary roles. This is true also of the world religions, both classical, primal and animistic. There is today a growing appreciation of the riches, cultural and spiritual, of various religions. This is also a phenomenon that marks the contemporary Church in its attitudes to the world and the world religions. Though not all antagonisms based on religion, culture, ideology and race are disappearing--for new winds of fundamentalism are blowing--there is no doubt that new currents of tolerance, mutual acceptance, coexistence, exchange, sharing and mutual enrichment are becoming stronger in the world of today.

b) The Need for a Renewed Mission Theology and Methods

It is in this context we must view the efforts of many theologians and missionaries to rethink the foundation of Christian mission theology and praxis, discover new insights and formulate a new mission theology, create new missionary attitudes, find new mission methods, set new mission goals and have new standards of measuring missionary work and its efficacy. Hence the efforts made by theologians to reinterpret the meaning of Christian mission today and the shape of Christian mission for the future are very laudable and indispensable to the Church.

In such a situation, there is no doubt, the concerns of the Church and the Magisterium to preserve and transmit the original content of revelation-faith and proclaim them to the world of today will also be appre-ciated. The concerns of the Church and the Magisterium are not to be seen as obscurantist, retrograde action, but rather as an act of fidelity to God's mission to the world in God's Son Jesus Christ and the Holy Spirit.

3. THE CENTRAL ISSUE IN MISSION
DEBATE TODAY: JESUS CHRIST
a) New Dimensions in Mission Theology

With The Vatican Council II (1962-65) decrees Ad Gentes and Evangelii Nuntiandi the Catholic Church, theologians and missionaries have to have a better perception of the complex aspects and dimensions of Christian Mission. Although the new aspects were not totally absent or foreign to the prior concept of mission and evangelization, their inner inter-relationship and connection with the central aspect of the proclamation of

Jesus Christ are now better perceived and appreciated. Thus evangelization is understood to be witnessing to the life of Jesus Christ. It is promotion of the Reign of God values of justice, peace and love. It is helping people of today to have a true God experience, an experience that makes them aware of their being children of the same God and father of all. It is human promotion, a kind of social humanism that promotes the true well-being of humans everywhere. It is liberative action that removes unjust, sinful, exploitative, social, cultural, political and economic structures that keep people in slavery of one kind or another. It is a kind of spiritual humanism that implies the promotion of previous human and spiritual values found in all religions.

All the above call for genuine dialogue with all religions and ideologies and authentic inculturation in order to promote human wholeness and the development of human potentialities. This human wholeness and well being would seem to be the common platform where all religions and ideologies of the contemporary world can meet, stand and speak a commonly intelligible religious and human language.

b) Implications of New Mission Theology

The implications of the above points would be that any opposing discourse, dogmatic or theological, is culture-bound, historically dated and tribalistic in its interpretation of religious truths. Religions and ideologies should, it is argued by some, shed such dogmatic, traditional pretensions and move on to the all-important question and problem of human salvation, wholeness and well-being. To be saddled with the theological hangovers of colonial mission theologies and methods would be obstructing the onward march of Christian mission in theory and practice.

Obviously, the above missiological position is not representative of all theologians and not everyone subscribes to all the new positions. But they are wide-spread, valuable and influential enough to be taken seriously by all Christians and call for a response.

c) The Central Issue in Contemporary Mission Theology

In the ultimate analysis, it is not the new aspects and dimensions of mission theology and evangelization methods that pose the problem. It is the central question of God's revelation in Jesus Christ-Spirit-events for the salvation of humankind and its relationship to world religions as identical or independent ways of human salvation in the sense understood by each religion. It is argued by some that the mystery of God is not exhausted in the revelation in Jesus Christ which is definitive, absolute and unique and constitutive of salvation only for Christians. Rather, the mystery of God is greater than Jesus and God has revealed Self in other ways through other religions that are equally constitutive of salvation for their followers.

The central issue, therefore, in today's missiological debate is the person of Jesus Christ and the implications of this truth for human salvation. The proponents of some mission theologies demand that the missiological preoccupations of the past centuries and the accompanying missionary goals and methods be jettisoned in favor of more tolerant, respectful, mutually acceptable, non-controversial, mutually enriching and salvific missiologies, goals, and methods.

Thus it is proposed by some that the unfounded ecclesiocentrism in mission theology and methods should be abandoned. Mission exists not to perpetuate and expand the Church. As a king of idolatry the Church should be demolished. The Church exists only to bring about the "Reign of God" which is a Reign of justice, peace and love.

Christocentrism, likewise, has plagued and vitiated mission theology, goals and methods of evangelization for centuries. Jesus' mission was not to promote his own "Reign" but his whole life was at the service of ushering in God's Reign. Christian mission has misunderstood and distorted Jesus' mission by making it an instrument of Jesus' Reign and not of the "Reign of God."

Again, some would say that theocentrism need not be the basis for mission today since considerable sections of the religious world have no reference to a personal God. The same is true of ideologies that have no transcendent reference, allegiance and worship patterns. These too need and are in search of salvation. Hence the ultimate meaning and salvation need not be found in God.

d) A New Foundation for Christian Mission

The common foundation for all missions, Christian and other, could then be reduced to soteriocentrism, understood as human well-being, wholeness, which in turn is salvation. Here all can concur, celebrate, strive for, collaborate and speak the same religious language. This will obviate the religious conflicts and miseries of the past, serve the true meaning and goals of mission, and the formulation and adoption of acceptable and effective methods of evangelization.

In the light of such radical theologies of mission, we have to ask: How can we reconcile them with Christian revelation and the traditional understanding of Jesus Christ as the Son of God and the fullness of God's salvific revelation; what is its significance for humankind's salvation, its relationship to other religions; what are its implications for Christian mission, missionary goals and methods? Thus the missiological problem today is ultimately a christological and soteriological problem.

4. AN UNCLARIFIED PRESUPPOSITION IN TODAY'S
CHRISTOLOGICAL-MISSIOLOGICAL DEBATE

A positive perception of all religions, their spiritual values and riches, prayer-experience and their salvific significance has led some Christian theologians to think of Jesus Christ as one of the many revelations of the mystery of God and hence one of the many ways of human access to God and salvation. But behind this position there lies an uncritical assumption that the universal salvific will of God, which is clear from the record of Christian revelation, and the specific salvific will and historical revelation of God in Jesus Christ and its universal and absolute significance for human salvation, are irreconcilable.

Since the majority of humankind belong to the general history of revelation and salvation of God, it must be affirmed that world religions are independent ways to salvation. Hence all religions are the result of God's revelation and God's way of salvation for humankind. God's revelation in Jesus Christ can then be affirmed as absolute and universal only for the Christian as a subjective truth, a mythos valid only for them.

This is a very questionable assumption. In reality, the God of creation and the Lord of the general history of salvation is also the God of historical revelation in Jesus Christ and salvation through faith in him. The unicity of God, the unity of creation and salvation and the unity of humankind lead us to believe that the two ways of revelation and salvation are intimately and essentially related. While there is distinction, there is also continuity and fulfillment. There is nothing inconsistent if the God who creates all things and wills the salvation of all peoples subsumes his universal salvific revelation and will into a specific revelation and will in his son Jesus Christ, which in turn constitutes an absolute, universal and definitive way of salvation for all, even to those who live according to the former. Not only is there nothing inconsistent, incompatible, divisive and intolerant in such a revelation and way of salvation, it is also eminently consistent, unifying and gracious on the part of God to call all humans to the same revelatory knowledge and salvation. Besides, God could create the universe and all human beings in view of God's self-revelation and self-communication in the son Jesus Christ. We are dealing with the unfathomable mystery of God and the manifold wisdom of God in God's communication in creation and human salvation to be climaxed in God's self-communication in historical revelation in Jesus Christ and the salvation offered through faith in him.

If God has spoken to humankind in Jesus Christ, as the entire Christian tradition has been witnessing to in life, worship and script, it is perfectly legitimate and even obligatory to believe that Jesus Christ has universal revelatory-salvific significance for all. There is no doubt that such truth is of the very essence of Christian revelation, faith, life, worship and theology. Tampering with it, whatever the difficulties and however well-intentioned the motives for doing so, will only mean tampering with the content of God's revelation and offer of salvation. Humans are free to accept or reject it but not to distort or vitiate it. Those who are unable to accept it, whether due to sociological or religious reasons, or philosophical difficulties or due to the absence of credibility of the Christians to mediate it, will certainly find their own ways to salvation, provided there is no resistance to God's general offer of salvation. In any case, truth is greater than the human mind and especially revelatory-salvific truth is not to be trimmed to fit the narrow frame of the human intellect.

Even our inability to define, articulate and formulate satisfactorily the relationship between God's revelation and offer of salvation in the general history of salvation and God's historical and personalistic revelation and offer of salvation in Jesus Christ is no reason to undervalue or wish away one or the other. It is part of the existential tensions of the mystery of God's revelation and offer of salvation so that no human person may glory in one's own salvific efforts and search and sink into a challengeless salvific security.

5. THE CENTRALITY, UNIQUENESS AND UNIVERSAL SIGNIFICANCE OF JESUS FOR HUMAN SALVATION

Humans look for meaning and wholeness, whatever may be the ways these are understood and expressed in cultural molds peculiar to particular peoples. Such a search for meaning and wholeness of life leads them to the ultimate, transcendent reality which most people call God or, similar names. The ultimate meaning and wholeness is Transcendence itself. God, the transcendent Reality, may also reveal Self historically and thus encounter humans in their search for ultimate meaning and wholeness. Such a revelatory-salvific encounter in history in no way denies human search and freedom since the Transcendent reality does not force itself upon humans and their freedom. It is always a gracious offer. God's graciousness and goodness are infinite so that God can wait and encounter humans who continue their search for meaning and wholeness till the end of their salvific journey and they realize for themselves that the God of creation, and the God of revelation and salvation in Jesus Christ is the one and the same God who offers meaning and wholeness to life.

Jesus Christ presented himself to humankind as their ultimate meaning, Logos, and life, from God. "Before the world was created, the World already existed; he was with God, and he was the same as God. From the very beginning the Word was with God, Through him God made all things. The Word was the source of life, and this life brought light (meaning) to humankind" (Jn 1:1-4). This is how his disciples perceived and understood him gradually and after his death-resurrection-Spirit event as all the New Testament writers testify too, though under varied imageries and languages. "I did come from the Father, and I came into the world; and now I am leaving the world and going back to the Father" (Jn 16:28). "You are the Messiah, the Son of the living God" (Mt 16:16). "We know that you know everything; you do not need someone to ask you questions. This makes us believe that you are from God" (Jn 16:30).

This revelation and offer of God to humankind in Jesus Christ has been authenticated by his life, teachings, death-resurrection and the giving of the Spirit to his disciples. This is part of the very essence of Christian faith. Such faith is no myth but founded on the life, teachings, works and especially the death-resurrection of Jesus and the giving of the Holy Spirit to all who accept him as God's offer of meaning and life. The Christian dogma of Jesus Christ as God and as human is to be understood as the formulation of the perception of Jesus by his disciples as God's definitive, unique and universal and historical offer of salvation for all. "In many and various ways God spoke of old to our fathers by the prophets; but in these last days he has spoken to us by a Son, whom he appointed the heir of all things, through whom all he created the world. He reflects the glory of God and bears the very stamp of his nature, upholding the universe by his Word of power" (Heb 1:1-3).

The Christian faith in Jesus Christ founded on historical facts does not negate or nullify human search for meaning and wholeness, the salvific riches and insights into the mystery of God and human existence, or the truth and grace that God has revealed and offered to them in the course of humankind's age-old search for him. It does not belittle or reject their expressions in faith, prayer, worship, conduct of life and culture. Many of them even and often do enrich believers in Jesus Christ in their faith-worship expressions. Believers in Jesus Christ can also be led to see the marvelous and mysterious wisdom and infinite graciousness of God to all, the intimate connection between God's general revelation and offer of salvation and their historical expression in Jesus Christ and praise the one Father of all and the unity of all humankind as God's family, heirs to the same gracious salvation and wholeness as the early Christian witnesses tell us: "It is clear that God gave those gentiles the same gift that he gave us when we believed in the Lord Jesus Christ . . . when they heard this they stopped their criticism and praised God saying, Then God has given to the gentiles also the opportunity to repent and live" (Acts 11:17-18). On the other hand, this conviction did in no way prevent Peter from baptizing the family of Cornelius.

While God's revelation and offer of salvation in Jesus Christ do not negate other searches and offers of salvation, he intended it as absolute, total and final for all humankind. This is clear from the life and death-resurrection of Jesus. Jesus presented himself as God's final and definitive salvific covenant with humankind. "Then he took a cup, gave thanks to God, and gave it to them. Drink it, all of you, he said; this is my blood, which seals God's covenant, my blood poured out for many for the forgiveness of sins" (Mt 26:27-28). Jesus Christ, therefore, has constitutive salvific significance for all. By his absolute obedience to God's will and total solidarity with and self-giving to all, Jesus Christ became the absolute and unique norm for all ultimate meaning and wholeness of life, whatever may be the expressions of such meaning and salvation in creeds, worships, community structures and philosophical, mystical or spiritual interpretations and formulations.

The ultimate meaning and purpose of all religions are openness to God and one's neighbor or at least to one's neighbor. Jesus Christ is the supreme expression of that core of all religiosity. He has, therefore, universal salvific significance, without though infringing upon human freedom. This is also the teaching of Vatican II: "All this holds true not for Christians only but also for all humans of good will in whose hearts grace is active invisibly. For since Christ died for all, and since all humans are in fact called to one and the same destiny, which is divine, we must hold that the Holy Spirit offers to all the possibility of being made partners, in a way known to God, in the paschal mystery" (Gaudium et spes--GS 22).

It has been the constant conviction and belief of the Church that Jesus Christ has universal salvific significance for all humankind. Through his incarnation, Jesus Christ has united himself with every human person and through his death and resurrection he has united all humans to his paschal mystery in ways known to God. Again Vatican II confirms this view (GS 22).

Jesus Christ is a twofold Logos, namely Word and Meaning. He is the ultimate meaning of God. He is God's ultimate meaning and revelation to humankind. He is also the ultimate meaning of human beings. He is the total openness to God and to humans and their total openness to God and to one another. Thus Vatican II says: "'It pleased God in his goodness and wisdom, to reveal himself and to make known the mystery of his will' (cf. Eph 1:9). God's will was that humans should have access to the Father, through Christ, the Word made flesh, in the Holy Spirit and thus become sharers in the divine nature (cf. Eph 2:18; 2 Pet 1:4)" (Divini verbum--DV 2).

6. THE ABSOLUTENESS AND UNIVERSAL SIGNIFICANCE OF THE CHRISTIAN MESSAGE FOR SALVATION

There was a time when some theologians claimed the Christian faith to be absolute for various socio-historical reasons in a triumphalistic sense, along with a generally negative appraisal of other religions and religionists. The absoluteness of the Christian message for hu-man salvation may have little to do with socio-historical reasons. It comes, rather from God's absolute and definitive offer of salvation in Jesus Christ. It is God's offer of salvation in Jesus Christ. It is God's offer of Self as truth and life: "The Word became a human being and, full of grace and truth, lived among us" (Jn 1:14).

This Self-offer of God has been accepted uniquely and absolutely by humans in Jesus Christ, who is truly human, in his incarnation and through his death and resurrection, whose real significance is the human total surrender to God's will and self-giving to one's neighbor. Such surrender and self-giving constitutes also the absoluteness and uniqueness of the Christian faith and message. It also constitutes human meaning and whole-ness, which we call salvation. The heart of the Christian message of salvation is sharing in the absolute surrender and self-giving of Jesus. As such it has universal and absolute significance for all, even those who strive to do so through the working of the Spirit of God in their hearts. Somehow they are also in Christ, baptized into the real significance of his death and resurrection though without the resultant creed and sacramental symbols, but in their lives.

For Christian faith, Jesus God's definitive and personal invitation to similar surrender and self-giving, overcoming the inborn resistance to God's will and deep-rooted selfishness whose power over humans cannot be under-estimated. It is also a message to humans that such surrender and self-giving cannot be accomplished by human search and efforts, but is a gracious gift achieved through the power of Jesus' death-resurrection and the Spirit released through it.

Jesus Christ is the personal and historical witness of human surrender to God's will and self-giving to others. He is not only a model for all humans to do the same. He also gives the power to do this by the gift of His Holy Spirit. Jesus is the pattern for human's self-surrender and self-giving and he communicates the power of grace to do the same.

Such witness and communication of salvific power and grace are unique in human history. But it does not take away or deny the grace and power of other efforts for salvation, or other ways in which the Spirit communicated to humans the same saving grace. It is, however, not a different grace and salvific power, but the same saving grace of Jesus Christ as he himself has said: "No one comes to the Father except through me."

We may ask, then, why this unique way, when other ways are there and equally good. To begin with, all other ways of salvation offered by God are part of God's unique plan of salvation. It is also the expression of God's irreversible self-offer, authenticated and personalistic and expressive of total human salvation, overcoming sin and finally death itself, and symbol of human's final communion with God, as in the incarnate and risen Lord Jesus Christ. All other ways are subsumed into this one, unique, and universally applicable way of salvation. It is this that gives meaning and substance to all other ways of salvation and all other mediations of salvation. Such unique and universally applicable testimony of God's irreversible revelation-salvation is not seen anywhere else in the horizon of human history.

The uniqueness, absoluteness and universal significance of the revelation-salvation in Jesus Christ gives no real ground for human pride, arrogance, superiority, boasting or intolerance, for it is a call to total "kenosis," self-emptying, letting God's rule take hold of the human heart and mind. It is to share in the "humiliation" even to the cross (Phil 2:5-11) and to become alive to God with a new life that looks to God (Rom 6:8).

The uniqueness and absoluteness of Christianity ought to give no real ground for exclusion or rejection of other religions, though in the course of history it has happened. All religions, in their original form also existed for the same end, though they too became instruments of power in the course of history. Christianity is and ought to be more and more a call to authentic religion as human's surrender to God and self-giving to others. All have the same divine vocation (GS 22) and Christianity offers its example and symbols to all in their attempt to fulfill the one divine-human vocation.

Far from generating an attitude of superiority, Christians are called to make the unique self-surrender of Jesus to God and his self-giving to others, their own as individuals and as Church, and thus become a sacrament of true religion to all others.

Jesus Christ gives concreteness and substance to what all religions are striving to achieve as Leslie Newbegin has put it:

> The central question is not "How shall I be saved?" but "How shall I glorify God by understanding, loving and doing God's will here and now in this earthly life?" To answer that question I must insistently ask: "How and where is God's purpose for the whole of creation and the human family made visible and credible?" That is the question about the truth--objective truth--which is true whether or not it coincides with my "values". And I know of no place in the public history of the world where the dark mystery of human life is illuminated, and the dark power of all that denies human well-being is met and measured and mastered, except in those events that have their focus in what happened under Pontius Pilate".[1]

7. THE PASCHAL MYSTERY OF JESUS CHRIST AND THE CHURCH

---

[1] Leslie Newbegin, "Religious Pluralism and the Uniqueness of Jesus Christ," *International Bulletin of Missionary Research*, 13 (1989), p. 54.

Conversion to God and salvation are not once for all events. They are a process by which humans are transformed into the image of God. The image of God has now been revealed in God's Son Jesus Christ. Thus to be transformed into the image of Jesus Christ is also wholeness and salvation. The same God calls humans "to become like his Son so that the Son would be first among the many brethren" (Rom 8:29).

Conversion and salvation are the process by which humans are assimilated into the image and likeness of Jesus Christ: Thereby we let God transform us inwardly by a complete change of our minds (cf. Rom 12:2).

The Church is nothing else but the community of believers who have accepted God's revelation and offer of salvation-life-wholeness in Jesus Christ, God's Son, and who strive to assimilate the paschal mystery of Jesus Christ into their personal and community lives and thus be transformed into the likeness of God as Jesus Christ himself. Thus Paul exhorts his Christians: "Your minds and hearts must be made completely new and you must put on the new self which is created in God's likeness and reveals itself in the true life that is upright and holy" (Eph 4:23-24).

The Church is a communion in the Holy Spirit, taken into the mystery of the life of the Holy Trinity. It is a fellowship because of the indwelling of the Spirit: "Surely you know that you are God's temple and that God's Spirit lives in you" (1 Cor 3:16). This is exactly what Jesus promised before his death and resurrection: "When that day comes, you will know that I am in my Father and that you are in me, just as I am in you" (Jn 14:20).

The Church is the result of the incarnation of the Word and the paschal mystery of Jesus Christ. It is much more than a historical and sociological phenomenon, and its exists only to proclaim God's offer of salvation in Jesus Christ to all humans and transform individuals and society into God's children, in the image of God's Son. Conversion and salvation are a slow movement towards the wholeness of life and the Church exists as its visible sign and instrument in proclamation, sacramental signs, worship and a life modelled on Jesus Christ. The Church, therefore, is not something optional. It is born of the paschal mystery of Jesus: "For it was from the side of Christ as he slept the sleep of death upon the cross that there came forth the wondrous sacrament of the whole church" (SC 5).

Jesus gathered a community of disciples and taught them to live as he lived. He gave them the Holy Spirit to bring about the transformation into his image as God's children: "For the Spirit that God has given you does not make you slaves and cause you to be afraid; instead the Spirit makes you God's children and by the Spirit's power we cry to God, Abba, Father" (Rom 8:15).

Jesus commanded his disciples to be witnesses of his life, death and resurrection to the ends of the earth, namely, to all humankind, and teach all to live according to his precepts, Jews and gentiles alike, without exception. The entire early Church in its oral, liturgical and scriptural tradition bears witness to this fact. Thus the apostles and the apostolic Church, the Church of the Fathers and the Church of the subsequent centuries confirm this understanding of Jesus Christ, and the Church's mission to the world. The early Fathers of the Church faced openly the problem of other religions and ways of salvation, and their views were surprisingly open and go beyond the single phrase extra ecclesiam nulla salus--and even that was interpreted narrowly during later centuries.

The mission of the Church is not based upon some isolated texts of Scripture but on the incarnation, life, death and resurrection of Jesus Christ and the giving of the Spirit to his disciples to go into the whole world, bear witness to him and his life, to proclaim his message and do what he did in his memory, namely, his submission to the Father and self-giving to his disciples through the sacramental symbols of baptism and of bread and wine.

All the Gospels end with a solemn commission to go into the whole world and proclaim the Good News of God's offer of forgiveness of sins and fullness of life by word, deed and witness of life. Thus Luke concludes his Gospel as follows: "Then he opened their minds to understand the Scriptures, and said to them 'This is what is written: the Messiah must suffer and must rise again from death three days later, and in his name the message about repentance and forgiveness of sins must be preached to all nations, beginning in Jerusalem. You are witnesses of these things.'" John, in a different language, says the same thing: "Jesus said to them again, 'Peace be with you. As the Father has sent me, so I send you.' Then he breathed on them and said: 'Receive the Holy Spirit. If you forgive people's sins, they are forgiven'" (Jn 20:21-23). Before his ascension Jesus promised his disciples the power of the Spirit to be his witnesses to the ends of the earth (cf. Acts 1:7-9). The bestowal of the Spirit on Pentecost day was also the solemn beginning of the mission of the Church.

As the Church springs from the Incarnation and paschal mystery of Jesus Christ, her mission and missionary motivation spring from the same sources. The fundamental methodology of doing mission today as always is also provided by the same paschal mystery of Jesus, though the concrete forms and shapes it takes and the methods used vary according to times and historical circumstances. The paschal mystery of Jesus reveals also the need and urgency of both Christian mission, even today in a climate of religious pluralism, and a positive evaluation of other religions. Indeed, the need and urgency of Christian mission are even greater today as we come to understand the close and essential connection between God's universal and cosmic plan of salvation and God's special plan of salvation. Indeed the

Church's experience of redemption in Jesus Christ gives it a profound insight into God's plan of salvation of all. It has nothing to fear from any authentic religion. It has much to contribute to them while it also learns from them about God's mysterious ways with them. In fact, Paul tells us in his letter to the Ephesians that God has made known to the Church "the mystery of his will according to his purpose which is set forth in Christ as a plan for the fullness of time, to unite all things in him, things in heaven and things on earth" (Eph 1:9-10).

There is no real contradiction, therefore, between God's universal salvific will and the specific, historical salvific revelation in Jesus Christ. As Paul put it: "His intent was that now, through the Church, the manifold wisdom of God should be made known to the rulers and authorities in the heavenly places" (Eph 1:11).

8. THE REIGN OF GOD, THE CHURCH AND CHRISTIAN MISSION
a) The Church and the Reign of God

There is a tendency today among some theologians and missiologists to speak of the building up of the Reign of God as the goal of all Christian missions. In the first place, this is no new discovery. This is exactly what thousand of missionaries, men and women, have been doing in the remote villages, jungles, mountains and valleys of Asia, Africa, Latin America and Oceania, sharing the life of the poor, giving them the benefits of literacy, health care and development, thus making their lives more worthy of humans. Exceptions do not erase the overwhelming testimony of the majority. We need only to ask the Harijans, the Tribals, the Campesinos and they will bear witness to who is building up the Reign of God in their midst. It is the missionaries who are really engaged in the work of building up God's Reign among God's people.

Secondly, in today's missiological debate, often the mission of the Church is reduced to building up God's Reign and promoting the values of the God's Reign, but both understood in a temporal sense. In general they reduce the Reign of God and the values of God's Reign to the earthly well-being of humans. "They would reduce her aims to a human-centered goal; the salvation of which she is a messenger would be reduced to material well-being" (EN 32).

But the biblical meaning of the Reign is wider than mere material well-being. It is God's rule and presence in the hearts of people. It is not an abstract concept, but concretely revealed in Jesus Christ. It is established primarily by the death-resurrection of Jesus, when he became irreversibly God's Reign. The proclamation of Jesus Christ is at the same time, the proclamation of God's Reign, and its values. He teaches all to let God's will rule over their hearts and become God's Reign. God's Reign must first be born in the hearts of individuals, and only then can human society become God's Reign and live by the values of God's Reign.

The Reign of God is primarily a spiritual reality in the New Testament, hence the role of Christian mission also is the Reign of God understood in its biblical sense.

Thirdly, the preaching of Jesus cannot be reduced to the imagery of God's Reign. God's Reign is not the only key concept in the New Testament. Discipleship and the Body of Christ are also important concepts in the New Testament. Thus Jesus spoke of his relationship with his disciples as that of the vine and the branches: "I am the vine, and you are the branches" (Jn 15:5). Paul expresses the same idea with the imagery of the body: "In the same way, all of us, whether Jews or gentiles, whether slaves or free, have been baptized into the one body by the same Spirit, and we have all been given the one Spirit to drink" (I Cor 12:13).

True, the Reign of God is not exhausted by the Church. Nor are the values of God's Reign found only in the Church. But the Church and the Reign of God are inseparably linked together. The Church, even if it fails to be fully God's Reign, is the concrete expression of the Reign of God. It is the community of those who accept God's rule in their hearts and seek to live as Jesus Christ did. The Church strives to be the Reign of God and promote its values. It proclaims the Reign of God and is its instrument in bringing it about in the world as Vatican II says: "It becomes on earth the initial budding forth of that Reign. While it slowly grows, the Church strains towards the consummation of the Reign and, with all her strength, hopes and desires to be united in glory with her King" (Lumen gentium--LG 5).

As Jesus is the revelation and the instrument of the Reign of God, the Church in a subordinate way is the revelation and instrument of the Reign of God. It exists only for the Reign of God: "Without doubt the Church has the Reign as her supreme goal, of which she on earth is its seed and beginning, and is therefore totally consecrated to the glorification of the Father" (Christifideles laici, 36).

The Reign of God, on the other hand, is not a purely spiritual and eschatological reality. It is equally an earthly reality. The Reign of God finds its expression in the values of justice, peace, freedom and human dignity for all. The promotion of the Reign of God and its values here on earth is an essential part of the mission of the Church. Without it, the Church's proclamation would lose its credibility and "sacramental" symbolic expression. Such values are not only symbols, but the beginnings of the Reign of God itself. Human promotion in all its wide variety and extension is vital to the mission of the Church in its service to the Reign of God.

The Reign of God, therefore, has spiritual eschatological and temporal dimensions. These are interdependent and essential elements of the Reign of God, and Christian mission cannot be reduced to any one of these without at the same time falsifying and distorting Christian mission and eventually making it ineffective and meaningless.

b) The Church and Religious Pluralism

The fact of religious pluralism is nothing new. Human existence has always been pluralistic from its very beginning. There never was a time when humankind was not pluralistic in its social structures, economic and political organizations, in its cultural expressions and religious creeds, worship and goals.

It was into this pluralistic world dominated mostly by the Hebrew, Roman and Greek cultures that God sent the Son in the fullness of time that God might offer salvation to all. While Jesus showed the greatest respect to every person, he was not ashamed to bear witness to his Father in Word, deed and in gathering together of a community of disciples.

Today's world is no different in its pluralistic situation. But the fact of religious pluralism and our new awareness of it cannot be an excuse for not proclaiming salvation in Jesus Christ. Our growing awareness of religious pluralism should help us to be tolerant, respectful, appreciative of other religions, and cultures but not relativize the message of salvation we have received from God in Jesus Christ or cease to proclaim and offer it as a way of salvation to all. We need to do mission in Jesus' way. The Gospel is the power of salvation for all peoples, and we have an obligation to all, the civilized and the uncivilized, the educated and the ignorant as Paul has put it (cf. Rom 1:15).

c) The Church, Dialogue and Mission

Dialogue is an essential part of Christian mission. Recent insights into the meaning of dialogue have helped the Church to see its mission in a new light and context. But there are different meanings and levels of dialogue.

God sending the Son into the world is an act of salvific dialogue with the humankind. Jesus' mission to the world was carried out in dialogue with the men and women of his time. But it was no neutral dialogue, but rather a dialogue that offered God's salvation and demanded an obedience of faith. Christian mission too cannot be reduced only to neutral dialogue.

Religious dialogue is not a meeting and sharing between two persons, but a meeting and sharing in order to listen to God and accept what God has to offer to us; dialogue cannot be a substitute for proclamation. The Christian way of dialogue is to do it in Jesus' way, receiving, sharing, respecting, but also giving the message of salvation in Jesus Christ.

No doubt, there are different kinds or levels of dialogue. We can enter into dialogue with other religionists in order to clarify our own religious positions, to enrich our religious experience with their religious experience, to enter into mutual collaboration in the promotion of human and spiritual values and to experience a conversion to our neighbor. We can also enter into dialogue with others as a means to evangelize as Jesus entered into dialogue with others, in order to reveal the Father and himself and thus offer fullness of life and salvation. There is nothing intellectually or morally unbecoming in it if it is done in respect and love for the other. It is part of the dialogue of salvation initiated even by God.

God so loved the world that God sent his only Son into the world. "For God loved the world so much that he gave his only Son, so that everyone who believes in him may not die but have eternal life" (Jn 3:16).

Jesus entered into dialogue with his contemporaries because he loved the world. We also enter into dialogue because we love God and our neighbor and want to share with them the joy of salvation we have found in Jesus Christ.

d) The Church, Mission, Conversion and Baptism

Conversion today is a much abused word. But its real meaning is always valid. By conversion we mean a change of heart. This can have different levels. Thus there is the conversion of the human person to God. We may speak of conversion to Jesus Christ. In fact, there are many who believe in and follow the teachings of Jesus without becoming Christians. But they have turned to Jesus Christ for the inspiration and the criterion of their lives. There is conversion to Jesus Christ in the Christian community with its sacraments and worship. There is also, finally, conversion to one's neighbor, even though one may have no religious or ecclesial affiliations.

Ultimately all conversion is to God; all other conversions are meant to lead to conversion to God. The Church is in fact the community of those who turn to God and want to continue being converted to God. In this sense, the Church needs constant conversion. But the Church also preaches conversion as Jesus gathered a community of disciples. Wherever it can, the Church also wants to promote conversion at every level. The mission of Jesus involved a conversion of heart and making people his disciples. Christian mission today implies also among other things, a similar conversion and gathering together the believing community through faith and baptism. Thus we see the apostles and disciples of Jesus proclaiming Jesus Christ in the power of the Spirit and gathering together communities of believers through repentance and baptism from the day of Pentecost onwards. Peter tells the people gathered in Jerusalem: "God raised this very Jesus from death, and we are all witnesses to this fact.... And when the people asked: 'What shall we do brothers?' Peter answered, 'Each one of you must turn away from his sins and be baptized in the name of Jesus Christ, so that your sins will be forgiven, and you will receive God's gift, the Holy Spirit'" (Acts 2:32, 37-38).

Christian mission has many dimensions, such as dialogue, human promotion, promotion of the values of the Reign of God and promotion of spiritual values found in all religions and ideologies. But there are two primary and essential elements: the proclamation of Jesus Christ and the gathering together of the believers in Jesus Christ, the Church. Without these primary elements, all other elements of Christian mission will lose their validity and cohesion. As Paul VI stated in Evangelii nuntiandi, there can be no true evangelization without the proclamation of the life, death and resurrection of Jesus Christ and the gathering together of the believing community through baptism.

9. CONCLUSION

Christian mission is based on God's plan to send the Son into the world and the saving Spirit to all who freely accept him. The salvation offered to humans in Jesus Christ is primarily a salvation from sin in all its individual and social manifestations and finally death itself. Such salvation has a religious, moral and spiritual content in the first place. It is not to be reduced to a purely economic, political or cultural liberation.

Human liberation and promotion of human dignity are essentially related to the spiritual salvation offered by God. They are the temporal expression of the eschatological salvation, the first fruits of the spiritual salvation, the necessary concomitants of the religious salvation. Without them, the religious salvation would lack credibility and substance.

Nonetheless, eschatological salvation offered by Jesus Christ through his death-resurrection cannot be arbitrarily reduced to its temporal expressions.

In God's offer of salvation of humankind, Jesus Christ is central. His mediation of salvation is unique and universal. The same God who creates all and gives revelation and salvation in ways known only to God, can and does subsume God's universal salvific will in the Son Jesus Christ, according to Christian faith. This is our faith and conviction, based on the life and testimony of Jesus Christ, especially his death and resurrection. We hold this humbly yet firmly, respectfully, yet unequivocally. We have the freedom to accept or reject it but we have not the right to relativize or syncretize it with other notions of ours against the cumulative witness of the early Church, the Scriptures and its twenty-centuries-old tradition.

The same God who wills the salvation of all wills also that all may come to the truth of Jesus Christ as the unique Savior of all (Jn 17:1-3; 1 Tim 2:3-4), even though we are not able to define satisfactorily how the grace of Jesus Christ is mediated to all.

The Church is the community of the believers in Jesus Christ, where he is accepted in faith, celebrated in worship and proclaimed in mission so that others may enter through conversion and baptism and find salvation since it is willed by God for the salvation of all and hence necessary (LG 14). The fact that God saves those who do not know Jesus Christ (LG 16) does not in any way take the necessity or urgency of proclaiming Jesus Christ for the Church is the universal sacrament of salvation (LG 48). It is only in the believing, worshipping and proclaiming community, the Church, that the people of every age and place can encounter Jesus Christ, his salvific revelation. Without the Church, the Christ-Spirit event, God's supreme revelation and salvific gift of life and wholeness to humankind cannot be mediated to the world.

The Reign of God, Jesus Christ, and the Church are not mutually exclusive realities but essentially related and interdependent and at the service of one another and the concrete expression and continuation of each other.

Our respect, love, and esteem for and sharing and collaboration with other religions and religionists need not lead us to dilute or distort our faith in the salvific revelation of God in Jesus Christ and his unique and universal significance. Doing so ultimately will be an act of disservice to the world and infidelity to God's will and gracious offer of salvation and impoverishment of the riches of God's salvific revelation.

What is required then in the contemporary world is not a relativized theology of mission and Christology, but that the Church strives to become truly Church, namely, God's Reign, as a clear sign, a forceful instrument and a convincing invitation to all to share in the unsearchable riches of God's salvific revelation in Jesus Christ.

AFTERWORD

EPISTEMOLOGY AND CHRISTOLOGY: THE UNDERLYING ISSUES

Leonard Swidler

I have found the articles written by this collection of scholars impressive in a very high degree. Apparently Cardinal Tomko has also, for if one compares his lead essay and responding essay, it is clear that his tone, attitude and emphasis moderated considerably in the latter.

Cardinal Tomko's lead essay, was written as the keynote address to a conference he initiated to focus on the issue of "Mission or/and Dialogue?" In it Cardinal Tomko tried to present the thinking of Christian theologians, missiologists and missionaries who are striking out in directions other than the traditional one which stressed the making of converts to the "one true church," the Catholic Church, and the "saving of souls." Although the Cardinal attempted to be as accurate and objective as possible in his presentation of this new thinking, it was clear where he stood. Moreover, because of his strong convictions and because of the fact that he saw his task as giving the charge to the conference he had launched, his tone was understandably one of advocacy.

Of course there is nothing at all wrong with advocacy if one is strongly convinced of the rightness of a cause. Many, if not all, of the writers in this volume also advocate a position more or less strongly. However, what is also characteristic of all of these essays--very much including both of Cardinal Tomko's essays--is that they also reflect the seriousness with which the authors take the arguments and reasoning of the various positions put forth concerning this at once crucial and complex question. For both those reasons the authors, beginning with Cardinal Tomko, are to be both gratefully thanked and read and pondered most earnestly.

I mentioned that the tone and emphasis of Cardinal Tomko's responsive essay had shifted considerably from those of his lead essay. It is obvious that he was persuaded that his interlocutors are serious, committed Christian thinkers and doers and that the arguments of many of them in the direction of dialogue--without any of them eschewing mission in the New Testament sense of bearing witness!--had a weightiness that demanded more due emphasis than he had perhaps given them in his conference address. Nevertheless, it is also clear that Cardinal Tomko has held onto his initial basic direction. He of course does not hold that "by no other name can you be saved than that of Jesus Christ."

Such a position was no longer possible for a Roman official, at least since the 1948 letter of the Holy Office to the Archbishop of Boston condemning such a position--to say nothing of the revolutionary statements of Vatican II on religious liberty and dialogue. Such a position of course was held, and promulgated in the most solemn way the popes knew how by the nineteenth-century Popes Gregory XVI and Pius IX, who referred to freedom of conscience as an "execrable error," a "deliramentum"!

As said, Cardinal Tomko, and none of the other authors here, hold such. No one here any longer holds an "exclusivist" position, that is, one which claims that only if a person becomes ex professo a Christian can s/he be "saved." Nevertheless, Cardinal Tomko, and a number of our responding authors, do hold to an "inclusivist" position, which insists that in some way whatever "saving" takes place in people's lives happens in Jesus Christ, is "included" in Jesus Christ. It seems to me that this need to insist on the "inclusivity" of Jesus Christ is essentially linked up with the Christology that is espoused.

It is interesting to note that almost all the present authors who tend to agree with Cardinal Tomko on this basic matter of outlook come from among the Protestants. I do not think that this was an accident of the choice of personnel. I have observed over many years that in the matter of interreligious dialogue, as distinct from intra-Christian ecumenism, there is a greater reluctance among Protestant theologians than among Catholic to move beyond an "inclusivist" Christology to a "pluralist" one (of course there are outstanding exceptions, like Paul Tillich toward the end of his life, Wilfred Cantwell Smith, John Hick--and some of our present authors). Perhaps this is because of a basic tendency to adhere tightly to the Reformation principle of "sola Scriptura." One might see a similar approach in many Catholics of the past, and present, with difference being that the "Scriptura" includes not just the Bible but also, and often primarily, the "Scriptura" of ecclesiastical documents, i.e., the "Traditio."

And yet, I think that such a fixing on the "Scriptura" as the decisive issue would fall short of finding the true foundation of this "inclusivist" approach to the question. All the world religions are based on texts, on "Scriptura," and this is doubtless one of the basic reasons why all the world religions have an absolutist quality about them: the "Scriptura" of each have somewhere along the line, and usually quite often, said that if you want to lead a true human life you MUST follow THIS true way. Among Jews, Christians, Muslims and Confucians the non-followers tended to be classified as "idolaters," "heretics," "infidels," "barbarians." Even the very permissive Hindus often admitted the right of Christians, Muslims, etc. to follow their own paths to enlightenment--but of course if they lived long, or often, enough they might come to the full enlightenment of the Hindu true understanding of reality. Even today many mild-mannered Buddhists will often let you know that whatever your solution to the conundrum of existence is, theirs is "beyond" that.

Not all Jews, Christians, Muslims, etc. hold such absolutist positions, however, and yet they understand themselves as loyal to, nourished from, their "Scriptura." There are doubtless many reasons for this, but I believe that a fundamental one in the contemporary scene is that in the past one hundred years or so we have been undergoing a fundamental paradigm shift in our understanding of the meaning of texts, of truth in general. The fact of this paradigm shift is no great discovery of mine, of course, although I too have written of it elsewhere.[1] However, the challenge of the new paradigm of the "deabsolutized" understanding of all truth, i.e., statements about reality, is increasing today, geometrically, in depth and breadth. Consequently the resistance to it is increasing proportionally--not unlike the increase in the resistance to the heliocentric theory as evidence for it increased in the hundred years from Copernicus to Galileo's fateful encounter with the Roman cardinals.

This "deabsolutized" understanding of truth--that all statements about reality are "not absolute," are always limited, always expressed from a particular perspective, always formulated in specific historical circumstances, always cast in particular, limited thought categories, always addressed to particular questions, etc., etc.--led to, or at least supported, a very important discovery in Christology which bears fundamentally on our issue here of

---

[1] I deal with the issue in an inchoative way in some earlier articles, e.g.: "Wahrheitsfindung im Dialog," Una Sancta (Spring, 1985), pp. 201-218; and books: "Interreligious and Interideological Dialogue: The Matrix for All Systematic Reflection Today," in: Leonard Swidler, ed., Toward a Universal Theology of Religion (Maryknoll, NY: Orbis Books, 1987), and Leonard Swidler, John Cobb, Paul Knitter, Monika Helwig, Death or Dialogue. From the Age of Monologue to the Age of Dialogue. Philadelphia: Trinity Press International, 1990. However, I treat it most thoroughly in my book After the Absolute. The Dialogical Future of Religious Reflection (Minneapolis: Fortress Press, 1990).

"mission or/and dialogue." That discovery can be simply described as realizing that in general there are different ways of perceiving and describing the world, and that in particular the way of the Bible, and Jesus and his first followers, was that of the Semitic world, a world in which metaphor, "picture language," was much more pervasive and decisive than in the Hellenic world where an abstract, ontological language was much more pervasive and decisive. (Indeed, as our very words tell us--philosophy, metaphysics, ontology, etc.--this abstract way of thinking, speaking, and asking questions, at least as far as the world west of the Indus river is concerned, was invented by the Greeks). This discovery led to the recovery of the Jewish- -the Jesus--way of understanding the Bible, and the understanding of Jesus. And this Jewish, this Jesus, way of understanding was not abstract, metaphysical, but concrete, metaphorical; it was not Greek but Jewish. Of course Hellenism was not without influence in the land of Israel at the time of Jesus--as the work of scholars like Martin Hengel bear out. Nevertheless, the root metaphors of the Jewish culture were Semitic, were cast in "picture-language" categories, and similarly determined their questions--and therefore answers. This fundamental cultural difference in how the world is perceived, spoken of and questioned had, and continues to have, a decisive influence on the development of Christianity as it moved from the Jewish world of the Jew Jesus (or rather, Yeshua) and his first (Jewish) followers of his "way" into the Hellenic post-70 world of the "Christian" (mostly Gentile) "Church." Greek-thinking Christians (and after 70, except for the "Ebionites" they were increasingly about the only Christians there were) wanted to know whether Jesus was a man or God, or neither, or both.

Those, however, were not Jewish questions or Jewish ways of speaking about Jesus, about Yeshua; Yeshua's first (Jewish) followers thought of him as the "anointed one," the messiah, a prophet, a teacher (rabbi), the son of God (as others were also children of God, as Jesus himself said), one having power or leadership qualities--mar in Aramaic, kyrios in Greek--etc. They did not think of him as the Second Person of the Blessed Trinity, as an hypostasis, as an hypostatic union, as "vere Deus et vere homo," etc. And yet, it is largely through that Greek-thinking lens that subsequent Christians have seen Jesus and his meaning; it is through that Hellenic glass that the texts, the "Scriptura" of the Bible, traditionally have been read and understood--and is consequently the source of the trouble in the encounter with other ways of understanding the meaning of life, of perceiving and speaking about what an authentic human life should be--which is what "salvation" means (salus, salutary, Heil, healthy, holy, [w]holy). If Jesus is not only a human being (homo), but also IS God (Deus), then of course his words and actions must be taken absolutely, must "include" all other "salvation."

However, if the fundamental view of the world and the consequent way of speaking about it of Jesus (Yeshua) and his first (Jewish) followers was not metaphysical, abstract, as it was for the (Gentile) Christians who shaped post-New Testament Christianity, but was basically metaphorical, concrete, then to read what Jesus and his first followers said and did in a way other than a metaphorical, concrete manner is to misunderstand, to distort, it. If someone wants to be a follower of Jesus, then the first question in this area s/he must ask is, how did Jesus understand and speak of himself and how did his first followers (all Jews) understand and speak of him? The answer to that question briefly is that Yeshua and his first followers understood and spoke of him Jewishly, that is, in metaphorical, "picture language." Obviously what Jesus and his first followers thought of Jesus is not the only appropriate question that can and should asked of what Jesus said and did and its meaning today, but clearly no questions or

answers can run contrary to that first, fundamental question and answer--
if one wants to claim to be a follower of Jesus, to be a Christian. For
example, if Jesus did not think of himself as God--as all New Testament
evidence indicates--how can his later followers do so, without falling into a
fundamental contradiction? It follows then, however, that if the Jewish--the
Jesus--way of understanding Jesus rules out stating that he IS God, then the
absolutist, inclusivist claims of Jesus' later followers fall away and the
"pluralist" approach makes sense.

Now I do not wish to suggest that every Christian thinker who takes
a "pluralist" approach necessarily follows my christological reflections
recorded in overly simplified form above. But I do want to argue that as
the paradigm of a "deabsolutized" understanding of truth finds ever wider
acceptance and penetrates ever more deeply into the understanding of our
most cherished "truths," a "pluralist" approach to religious truths will
increasingly prevail. I also want to argue that for us Christians this
paradigm shift and consequent re-thinking and re-search ineluctably leads us
to re-understand the meaning of the Jew Jesus, that is, our Christology, and
in that re-understanding the Jewishness of Jesus, and his first followers, will
play a decisive role.

Beyond that, I am also convinced, dialogue not only with Judaism,
vital for Christians as that is, but also dialogue with other religions,[2] and
ideologies--and most especially with modern critical thought--will help us
understand ourselves, the world, and its Source increasingly deeper, richer
and more meaningfully, which in turn will help us live more (w)holy, human
lives, interiorly and exteriorly, individually and communally.

---

[2] See my Yeshua: A Model for Moderns (Kansas City: Sheed & Ward, 1988), pp. 28-33, where I spell
out in some detail how the Christian dialogue with Buddhism suggests a solution to apparent contradiction
of "human" and "divine" talk in the Gospels, which contributed to the doctrinal formulations of the of the
early ecumenical councils--while trying to take seriously both the Gospels and the councils and what the
latter were trying to communicate.

* * *

It is with that fundamental conviction that my colleague Paul Mojzes and I launched this project. We want again to thank Cardinal Tomko for so graciously granting permission to reproduce his initial essay and for taking the time and energy to enter into serious dialogue with the many authors here, and we want to thank as well as the respondents themselves.

It is our hope that there will be many readers who, along with all of us authors of this volume, will also engage in reflection and dialogue on this vital question of the proper Christian attitude toward non-Christians: Mission or/and Dialogue? It is obvious that for us authors the correct answer is: Mission AND Dialogue. It is the relationship between the two, however, that needs much more dialogue.

AUTHORS

Gerald H. Anderson (United Methodist) is Editor of the International Bulletin of Missionary Research, and Director of the Overseas Ministries Study Center, New Haven, Connecticut. A minister of the United Methodist Church, he was a missionary in the Philippines, 1960-70, where he was Professor of Church History and Ecumenics at Union Theological Seminary, near Manila. He obtained his doctoral degree at Boston University.

Maria Clara Lucchetti Bingemer (Catholic) holds bachelor's degrees in journalism and theology and a master's in theology from the Pontifical Catholic University in Rio de Janeiro, and a doctorate in theology (1989) from the Pontifical Gregorian University in Rome. She is Assistant Professor of the Theological and Human Services Center in the Theological Department of the Pontifical Catholic University in Rio de Janeiro. She also serves as Assistant Professor at Santa Ursula University, as Academic Assistant at the Brazilian Development Institute, and as coordinator for publications on women and religion at the Institute of Superior Religion Studies--all in Rio de Janeiro. She has served as the Latin American coordinator of the Ecumenical Association for Third World Theologians and as a technical assistant to the National Conference of Brazilian Bishops. In addition to several articles and chapters in books, she has co-authored two books: Escatologia Crista (with J. B. Libanio; Vozes, 1985), and Maria Mae de Deus e Mae dos Pobres (with I. Gebara; Vozes, 1987).

Denise Lardner Carmody (Catholic) received her Ph.D. from Boston College in 1970. She has taught at Boston College, the College of Notre Dame of Maryland, Pennsylvania State University, and Wichita State University. At present, she is University Professor and Chair of the Faculty of Religion, University of Tulsa. Author of scores of books, her most recent ones include: Prayer in World Religions (Orbis, 1990) and Religious Woman: Contemporary Reflections on Eastern Texts (Crossroad, 1991).

Kenneth Cragg (Anglican) has held a number of academic posts and ecclesiastical offices in England, the Middle East (Bishop of Cairo), West Africa and the U.S.A. He has published a number of books dealing with issues in Muslim/Christian relationships, the most recent of which is Readings in the Qur'an (Harper & Row, 1988), which attempts a modern-idiom translation and arranges the Qur'an in its eight broad themes as an aid to new readers, with an introductory discussion of its role in the interreligious situation today. He has also published translations, from the Arabic, of Muhammad Abduh, Taha Husain, and Kamil Husain.

Gavin D'Costa (Catholic) is Senior Research Fellow in Religious Studies at the West London Institute of Higher Education. He is an Indian Roman Catholic who has studied at the universities of Birmingham and Cambridge. Among his publications are Theology and Religious Pluralism (1986), John Hick's Theology of Religions (1987), and most recently he has edited Christian Uniqueness Reconsidered: The Myth of a Pluralistic Theology of Religions (Orbis, 1990). He serves on the British Council of Churches and the Roman Catholic Committees for Other Faiths in Britain.

Claude Geffré (Catholic), Th.D. Professor and Rector of the Dominican Faculty of Sauchoir, France, has also since 1968 been Professor of Theology and Religious Studies at the Insitute Catholique of Paris. He is likewise the Director of the Collection "Cogitatio Fidei" of Éditions du Cerf. His publications include, Un nouvel âge de la théologie (1972 and 1987), Le Christianisme au risque de l'interprétation (1983 and 1988), and the articles "Dieu" and "Théologie" in Encyclopaedia Universalis, "Sécularisation," in Dictionnaire de Spiritualité (1989) and "Religio" in Catholicism (1990).

Robert W. Huston (United Methodist), for twenty-five years the chief ecumenical staff officer for The United Methodist Church (retired September, 1990), served for two periods on the Central Committee of the World Council of Churches. He has also served on the National Council of Churches general board since 1966 and on its Executive Committee and on the executive committee of the Consultation on Church Union. A pastoral minister for nineteen years in Tacoma, Washington and Boston, his doctorate in Ecumenics and Social Ethics is from Boston University, and he studied at one of the first Graduate School of Ecumenical Studies programs at Bossey, Switzerland. A graduate of the University of Puget Sound and a former junior officer in a commercial bank, he served 42 months on aircraft carriers in World War II. He now serves as Associate Minister of the Huntington/Cold Spring Harbor United Methodist Church, Huntington, NY.

Paul F. Knitter (Catholic), before moving to Xavier University in Cincinnati in 1975 where he is currently Professor of Theology, was a member of the Society of the Divine Word and taught at Catholic Theological Union in Chicago. He received a Licentiate in theology from the Pontifical Gregorian University in Rome (1966) and a doctorate from the University of Marburg (1972). Most of his research and publications have dealt with religious pluralism and interreligious dialogue. He is General Editor of Orbis Books' series "Faith Meets Faith" and has also authored No Other Name? A Critical Survey of Christian Attitudes toward World Religions (1985) and edited with John Hick The Myth of Christian Uniqueness: Toward a Pluralistic Theology of Religions (1987). He is at present working on a book exploring the relationship between interreligious dialogue and the theology of liberation.

Thomas F. Livernois (Lutheran) is an ordained minister in the Evangelical Lutheran Church of America (ELCA). He holds an S.T.D. degree from the Lutheran School of Theology. For two years (1988-1990) he was an Associate Director in the Office for Ecumenical Affairs of the ELCA. Prior to that he served a congregation in Neuchâtel, Switzerland. He has also taught at Susquehanna University in Selinsgrove, Pennsylvania.

Professor **Paul Varo Martinson** (Lutheran) was born in central China of missionary parents. After completion of college and seminary he served for a term with the Lutheran Church in Hong Kong. After completion of doctoral studies in History of Religions at the University of Chicago, Divinity School he was called to Luther Northwestern Theological Seminary, St. Paul, Minnesota, where he teaches in the area of World Religions and Christian Mission.

Melanie A. May (Church of the Brethren) is Ecumenical Officer of the Church of the Brethren, a position she has held since 1985 and will leave in January, 1991. A member of the World and National Councils of

Churches' Commissions on Faith and Order, she is the author of <u>Bonds of Unity: Women, Theology and the Worldwide Church</u> (Scholars Press, 1989) and is an Associate Editor of the <u>Journal of Ecumenical Studies</u>.

Robert Terrence McCahill (Catholic) is a Maryknoll missioner who has lived in three widely separated district towns during fifteen years in Bangladesh. "Brother Bob," as he is known to Muslims and Hindus among whom he lives and serves, tries to build trust and make signs. Befriending and accompanying seriously ill persons, he attempts to illustrate Christian living to persons unacquainted with Christians. Due to God's initiative he is in love with God, has deep respect for Islam and Hinduism, considers humankind our family, and enjoys bicycling to many villages.

Michael B. McGarry (Catholic) is a member of the Paulist Fathers. His graduate studies were at the University of St. Michael's College (Toronto); he also studied at the Hebrew University (Jerusalem). The author of <u>Christology After Auschwitz</u>, he has worked in Catholic-Jewish relations for many years. Currently, he is the Rector of St. Paul's College (Washington), the major seminary for the Paulist Fathers. He also serves on the Advisory Committee to the Secretariat for Catholic-Jewish Relations of the National Conference of Catholic Bishops.

Paul Mojzes (United Methodist) is professor of religious studies at Rosemont College in Rosemont, Pennsylvania, and Co-Editor of the <u>Journal of Ecumenical Studies</u>. A native of Yugoslavia, he studied at the University of Belgrade Law School and Florida Southern College and received the Ph.D. degree from Boston University in 1965. He is an ordained United Methodist minister. Both his parents were Methodist ministers in

Yugoslavia, a condition resembling missionary activity. He has participated in numerous interreligious dialogues. He has published Christian-Marxist Dialogue in Eastern Europe (Augsburg, 1980) and Church and State in Postwar Eastern Europe (Greenwood, 1986).

Raimundo Panikkar (Catholic) partakes of pluralistic traditions: Indian and European, Hindu and Christian, sciences and humanities. He has lived and studied in Spain, Germany, Italy, India, and the U.S., and holds doctorates in philosophy, science, and theology. He was ordained a Roman Catholic priest in 1946. Now Professor Emeritus of Religious Studies at the University of California, Santa Barbara, he spends most of his time in India and in Spain, where he lives in the mountains of Catalunya (place of pure emptiness), trying to learn the Wisdom of Life. Previously, he taught Sanskrit at the University of Madrid, philosophy in Rome, indology in Bangalore, and comparative religion at Harvard. He has published about 300 major articles on topics from the philosophy of science to metaphysics, comparative religion, and indology. Among his thirty books are: The Silence of God: The Answer of the Buddha (Orbis, 1989); The Intrareligious Dialogue (Paulist, 1978; 2nd ed., Asian Trading Corp., 1984); Myth, Faith, and Hermeneutics (Paulist, 1979; 2nd ed., Asian Trading Corp., 1983); and Blessed Simplicity: The Monk as Universal Archetype (Seabury, 1982).

Samuel Rayan (Catholic) was born in Kerala, India, and entered the Society of Jesus in 1939. Following studies in India and ordination to the priesthood in 1955, he received a doctorate in theology from the Gregorian University of Rome. From 1960 to 1972, he was chaplain to a movement of Catholic university students. Since 1972, he has taught systematic theology on the faculty of the Vidyajyoti Institute of Religious Studies in

Delhi. From 1968 to 1983, he served on the World Council of Churches' Commission on Faith and Order, and is active in the Ecumenical Association of Third World Theologians. In 1978, Orbis Books published his The Holy Spirit: Heart of the Gospel and Christian Hope. Two of his booklets have been published in India: The Anger of God and In Christ: The Power of Women, as have many articles in books and periodicals. His present interest is in the theology latent in peoples' struggles against every sort of oppression.

Leonard Swidler (Catholic) has a Ph.D. in History and Philosophy from the University of Wisconsin and a S.T.L. from the Pontifical Catholic Theology Faculty of the University of Tübingen. He has taught in universities in Germany, Poland, China, and the United States and has been Professor of Catholic Thought and Interreligious Dialogue at Temple University since 1966. He is the co-founder and Editor of the Journal of Ecumenical Studies and the author/editor of more than forty books and 150 articles. His recent books include: After the Absolute. The Dialogical Future of Religious Reflection, 1990; with John Cobb, Paul Knitter, Monika Hellwig, Death or Dialogue. From the Age of Monologue to the Age of Dialogue, 1990; with Gerard Sloyan, Lewis Eron, Lester Dean, A Jewish-Christian Dialogue on Jesus and Paul, 1990; with Paul Mojzes, eds., The Other. Attitudes of Religions and Ideologies towards the Outsider, 1990); with Seiichi Yagi A Bridge to Buddhist-Christian Dialogue, 1990.

Norman E. Thomas (United Methodist) is Professor of World Christianity at the United Theological Seminary, Dayton, Ohio. He received his degrees from Yale University and the Ph.D. from Boston

University. He served as a missionary in Africa, and was director of the Director of Mission and Evangelism Program at Boston University. He is the author of a number of articles on religion and social change in Africa and edited Rise Up and Walk. He is the book editor of Missiology. Since 1988 he has been a member of the Executive Committee of the International Association for Foreign Mission Studies.

Jozef Cardinal Tomko (Catholic) was born in Udavske, near Kosice, in Czechoslovakia in 1924. He studied in Bratislava and then went to Rome where he obtained three doctoral degrees from various universities. Ordained as a priest in 1949 and consecrated as titular of the archdiocese of Doclea and bishop in 1979, he was created a cardinal in 1985. He is the Secretary-General of the Synod of Bishops and the Prefect of the Congregation for the Evangelization of Peoples. Cardinal Tomko resides in Rome and was recently able to visit his native Slovakia. Among his publications is the book, Il Sinodo dei vescovi: Natura, metodi e prospettive.

Hans Waldenfels (Catholic), born in 1931 at Essen, Germany, entered Society of Jesus in 1951, studied philosophy in Pullach, Munich, theology in Tokyo, Rome, Münster. He took a degree in theology at the Pontifical Gregorian University, Rome, finished his Doctor Habilitation in Theology at the University of Würzburg. Since 1977 he has been Director of the Seminar for Fundamental Theology and Professor of Fundamental Theology, Theology of Non-Christian Religions, and Philosophy of Religion at the University of Bonn, Germany, where he was twice the Dean of the Faculty of Theology.

RELIGIONS IN DIALOGUE